FRUITS &

VEGETABLES

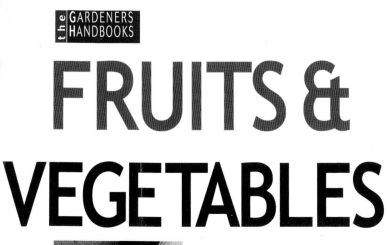

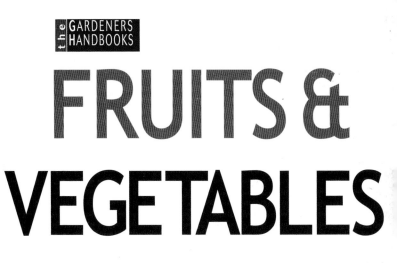

the GARDENERS HANDBOOKS

FRUITS &
VEGETABLES

CONSULTANT EDITOR
Judy Moore

WELDON OWEN

Conceived and produced by
Weldon Owen Pty Ltd
59-61 Victoria Street, McMahons Point,
Sydney NSW 2060, Australia
Copyright © 2003 Weldon Owen Pty Ltd
Revised edition copyright © 2010 Weldon Owen Pty Ltd

WELDON OWEN PTY LTD
CHIEF EXECUTIVE OFFICER Sheena Coupe
CREATIVE DIRECTOR Sue Burk
SENIOR VICE PRESIDENT, INTERNATIONAL SALES Stuart Laurence
VICE PRESIDENT, SALES: UNITED STATES AND CANADA Amy Kaneko
VICE PRESIDENT, SALES: ASIA AND LATIN AMERICA Dawn Low
ADMINISTRATION MANAGER, INTERNATIONAL SALES Kristine Ravn
PRODUCTION MANAGER Todd Rechner
PRODUCTION COORDINATORS Lisa Conway, Mike Crowton
PUBLISHING COORDINATOR Gina Belle

LIMELIGHT PRESS PTY LTD
PROJECT MANAGEMENT Helen Bateman/Jayne Denshire
PROJECT EDITOR Lynn Cole
PROJECT DESIGNER Katie Ravich
CONSULTANT EDITOR Judy Moore

REVISED EDITION
PROJECT COORDINATOR Natalie Ryan
DESIGNER Christina McInerney
CONSULTANT EDITOR Annelise Evans

ISBN 978-1-921530-84-5

Printed by Toppan Leefung Printing Limited

Printed in China

A Weldon Owen Production

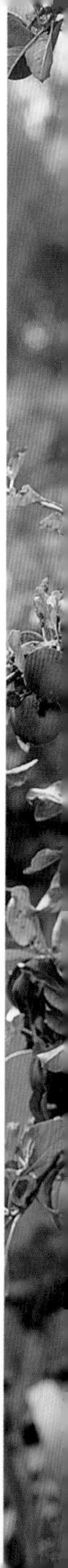

CONTENTS

8   HOW TO USE THIS BOOK

10   PLANNING YOUR GARDEN

Consider Your Climate 12
Garden Planning 16
Fruit Trees and Soft Fruit in Your Garden 22

26   TAKING CARE OF THE SOIL

Knowing Your Soil 28
Compost 34
Fertilizers 40
Mulches 50

54   PLANTING YOUR GARDEN

Choosing Plants and Seeds 56
Sowing Seeds 64
Planting Outdoors 66
Frost Protection and Extending the Season 68
Favourite Fruits and Nuts at a Glance 72
Planting Your Fruit Garden 74

80 MANAGING YOUR GARDEN

Garden Care for Four Seasons 82
Managing the Vegetable Garden 86
Easy-care Fruit Trees and Soft Fruit 90
Effective Watering 94
Pruning Basics for Fruit Crops 96
Dealing with Pests and Diseases 100
Dealing with Weeds 102
Controlling Weeds in the Vegetable Garden 108
Controlling Weeds in the Fruit Garden 110

112 PLANT DIRECTORY: VEGETABLES

Herbs for the Kitchen Garden 240

246 PLANT DIRECTORY: FRUIT

308 INDEX

How to Use This Book

This valuable guide will lead you gently through the process of planning and caring for your garden. Whether you are a novice or a more experienced gardener, you'll discover how to get the best results from your soil, whatever the size or design of garden you have chosen.

Colourful photographs give you guidance and inspiration in planning and planting your garden.

There are many helpful illustrations in the book, showing such things as tools, techniques and plant parts.

almonds and cherries, make handsome decorative features on a wall or trellis. Use freestanding trees singly as specimens or include them in a small copse or orchard. Or try an extra-showy type such as weeping 'Warwickshire Draper' plums, Downie' or a quince tree, with handsome columnar cherry 'Sylvia', crab apple 'John fruits and rose-like flowers.

REWARDING CHOICE
With proper care, nut trees, such as this walnut, yield good harvests of fresh creamy nuts that taste far better than any you can buy. Walnuts don't usually need much pruning.

BRILLIANT COLOUR
Fruits such as elderberries (above) and currants provide colour as vivid as any flower.

BORDERS AND PERENNIAL PLANTINGS
Low-growing fruit bushes, compact blackcurrants, shrubs for structural plant mixed borders. Creeping plants, including lowbush and strawberries, fit easil foreground of a flower or They also make interesting as long as they get their fair sunshine and a little help fro beat the weeds.

WALLS, FENCES AND TRELLI
Climbing fruits, such as grapes can cover arbours or trellises, su sitting areas, highlighting special or screening off utility areas. Esp trees (those trained to grow flat a wall or trellis) can form a living that's both unique and productive.

Fruiting plant come in a range sizes, so there's a one kind for any s of garden. Before y buy, make sure your have enough space allow each plant to grow up and out without crowding.

POINTERS FOR AN EASY-CARE EDIBLE GARDEN
Don't wait until your fruit trees are delivered to decide where to put them. An attractive, easy-care garden requires advance planning, starting with careful plant and site selection.
Choose problem-resistant plants Look for cultivars that are naturally resistant to the pests and diseases that are common in your area. (Local growers and horticultural societies can tell you which problems to watch out for; catalogue descriptions will list the problems a particular cultivar can resist or tolerate.)
Plan for plant size Think carefully about how large a tree you can handle. With trees over 1.8 m (6 ft) high you will need a ladder to harvest or prune; that will slow you down and be more strenuous.
Consider the water supply Try to plant near a water supply that you can tap into without much trouble. Otherwise, you may be spending lots of time-hauling buckets of water or lugging long hoses around. If dry spells are common in your area, you may want to install a permanent irrigation system before you plant. This can save you hours of work and provide excellent results.

24 PLANNING YOUR GARDEN

BORDER GUARDS
With their prickly stems and bushy habit, brambles are excellent as barrier plants, with delicious fruit as an added bonus.

FRUIT TREES AND SOFT FRUIT IN YOUR GARDEN 25

Clear and easy-to-follow pointers, or step-by-step instructions to show you how to proceed.

General information about various aspects of gardening.

Photographs of individual plants, showing what they look like when grown in the right conditions.

Botanical name

Family name

Hardiness of plant pages 308/309.

Common name

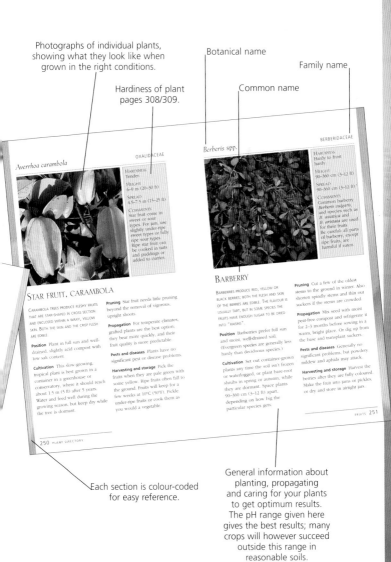

Averrhoa carambola

OXALIDACEAE

HARDINESS
Tender.

HEIGHT
6–9 m (20–30 ft)

SPREAD
4.5–7.5 m (15–25 ft)

COMMENTS
Star fruit come in sweet or sour types. For jam, use slightly under-ripe sweet types or fully ripe sour types. Ripe star fruit can be cooked in tarts and puddings or added to curries.

STAR FRUIT, CARAMBOLA

CARAMBOLA TREES PRODUCE FLESHY FRUITS THAT ARE STAR-SHAPED IN CROSS SECTION AND ENCLOSED WITHIN A WAXY, YELLOW SKIN. BOTH THE SKIN AND THE CRISP FLESH ARE EDIBLE.

Position Plant in full sun and well-drained, slightly acid compost with low salt content.

Cultivation This slow-growing, tropical plant is best grown in a container in a greenhouse or conservatory, where it should reach about 1.5 m (5 ft) after 5 years. Water and feed well during the growing season, but keep dry while the tree is dormant.

Pruning Star fruit needs little pruning beyond the removal of vigorous, upright shoots.

Propagation For temperate climates, grafted plants are the best option; they bear more quickly, and their fruit quality is more predictable.

Pests and diseases Plants have no significant pest or disease problems.

Harvesting and storage Pick the fruits when they are pale green with some yellow. Ripe fruits often fall to the ground. Fruits will keep for a few weeks at 10°C (50°F). Pickle under-ripe fruits or cook them as you would a vegetable.

Berberis spp.

BERBERIDACEAE

HARDINESS
Hardy to frost hardy.

HEIGHT
90–360 cm (3–12 ft)

SPREAD
90–360 cm (3–12 ft)

COMMENTS
Common barberry *Berberis vulgaris*, and species such as *B. asiatica* and *B. aristata* are used for their fruits. Be careful: all parts of barberry, except ripe fruits, are harmful if eaten.

BARBERRY

BARBERRIES PRODUCE RED, YELLOW OR BLACK BERRIES, BOTH THE FLESH AND SKIN OF THE BERRIES ARE EDIBLE. THE FLAVOUR IS USUALLY TART, BUT IN SOME SPECIES THE FRUITS HAVE ENOUGH SUGAR TO BE DRIED INTO "RAISINS".

Position Barberries prefer full sun and moist, well-drained soil (Evergreen species are generally less hardy than deciduous species.)

Cultivation Set out container-grown plants any time the soil isn't frozen or waterlogged, or plant bare-root shrubs in spring or autumn, while they are dormant. Space plants 90–360 cm (3–12 ft) apart, depending on how big the particular species gets.

Pruning Cut a few of the oldest stems to the ground in winter. Also shorten spindly stems and thin out suckers if the stems are crowded.

Propagation Mix seed with moist peat-free compost and refrigerate it for 2–3 months before sowing in a warm, bright place. Or dig up from the base and transplant suckers.

Pests and diseases Generally no significant problems, but powdery mildew and aphids may attack.

Harvesting and storage Harvest the berries after they are fully coloured. Make the fruit into jams or pickles, or dry and store in airtight jars.

Each section is colour-coded for easy reference.

General information about planting, propagating and caring for your plants to get optimum results. The pH range given here gives the best results; many crops will however succeed outside this range in reasonable soils.

Part One

PLANNING YOUR GARDEN

CONSIDER YOUR CLIMATE

M ore than any other single factor, climate influences the selection of plants you can grow. The term describes the interaction of air temperature, moisture, wind and other factors.

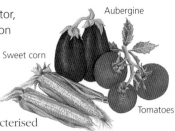

Sweet corn

Aubergine

Tomatoes

Spinach

Summer squash

Our temperate climate is characterised by alternating periods of moderately wet and dry weather, with predictable winds. Fortunately, most of the vegetables and many fruits that you are familiar with are well suited to this temperate climate.

However, there are regional differences that you should consider when planning your edible garden. Northerly areas tend to have longer winters than in the south, so may need to sow a couple of weeks later. The western coast is usually wetter and milder than the eastern coast, and the South-west enjoys a very mild, almost frost-free climate. Even in your own locality or garden, there will be "microclimates", which may differ from the average by being drier, wetter, cooler or warmer than the surrounding area. Frost pockets or slopes exposed to wind are areas to avoid if possible; if necessary you may need to take action to mitigate the effects of such conditions.

OBSERVE SUN AND SHADE PATTERNS
Most crops require ample sunlight to yield a generous supply of produce. Start your sun-and-shade survey as soon as you can —today, if possible. Try to watch the light

---

TENDER OR FROST–TENDER CROPS

Aubergine, chilli pepper, courgette, cucumber, lettuce (some), lima bean, melon (sweet), okra, pak choi, peanut, potato, pumpkin, runner bean, summer squash, sweet corn, sweet pepper, sweet potato, Swiss chard (spinach beet), tomato.

patterns through one whole growing season before doing any planting. A site that is sunny in early spring or autumn may be in deep shade by midsummer. On one sunny day a month, for at least several months before planting, watch your proposed sites through the day. Record when the sun first strikes the ground and when shadows take its place.

Your fruits and vegetables have three basic, climate-dependent requirements: a suitable temperature range, a favourable frost-free period and an adequate supply of moisture. Monitor the weather in your area, and be prepared to take action if your plants aren't getting the conditions they need to grow to their best.

RAISED BEDS

These are the ultimate in outdoor, custom-built plant containers. They require an initial investment of energy, but you'll save both time and labour later. Raised beds are productive and working on them is easier on your back.

Broccoli   Asparagus

Onions

Radish

GROWING SEASON

In our temperate climate, the main growing season begins after the last frost in spring or, in some areas, early summer, and ends when frosts begin again in autumn. But gardening activity begins before the technical start of the growing season and continues beyond the end. Frost occurs when the air temperature falls below 0°C (32°F) during the night, after dew has formed. The result is a lacy, white coating of water crystals on leaves the following morning. Frost damage may seem to be limited to the surface, but the plant's interior is also affected. Sensitive plants may die when exposed to frost in the spring or autumn. Many tender perennials that originate from warmer climates, such as tomatoes or chilli peppers, are therefore grown as annual vegetables.

Hardier vegetables, such as those belonging to the cabbage, or brassica, family, will tolerate some frost damage. They make useful winter crops and some taste better after being exposed to cold. Using hardy cultivars and cover such as cloches makes it possible to grow some crops for most of the year.

HARDY OR FROST-TOLERANT CROPS

Beetroot, broccoli, Brussels sprouts, cabbage, cauliflower, chicory, Chinese cabbage, corn salad (lamb's lettuce, mâche), kale, kohlrabi, Romaine or cos lettuce (some), mustard (most), onion, parsnip, radish, spinach, turnip.

SHADE CROPS

There are a few vegetables that can tolerate partial shade. Choose crops that fit your conditions from the following list: cabbage, corn salad (lamb's lettuce, mâche), endive, horseradish, lettuce, pea, radish, rhubarb, rocket, spinach, Swiss chard (spinach beet).

PRODUCTIVE AND BEAUTIFUL
This mixed cottage garden demonstrates what can be done with a well-sited space.

Garden Planning

When planning your garden, think about how much time you want to spend in it. The amount of work your garden requires will depend on its size and will vary with climate and seasons.

Site Selection

Consider also how much fresh produce you want. You may need only a small vegetable garden near the kitchen to meet your day-to-day demands for organically grown vegetables. Or you may decide to dedicate a substantial area to growing fruits and vegetables so that you'll have enough produce to freeze or store for later consumption.

Topography

Slopes and contours influence the way you arrange your garden. Cold air flows like water down a slope until it is blocked by a solid barrier, such as a wall or uphill slope, forming a frost pocket—avoid such a site if you can. If planting on a slope, place the rows or beds across it. If rows run up and down the slope, water will trickle down the slope instead of penetrating the soil to reach plant roots. Also avoid low-lying areas, where poor air circulation makes plants more susceptible to disease.

Since most vegetables need at least 2.5 cm (1 in) of water each week, be prepared to water your vegetable patch during dry periods. Make sure you can reach the site with a garden hose or irrigation system, or be prepared to carry

POTS OF GOODNESS

For a small household, just a few heads of cabbage and some fresh salad greens, planted successively in containers, may be all that you need. This is far better than building a garden that is too big and that will be a chore for you to look after.

water by hand. Avoid gardening in low areas prone to flooding, and on high areas with too much drainage.

OBSTACLES AND ACCESS

Locate your garden in a place that's easily accessible, both to you and to vehicles that will deliver materials you may need later, such as soil or compost. Avoid areas that have had heavy foot or vehicle traffic, because this activity compacts the soil and damages its structure. Paths should be wide enough for a wheelbarrow. As you choose a site, look for hidden obstacles such

HINTS ON CROP ROTATION

Wait 3–5 years before growing the same, or closely related, vegetables in the same spot.

Include soil-improving crops such as rye or clover between early and late crops, or between autumn and spring crops.

Grow legumes, such as clover or peas, the year before grasses, such as sweet corn.

Grow light feeders (such as root crops) before heavy feeders (tomatoes, peppers, cabbages and most leafy vegetables).

Make heavy compost applications to heavy feeders during the growing season.

Make light compost applications to light feeders during the growing season.

HIGH YIELDS

Before planting a fruit and vegetable garden on this scale, think about how much produce you actually need. Freezing and bottling are time-consuming and must be done when the crops are ready, whether or not that fits in with your schedule.

as septic tanks, tree roots, drainpipes and electricity cables, and avoid these areas.

LIGHT

Most plants need 6–12 hours of sunlight each day. Pick a site well away from trees and buildings that cast shade for more than half the day. If you have a city garden nestled among tall buildings, you may be limited to shade-tolerant plants. Given a favourable position, the soil in your garden will warm quickly and you may be able to plant early.

A SIMPLE PLAN

With structured beds, organizing crop rotation is fairly easy. Each year, move your crop over to the next bed in the sequence. Set aside a separate bed for perennials, such as asparagus and rhubarb. Sketch a plan of the bed each year so you're not relying solely on your memory.

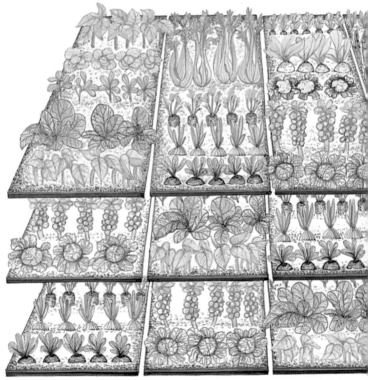

Plot A   Plot B   Plot C

DEMARCATION

This ornamental red cabbage would make an attractive border to separate sections of your garden.

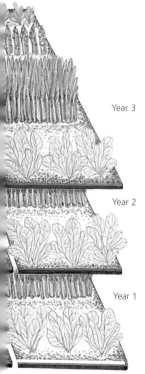

Year 3

Year 2

Year 1

Plot D (permanent bed)

TURN LAWN INTO A VEGETABLE GARDEN

Use a spade to remove the turf. Slip the blade forward just under the surface to slice through the roots.

Or solarize the area to kill both grass and weeds by covering it with black plastic for several months during summer.

Or simply mulch the area thickly. It may take a month or two to smother the grass completely. Then dig over the area.

Perhaps the ultimate in space saving, espalier training can also provide your ripening fruit with additional warmth from a sunny wall or fence.

WIRE CAGES

An alternative to staking for plants such as tomatoes is this cage system. You can also grow climbing crops such as cucumbers or squashes this way, with the cage upright, or turn the cage on its side and secure it with several stakes. Plant inside the cage; the climbers will loop around and form a horizontal tube. This works well for heavier crops, such as melons.

Means of Support

Training plants to grow vertically, instead of horizontally, saves space and makes cultivating and harvesting easier. Because fruits aren't in contact with the soil, they're less likely to succumb to soil-borne pathogens. Staked plants are also very tidy and leave you more room for special techniques such as interplanting and companion planting. You can purchase stakes made of wood, metal, plastic or bamboo in a variety of heights to fit the needs of the plant.

No matter what method you use, have your support system in place before you plant. Climbers such as peas and beans attach themselves by wrapping tendrils or twining stems around the support. Plants such as tomatoes or sweet peppers need more help. Tie loosely to the stake with garden twine or scraps of soft cloth.

Supporting Fruiting Canes

Start by setting sturdy 1.8-m (6-ft) posts every 6 m (20 ft) along the planting row. Then construct the support in one of these configurations.

A T-trellis makes picking easy for summer-bearing loganberries and raspberries, as well as blackberries. Put one cross arm about three-quarters of the way up each post so it resembles a T. Run wire from the end of each cross arm to that of the opposite post to support both sides of the plants.

A hedgerow trellis is used to hold canes upright between the wires. Add two cross arms to each post, one at the top and another about halfway down. Run wires between the ends of opposite arms. After cutting out the fruited canes after harvest, tie the remaining shoots to the bottom wires. When the shoots are tall enough, tie them to the top wires, too.

STOUT STAKES

Staking improves plant health, since better air circulation promotes drying and lessens the chance of disease. Sturdiness is more important than the appearance of the stakes, since your plants will become heavy with fruit as the season progresses.

TRAINING WIRES

This simple structure provides wires or strings for plants such as beans and cucumbers to climb up. Just remember not to place it where the growing plants will cast shade over their smaller neighbours.

Fruit Trees and Soft Fruit in Your Garden

It's surprising that fruiting plants have been neglected for so long in garden design. Most have two irresistible features: attractive flowers and edible fruits.

Many have other features as well, such as showy autumn colour or interesting bark. The options for including edibles in your garden are limited only by the space available. Here are some ways to use these beautiful and productive plants.

Shrubs and Hedges

Fruit- and nut-bearing bushes, such as some hazelnuts, elderberries, currants and highbush blueberries, form large shrubs substantial enough to edge the boundary of your property, mass into an informal hedge or naturalize. Prickly shrubs, such as raspberries, blackberries and gooseberries, make a barrier that the neighbourhood children, dogs and other animals won't be quick to push through.

Trees

If you're installing a new garden layout or renovating an old one, consider growing a fruit tree. Apples, pears, plums, cherries, walnuts and other full-sized fruit and nut trees provide height and structure plus a useful crop. Trained fruit trees, such as peaches, dwarf apples,

CONTAINERS

Decks and patios can be fruitful when you grow suitable edibles in containers. Strawberries look superb cascading out of hanging baskets or strawberry pots. Dwarf citrus trees, trailing tomatoes and herbs are also good candidates for container culture.

APPLE-BLOSSOM WALK

A fruiting pergola is a striking feature in a garden.

almonds and cherries, make handsome decorative features on a wall or trellis. Use freestanding trees singly as specimens or include them in a small copse or orchard. Or try an extra-showy type such as weeping 'Warwickshire Draper' plums, columnar cherry 'Sylvia', crab apple 'John Downie' or a quince tree, with handsome fruits and rose-like flowers.

REWARDING CHOICE
With proper care, nut trees, such as this walnut, yield good harvests of fresh, creamy nuts that taste far better than any you can buy. Walnuts don't usually need much pruning.

POINTERS FOR AN EASY-CARE EDIBLE GARDEN

Don't wait until your fruit trees are delivered to decide where to put them. An attractive, easy-care garden requires advance planning, starting with careful plant and site selection.

Choose problem-resistant plants Look for cultivars that are naturally resistant to the pests and diseases that are common in your area. (Local fruit growers and horticultural societies can tell you which problems to watch out for; catalogue descriptions will list the problems a particular cultivar can resist or tolerate.)

Plan for plant size Think carefully about how large a tree you can handle. With trees over 1.8 m (6 ft) high you will need a ladder to harvest or prune; that will slow you down and be more strenuous.

Consider the water supply Try to plant near a water supply that you can tap into without much trouble. Otherwise, you may be spending lots of time hauling buckets of water or lugging long hoses around. If dry spells are common in your area, you may want to install a permanent irrigation system before you plant. This can save you hours of work and provide excellent results.

BRILLIANT COLOUR

Fruits such as elderberries (above) and currants provide colour as vivid as any flower.

Borders and Permanent Plantings

Low-growing fruit bushes, such as compact blackcurrants, make great shrubs for structural plantings or in mixed borders. Creeping fruit-bearing plants, including lowbush blueberries and strawberries, fit easily in the foreground of a flower or shrub border. They also make interesting ground covers, as long as they get their fair share of sunshine and a little help from you to beat the weeds.

Walls, Fences and Trellises

Climbing fruits, such as grapes and kiwis can cover arbours or trellises, shading sitting areas, highlighting special views or screening off utility areas. Espaliered trees (those trained to grow flat against a wall or trellis) can form a living fence that's both unique and productive.

Fruiting plants come in a range of sizes, so there's at least one kind for any size of garden. Before you buy, make sure you have enough space to allow each plant to grow up and out without crowding.

BORDER GUARDS

With their prickly stems and bushy habit, brambles are excellent as barrier plants, with delicious fruit as an added bonus.

Part Two

TAKING CARE OF THE SOIL

KNOWING YOUR SOIL

Good soil is the gardener's key to success. Since it influences your plants' growth, health and yield, it deserves your first consideration. The golden rule is to treat your soil well.

SOIL COMPOSITION

Soil is actually a mixture of minerals, water, air and organic matter. Average soil contains about 45 per cent mineral matter, 25 per cent air, 25 per cent water, and 5 per cent organic matter.

Soil texture refers to the fineness or coarseness of your soil's mineral matter. Texture is determined by the relative proportions of sand (very coarse), silt and clay (very fine); it influences fertility, water retention and air circulation within the soil. The ideal garden soil is a loam, composed of about 40 per cent sand, 40 per cent silt and 20 per cent clay. The spaces between soil particles, called pore spaces, hold water, air and dissolved nutrients. If the spaces are large, as between sand particles, the soil is unable to retain sufficient water or nutrients.

The way sand, silt and clay particles join together is called soil structure. Both sand and compacted clays have no structure. In-between these extremes, various proportions of sand, silt, clay and organic matter are arranged as larger clumps, called aggregates. Soil structure is especially important because it influences the pore spaces, which in turn

HOME LITMUS TEST

Using a kit like the one above is an easy way to get a rough idea of your soil's acidity or alkalinity. Put some soil in the clean container and stir in distilled water. Let it stand for an hour, then place a strip of litmus paper in the mixture and leave it in for at least 60 seconds. Remove the paper and rinse with distilled water. Match the colour of the paper to the chart that came with the kit.

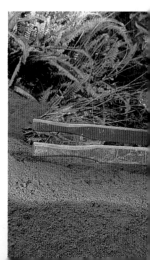

influence water content and drainage, movement of air in the soil and the release of nutrients. The ideal soil has a crumbly, granular structure that allows water to drain and oxygen and carbon dioxide to move freely from the air into the pore spaces. A light, loose soil structure is known as "friable". Adding organic matter will improve the structure of all soil types.

AIR AND WATER IN THE SOIL

Plants take in the oxygen they need from the air in the soil, so it is critical for vigorous plant growth. Oxygen is also critical for healthy soil and the well-being of soil organisms, such as earthworms. Air also contains gaseous nitrogen, which specialized bacteria convert into a form that your vegetables can use.

A steady supply of water is vital for the health of almost all plants. Plant roots absorb water and dissolved minerals from pore spaces in the soil. A good garden soil will hold enough water for plant growth while letting excess water drain down to deeper layers. While most

CHECK YOUR SOIL pH

Soil pH, the relative measure of how acid or alkaline your soil is, can affect nutrient availability for plants. It is measured on a scale from 1.0 (strongly acid) to 14.0 (strongly alkaline). Most plants thrive within a range of 6.0–7.0, from slightly acid to neutral. Nutrients tend to be most accessible to plant roots at this pH range. If you suspect your soil is extremely acid or alkaline, it's wise to test it using a proprietary soil-testing kit, or use a soil-analysis service. If the results confirm your suspicions, you can make small changes to your soil's pH by incorporating compost or soil improvers, such as powdered sulphur to lower pH or ground limestone to raise it. But by far the best solution is to select plants that do well in your natural conditions.

HEALTHY SOIL
Good friable soil is a pleasure to work with. Careful digging and regular additions of organic matter will keep it healthy.

vegetables prefer well-drained soil, there are a few, such as celery and watercress, that can tolerate more moisture. Raised-bed gardening can help if you need to improve the drainage of your garden beds (see page 13).

Organic Matter

Soil organic matter refers to the decomposing remains of plants and animals. Organic matter is important because it attracts and holds important plant nutrients in the soil. It is critical for soil structure because it provides the "glue" that holds individual particles of minerals together as aggregates. When organic matter has decomposed, its stable remains are called humus. The organic matter content of your soil is influenced by many factors, including climate, vegetation, drainage, soil organisms and cultivation. Generally, wetter climates and healthy populations of soil microbes help to create soil with a high content of organic matter. High annual temperatures, less vegetative

Little Helpers

Your allies in the battle for good soil structure are the small creatures that crawl through your soil. Earthworms are perhaps the most famous soil builders. Their tunnelling loosens and aerates compacted soil, and the organic matter they drag down encourages stable soil granules. Rodents churn the soil as they dig and mix organic matter into the subsoil. Plant roots also improve soil structure by adding organic matter below the surface as they break down. Plus, the tiny passages left by the decayed roots allow water and air easier access to lower soil layers, in turn encouraging even more micro-organisms and plant growth.

PROTECT YOUR SOIL

Good soil looks dark and has a crumbly texture, with visible organic matter.

growth and intensive cultivation lessen the ability of soil to accumulate organic matter.

Soil Nutrients

The amount and type of soil nutrients that are available to your plants depend on the interaction of many factors, including soil texture, structure, moisture, organic matter and pH. Fine texture, loose structure, ample moisture, high organic matter content and near-neutral pH are all conditions that make the most nutrients available to your plants.

DO NO HARM

Before you start digging in spring, or after heavy rain, wait until the soil has dried out a bit, or you will damage its structure.

A Hands-on Test for Soil Texture

To check if your soil is sandy, silty or clay, take a chunk of soil about the size of your thumb. Moisten it enough so that you can roll it into a ball. Flatten the ball between the pad of your thumb and the side of your bent index finger. Push your thumb forward repeatedly, pressing the soil outward to form a ribbon. The longer the ribbon, the more clay is in the soil. A heavy clay will make a ribbon 2.5 cm (1 in) long; a sandy soil might not make a ribbon at all. To confirm your findings, put the ribbon in your palm and add enough water to make a runny paste. Rub the index finger of your other hand around in the mud in your palm. If it feels gritty, the soil is sandy. If it's smooth, the soil is silty. If it's on the sticky side, you've got clay.

SPARE YOUR BACK
Here are some tips that can help save your muscles next time you turn the soil. First, insert the spade into the soil so the blade is straight up and down.

1. Keeping your back straight and your foot on the upper edge of the blade, use your weight to push the blade into the soil.
2. Bend both your waist and knees as you slide the spade under the soil, then straighten up to lift the load.
3. Turn your whole body before depositing the soil—don't just twist your torso as you fling the soil to the side.
   It's easy, in your rush to finish, to ignore pain. But pain has a purpose: it's telling you to take a break. You'll get more done and feel better if you take regular breaks, before you feel any pain.

To check the nutrient content of your soil, it may be worthwhile to get a lab test of your soil before you plant your crops. It's often a good idea to test the soil in a newly created bed, or in a bed that has been producing for many years. You can get your soil tested by horticultural organisations such as the Royal Horticultural Society (RHS) or a private soil-testing lab. They will provide you with a statement indicating any nutrient deficiencies or excesses, along with recommendations for fertilizers to correct the imbalances. Make sure you ask for recommendations for organic fertilizers. You may want to test the soil again in a few years to monitor the results of your gardening practices and make any necessary adjustments.

WHEN TO WORK THE SOIL
Each time you work the soil, you have a chance to either destroy or maintain good structure. If you dig when it's too wet, the soil forms clods that are hard to break apart once they dry. And walking

around on wet soil while you're digging promotes compaction, another factor that can ruin good soil structure. If you work the soil when it's too dry, the clumps of soil disintegrate, leaving powder that can blow away in the wind or be carried off by the next rainfall.

Even if you don't affect the structure, there are other good reasons to avoid working very wet and very dry soils. Wet soils stick to everything—your shoes, your tools and the dog keeping you company. Dry, crusty soils make it hard to push a spade into the ground, so digging is twice as much work as it needs to be.

SHOULD YOU DIG IN SPRING OR AUTUMN?

In most cases, and particularly on heavy clay soils, your odds of finding soil in just the right condition for digging are better in autumn than spring. Rains are usually less frequent then, so the soil gets more time to dry out. If the soil is too dry, just water it and wait a day or two. Freedraining, light soils, such as sandy or chalky soils, will still be workable in spring.

Autumn digging is a bad idea if you garden on a slope because it exposes loose soil to erosion. Because slopes drain faster than level soils, you may be able to work them in spring when other soils are still too moist. If you do dig in autumn, cover the soil with a thick mulch or grow a green manure over the winter.

SIMPLE READINESS TEST

To check whether the soil is at the right stage for digging, pick up a handful of soil and squeeze it. Open your hand. If the soil stays in a firm ball in your palm, it's too wet to work. If it falls apart, it's too dry. If it holds together until you poke it with your finger, it's just right.

Compost

Composting is an excellent way to manage garden and kitchen wastes and make your own fertilizer. It is a good source of organic matter and nutrients for plants.

Compost improves soil structure and water retention and research shows that it contains beneficial micro-organisms that suppress plant pathogens in soil.

How to Make Fast, Hot Compost

1. Start saving all the organic wastes you normally throw away—leaves, grass clippings, kitchen scraps, rotted straw and other organic wastes. Decomposition is most efficient if tougher materials are shredded. A lawn mower will shred leaves and other light materials. Use a shredder for woody prunings and tree bark. Newspaper should be shredded to fine pieces or scrunched up into loose balls. Avoid adding oils, meat scraps and bones,

BREWING COMPOST TEA

To make a good liquid fertilizer, put a spadeful of compost in a cheesecloth or hessian bag. Tie the bag closed and suspend it in a container of water. Keep it covered for a few days. Once it has steeped, use the liquid to drench the soil at the base of plants you want to feed. Or dilute the liquid with water until it is the colour of weak tea, then spray it on plant leaves. Because the nutrients are dissolved in water, the plants can take them up immediately for a quick burst of energy. (Reuse the "tea bag" several times, then add the soaked compost to the garden.)

RECYCLING SCRAPS

Keep a small bin handy by your kitchen to collect compostable food scraps.

FAST, HOT COMPOST

Build up the layers of your compost heap with equal amounts of high-carbon and high-nitrogen materials (see page 37).

Sprinkle water generously over each layer to keep the pile moist and encourage decomposition of the material.

Aerate the compost heap by turning it over every couple of days with a garden fork. This hastens microbial activity.

COMPOST FOR BUSY PEOPLE

For easy access, put your compost heap on a level, well-drained spot close to the vegetable garden. Some gardeners build elaborate, multi-bayed compost bins, but you can just dump your stuff in an open heap. Besides kitchen scraps, toss in pulled annual weeds (if they don't have seeds), grass clippings, fresh cow or horse manure, sawdust, shredded paper from the office shredder and just about any plant or plant derivative. Don't add diseased plants because the bacteria, fungi or viruses might survive and spread.

Turn the heap every so often with a fork; the more often you turn it, the more air gets in and the faster the soil organisms can break it down.
If you're chronically pressed for time, buy a cheap fork and leave it near the compost heap so you can turn it when the mood strikes, not at those less-frequent times when you remember to bring the good fork from the shed. When your compost is dark and crumbly (in a few weeks or months), it's ready to use.

because they attract scavenging animals and slow the decomposition process. Do not add human or pet faeces, or pesticides, or herbicide-treated grass clippings.

2. Choose a spot near the vegetable garden for composting and store ingredients in heaps or bins. Containment is not important, but walls will keep the area neat and the dog out.

ULTRA TIDY
Multiple, sturdy bays are great for composting. As the heap ages, fork it into the next bay and start a fresh batch in the first bay. Put a sliding door on each bay if you wish.

COMPOST TROUBLESHOOTING

If your compost heap doesn't heat up, add more high-nitrogen material (see opposite). If the compost is dry, add water, or try turning the heap.

If the heap smells bad, add more high-carbon material (see opposite). If it is too wet, turning may help to add more air.

If the finished compost is covered with seedlings, your compost has not heated up enough and seeds of weeds and other plants have survived. Either avoid adding materials with seeds or make sure that they're in the centre of a hot compost heap.

If woody stems, prunings and dry leaves have not broken down, try shredding or chopping them into smaller pieces before adding them to a new heap. Adding more high-nitrogen ingredients can help balance these high-carbon materials.

TOP-DRESSING

Apply compost to a depth of 2.5–5 cm (1–2 in) over your garden soil each year or use it to mulch rows of plants. If soil tests indicate a nutrient imbalance, sprinkle the appropriate fertilizers over the soil before adding the compost, or add fertilizer to the compost itself. You can dig the compost in, or leave it on top as a mulch.

Or purchase a ready-made compost bin or tumbler.

3. You'll need enough raw materials to make a heap roughly 90 cm (3 ft) on each side; smaller heaps won't heat up as efficiently. Build the heap by stacking the materials layer upon layer, using any kind of garden fork. Alternate materials that are high in carbon (brown, woody materials such as sawdust, straw and newspaper) with layers of material high in nitrogen (green, soft materials such as fresh grass clippings, kitchen scraps, weeds and manure).

Use about equal volumes of each. A heap with too much carbon remains cool and breaks down more slowly. Too much nitrogen can create odour problems.

As you work, add several spadefuls of garden soil to innoculate the heap with the right decomposer organisms. Just sprinkle soil on top of alternate layers. You can add dry mineral fertilizers, too, if your soil needs them. If you are adding insect-infested plant material to your heap, make sure you put it in the centre, where temperatures will be high enough to kill the pests.

4. Keep the heap moist, but not soggy. As you build the heap, sprinkle the layers with water if the materials are dry. Keep the layered heap covered with an old compost sack to help maintain the right amount of moisture. Conditions that

TURN, TURN, TURN
Forking over the compost heap helps the microbes with their task. A hot compost heap can be ready to use in 2–6 weeks. You'll know it's ready when the temperature has stabilized and the individual materials you added at the beginning are no longer recognizable.

Worm castings are a rich source of organic matter. Buy a commercial worm bin and follow the instructions that come with it to keep your worms healthy and ensure a constant supply of this powerful soil supplement.

are too wet or too dry will change the rate of decomposition, and your compost might not be ready when you want it.

5. To work properly, organisms that hasten decomposition require oxygen. The simplest way to aerate the heap is to turn it every day or two. Invert the heap, one forkful at a time, with your garden fork, next to the original heap. Materials originally on the outside should end up in the middle. Fluff the heap as you go, sprinkling with more water as needed.

Aeration hastens microbial activity, which increases the temperature of the heap. Turning every day or two helps maintain a constant temperature. Use a compost thermometer to monitor the temperature, which should stay below 71°C (160°F), since higher temperatures will kill important decomposer organisms. If the heap gets too cool, turning it will raise the temperature. If the temperature gets too high, let the heap stand for a few days without turning it over, or add a small amount of water.

TYPES OF WORM BIN

Basically a worm bin is a simple box with a drainage system to collect liquid waste. Several designs are commercially available, but you could also make your own. Buy red brandling worms that are bred for worm bins. Garden earthworms are not suitable.

FERTILIZERS

Plants need 16 chemical elements for healthy growth, some in greater amounts (macronutrients) than others (micronutrients or trace elements). Each of these elements performs a particular role.

FERTILIZERS OR CONDITIONERS?

A fertilizer is a material that contains significant amounts of the chemical elements that plants need to grow, such as nitrogen, phosphorus and potassium. It may also contain material that improves the soil, such as organic matter. But its primary function is to add nutrients. Bonemeal, poultry pellets and seaweed meal are examples of organic fertilizers.

A conditioner improves the soil physically, usually its structure or drainage, or enhances microbial activity. It may contain some nutrients, but not enough to be called a fertilizer. Garden compost, grass clippings, lime and leaf mould are examples of soil conditioners. The material you use depends on what effect you want. Fertilizers provide a general nutrient boost during the growing season and are useful for correcting specific nutrient deficiencies. Conditioners are important for long-term soil health, because they add organic matter and humus. Work these in before planting, or use as mulches, but don't count on them to provide enough nutrients to support hungry plants. Build up the soil humus and use a balance of fertilizers and conditioners and your plants will have all the nutrients they need.

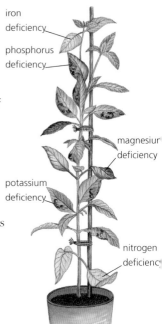

iron deficiency
phosphorus deficiency
magnesium deficiency
potassium deficiency
nitrogen deficiency

DEFICIENCIES

Thankfully, plants rarely show all these nutrient deficiencies at once. If you see any of these symptoms, try a seaweed spray for a quick fix, then improve the soil with well-rotted garden compost or a supplement for a long-term solution.

A BEAUTIFUL CROP

These kohlrabis (right) look as if they have everything they need to thrive.

Nitrogen for Lush Leaves

If you've ever fertilized a lawn, you know what a dramatic effect nitrogen has: it gives plants a deep green colour and stimulates leafy growth. It is one of the three primary macronutrients that plants need and is probably the nutrient you'll have to add most often, because it easily washes out of the soil.

Most of the nitrogen in the soil is bound up in organic matter. It is slowly released and converted to a form plants can use, which is dissolved in the water held between soil particles. Unlike many nutrients, the form of nitrogen dissolved in the soil solution leaches readily from the soil. That's why nitrogen is sometimes in short supply, especially in quick-draining, sandy soils or in those where it is used up by vigorous plants.

Good Organic Sources of Nitrogen

Well-rotted farmyard manure (usually a mix of cow dung, straw and urine) contains about 0.5 per cent nitrogen; horse manure has more nutrients. They make good soil conditioner. Pelleted chicken manure contains 2–5 per cent nitrogen and is handy for dressing borders and lawns. Spent mushroom compost contains about 0.7 per cent nitrogen, and may be more alkaline than acid. Seaweed meal is often applied in solution; it has 2 per cent nitrogen, and is rich in trace elements. Traditional soil fertilizers include blood, fish and bone, which is powdered for use as a base dressing—it contains 3.5 per cent nitrogen. Dried blood contains 10 per cent nitrogen and hoof and horn 12 per cent nitrogen.

GREEN MANURE
Dig a crop of clover into your soil. As it decays, it will release nitrogen in a form accessible to other plants.

ADDING EXTRA NITROGEN

You can add nitrogen to the soil in several ways. If you have naturally fertile soil, it's enough just to add well-rotted garden compost or manure each year to replace the nitrogen that plants remove. These balanced materials will provide a steady supply of nitrogen to growing plants throughout the season.

If your plants need extra nitrogen, you can use a more concentrated source. Depending on the fertilizer you choose, the nitrogen may be available right away, but it may last only a short while or be released gradually over a long period. See "Good Organic Sources of Nitrogen" (opposite) for materials you could add.

Growing a green manure crop of clover, alfalfa or some other legume is a useful way to add extra nutrients to the soil in your vegetable garden. Legumes host beneficial soil bacteria on their roots. These bacteria draw nitrogen gas from air in the soil and convert it to a form that both they and the plants can use. When you work legumes into the soil, the decaying roots release nitrogen that other plants can absorb.

AN EXCEPTION
If you add nitrogen to pea and bean crops, you may actually reduce your harvest.

HOLD THE NITROGEN
To get the best yield of beautiful tomatoes from your plants, hold off on the nitrogen. It promotes the growth of lush leaves at the expense of the fruit.

Phosphorus for Roots and Fruits

Plants need large amounts of phosphorus, which, like nitrogen, is one of the primary elements. Crops use it to produce flowers and fruits and to form seeds. It also helps them to mature, counter-acting the effects of too much nitrogen. Roots, especially the fibrous roots that spread out to absorb water and nutrients, need phosphorus to develop. Phosphorus makes stems strong and improves the quality of your vegetables; it also improves their resistance to disease. A lack of phosphorus limits how well your plants are able to absorb other nutrients, especially nitrogen.

A VITAL ELEMENT

For great crops, remember that phosphorus plays a crucial role in forming healthy roots and strong stems. It also helps in seed formation. Where there is a deficiency, fruits and seeds set and mature late.

Supplying Phosphorus

Most garden soils in the UK have sufficient phosphorus, but soil converted from old pastureland may be deficient. In very acid or alkaline soils with an extreme pH, the phosphorus reacts with soil chemicals, such as aluminium, calcium, manganese and iron, to create compounds that plants can't absorb. If you add phosphorus to very acid or alkaline soil, much of it binds to these chemicals.

To make more phosphorus available to plants, adjust the pH to near neutral (see page 29). In acid soils, this means adding lime. In alkaline soils, add sulphur. The pH changes slowly, so test your soil once or twice each year for several years, taking samples in the same month each time. Next, add a phosphorus fertilizer, both to increase the supply in the soil and to replace the phosphorus that crops remove (see "Good Organic Sources of Phosphorus," below). Since micro-organisms help to make phosphorus more readily available, add phosphorus to your compost rather than directly to the soil.

Because phosphorus doesn't dissolve readily, it doesn't move down through the soil, so dig it in where it's needed, in the root zone. It's best to correct major phosphorus deficiencies before planting, especially for more permanent features such as trees. When it is cold, even soil that has plenty of phosphorus may not supply your plants with what's needed. In permanent plantings, rake off heavy mulches in spring to help soil warm up. Try a temporary black plastic cover to warm the soil before planting vegetables.

SURE SIGN

Among common signs of phosphorus deficiency is a purplish cast to the leaves, especially on seedlings. Plants may be stunted, including the roots, and the leaves may have yellow streaks. Other signs are skinny, brittle stems.

GOOD ORGANIC SOURCES OF PHOSPHORUS

Animal manures contain phosphorus, nitrogen and potassium. Poultry manure has the highest content of phosphorus at about 14 per cent total. About 2 per cent is available at any time. Bonemeal, made from ground animal bones, has 11 per cent phosphorus. Raw bonemeal releases phosphorus more quickly than rock phosphate, but wear gloves and take care not to inhale when applying it. Liquid seaweed gives a quick shot of phosphorus when sprayed on plants or watered into the soil. The effect isn't long-lasting, but can be a big help for young plants forming roots, plants setting fruit and plants showing symptoms of a phosphorus deficiency. Rock phosphate is an alternative to animal products such as bonemeal, but takes longer to release its phosphorus. The more finely ground the rock, the more quickly the phosphorus is released. Rock phosphate is about 32 per cent total phosphate, but only about 3 per cent is available at any one time.

GOOD ORGANIC SOURCES OF POTASSIUM

Rock potash, from ground feldspars and other rocks, contains about 8 per cent potassium. Greensand, with 7 per cent potassium, is mined from ocean beds that have lifted and dried over time. Both are slow-release potassium fertilizers. Seaweed meal, which is dried, ground seaweed, contains 2–3 per cent potassium in a relatively available form, as well as beneficial trace minerals. Seaweed fertilizer is also available as a solution as a foliar feed and for containers as a growth tonic. Wood ash has 2-8 per cent potash and is soluble, but also alkaline, so is best cycled through the compost heap first.

POTASSIUM FOR HEALTHY GROWTH

Although potassium doesn't get as much attention as the other primary nutrients, plants use as much of it as they do nitrogen and about four times as much as they do phosphorus. Potassium makes plants vigorous by helping them to develop strong root systems and resist disease. It regulates how plants absorb nitrogen, sodium and calcium. Potassium

TELL-TALE SIGNS

If plants don't get enough potassium, they will be stunted and yield poorly, unlike true dwarf cultivars. Potassium deficiency can cause leaves to develop irregular yellow splotches, starting at the bottom of the plant and working upward. In more severe cases, leaves are dry and scorched at the edges. Be aware, however, that other problems can cause similar symptoms.

also balances the tendency of nitrogen to cause leafy growth and of phosphorus to encourage fruiting. Plants use potassium in photosynthesis and it is part of the process that moves newly photosynthe-sized sugars from the leaves to the roots, then converts them to starches.

KEEPING A PROPER LEVEL

Most soils, except those composed mostly of sand, are high in total potassium. The problem is that, like phosphorus, much of it is unavailable. Some 90 per cent is in rock minerals, such as mica and feldspar, which resist weathering. Fortunately, if you add potassium to the soil, plants can absorb it readily until it is leached away.

The trick to keeping potassium at the right level is to apply it twice a season, half a dose each time, rather than putting it on all at once. This way, your plants get just what they need.

HEALTHY CROPS

A good balance of soil potassium will promote strong, healthy growth in all your crops. It is especially important in tuber formation, and crops such as potatoes (see below) require high amounts of this element to form starches.

Secondary Macronutrients

Besides nitrogen, phosphorus and potassium, plants need large doses of calcium, magnesium and sulphur. **Calcium** helps plants absorb nitrogen and create proteins. Without it, new leaves and end branches are deformed; the upper leaves curl upward and turn yellow around the edges, then dry and fall off. Stems are hard and roots are brown and stubby. Blossom-end rot, where the bottoms of fruits turn brown or black, is a common symptom of calcium deficiency in tomatoes and sweet peppers. Drought can cause calcium deficiency because plants can't absorb it from the dry soil. Excess potassium can also limit available calcium.

Limestone is the main source of calcium. Limestone also neutralizes soil acidity, making it a useful addition to acid soils but something to avoid on alkaline soils. Add gypsum to alkaline

ZINC DEFICIENCY

Although not required in large amounts, an absence of trace elements such as zinc can cause problems. Above we see the typical yellowing between dark green veins and the leaves starting to roll along the edges that indicate a lack of zinc.

soil that is calcium-deficient. Calcium is also found in fertilizers that supply other nutrients, such as rock phosphate, bonemeal, seaweed meal and wood ashes. **Magnesium** is part of the chlorophyll molecule, which makes plants green and is essential for photosynthesis. Without it, plants are chlorotic—the leaves are pale with dark green veins. Correct a magnesium deficiency in an acid soil by adding dolomitic limestone, containing magnesium carbonate. In alkaline soils, you could use Epsom salts, which is magnesium sulphate.

Sulphur is part of the proteins that plants build. Plants with a sulphur deficiency are small, pale and spindly. Sulphur also makes soils acid. Deficiencies are rare. Adding ample quantities of organic matter will usually supply all the sulphur your plants need. To lower your soil's acidity, use ground sulphur, also known as flowers of sulphur.

MAGNESIUM DEFICIENCY

Mottling and dead spots on leaves, which may be brittle and curl up, indicate a lack of magnesium. Fruit matures late or not at all. Deficiencies are more common late in the season and in soils with too much potassium or calcium.

SEAWEED

In its fresh form or prepared as an extract, seaweed is an excellent source of calcium and trace elements, or micronutrients, such as iron, zinc, copper and boron.

Mulches

Mulching retains soil moisture, controls weed growth, provides a barrier against soil-borne diseases, protects soil from erosion and keeps your harvest clean. Its importance cannot be overestimated.

Organic Mulch

Organic mulches are plant residues, such as garden compost, bean haulms, grass clippings, shredded leaves, newspapers, pine needles, sawdust, straw and wood chips. Their decomposition enhances soil productivity, enriches the soil with nutrients and supplies organic matter to improve the soil structure.

Organic mulches encourage and shelter beneficial organisms at the soil surface and just below it. Thick layers of mulch act as a cushion, reducing soil compaction. And at the end of the season, you don't have to remove them, because they decompose naturally. Ideally,

SHREDDED LEAVES
Run autumn leaves through a shredder to make a lightweight insulating mulch that is just the thing for protecting late-season crops.

GRASS CLIPPINGS
Use both fresh and dry grass clippings, hay or similar material to mulch around all kinds of plants. Because they contain balanced amounts of carbon and nitrogen, they won't draw nitrogen from your soil as they break down.

organic mulch should be applied before annual weeds (such as chickweed) have a chance to germinate and the perennials (such as couch grass) emerge.

The best time to mulch in most gardens is in spring, once the soil has warmed up after winter, but before it starts to dry out in the warmer weather. Mulching at that time encourages crop growth at the start of the growing season and suppresses weeds that might compete with seedling crops. As the mulch breaks down, it will provide extra nutrients for hungry crops such as potatoes. Topping up the mulch in autumn provides some protection from frosts for crops left in the ground such as root vegetables and stops winter rains washing nutrients out of the soil.

Build a mulch layer 7.5–10 cm (3–4 in) thick. Keep the mulch about 10 cm (4 in) away from plant stems. This avoids encouraging rot in the plant stems, and also promotes surface aeration, which helps to lessen the chance of disease and problems from slugs and snails.

BARK MULCHES

Wood or bark chips may contain wood that has been treated with chemicals that could harm plants. If you chip your own wood, let it sit outside for a few months before using it, so that any natural substances harmful to plants are leached out. Turn the pile every few weeks to keep chips from going "sour". Cypress bark can be toxic to young plants.

TWICE AS EFFECTIVE
Compost works best when it is topped with a thin layer of a longer-lasting mulch, such as shredded bark, wood shavings or similar materials.

LANDSCAPE FABRICS

Black plastic and woven materials used as a mulch should be put in place early in the season. Lay it down several weeks before planting, to warm the soil. Landscape fabrics can go on anytime before planting. Create planting holes by cutting crosses in the fabric.

ORGANIC HABITAT

Organic mulches enrich your soil as they break down. They also provide the kind of environment that worms, friendly bacteria and other beneficial garden creatures thrive in, so there are benefits all round.

STRAW

Fresh straw is a traditional organic mulch for crops such as strawberries and melons because it keeps the fruits clean and free from rot, although it can harbour slugs and snails.

BARK CHIPS

These make a long-lasting, weed-suppressing mulch. They're often used for paths and in permanent plantings, such as around your fruit trees and bushes. However, they tend to get scattered, leading to more work keeping areas near mulched beds clean.

A light-coloured mulch such as straw reflects light and keeps soil cool. Dark-coloured mulches help to warm the soil.

You may have to improve some types of organic mulch. For example, pine needles and leaves are acidic and can be neutralized with lime. (As a general rule, apply 2.2 kg [5 lb] of lime per 9.3 sq m [100 sq ft] to raise the pH of soil by 1 point. Sandy soils generally need less lime to raise the pH; clay soils need more.) If you use seaweed, rinse away the salt first. If you're uncertain of the nutrient value of a mulching material, test your soil annually so you know what changes are taking place.

INORGANIC MULCHES

These mulches include those materials that don't improve soil, such as plastic or gravel. Gravel isn't practical in most vegetable gardens, but black plastic is widely used because it warms the soil early for the fastest crops. Landscape fabrics are similar to black plastic, but have tiny pores to let water and air in. Gardeners might find both black plastic and landscape fabric expensive, but they can last several seasons if you remove and store them each autumn.

If you decide to use black plastic or similar landscape fabrics, make sure you purchase the right width and length for your beds or rows. To determine the right width, measure across beds and rows, then add at least 15 cm (6 in) to each side. After you lay it out, anchor the sides with soil, rocks or boards. Cut holes for planting. At the end of the season, remove and store the fabric until next season, if it's still in good condition.

Part Two

PLANTING YOUR GARDEN

CHOOSING PLANTS AND SEEDS

Make a list of the plants you want to grow, along with an estimate of the number or amount of seed for each. Refer to your list when at the garden centre or ordering from catalogues.

A STEP AHEAD

Trays of healthy seedlings save you some time, which may justify their extra expense, especially if your growing season is short.

BUYING PLANTS

When buying vegetable seedlings, look for healthy, green plants with lush foliage. Reject tall, leggy seedlings in favour of short, sturdy plants. Upright, annual vegetables, such as sweet peppers, tomatoes or broccoli, that are planted individually, should be limited to one seedling per pot or module. An extra seedling may look like a bargain, but it's easy to damage both plants if you attempt to separate them, and the vigour

FOOLPROOF VEGETABLES

There is really no such thing as a "foolproof" vegetable. They all need good soil preparation and regular care. But there are some relatively easy-to-grow crops that make good confidence builders for the novice gardener. Some of the most dependable are listed below, along with some growing hints.

Bean, runner Needs supports.
Beetroot Keep soil evenly moist.
Garlic Plant autumn, harvest summer.
Lettuce Best in cool weather.
Onion Grow from young bulbs, or "sets".
Radish Sow from spring.
Squash, summer Apply compost.
Swiss chard Pick leaves regularly.
Tomato, cherry Needs ample water.

MINIATURE AND BABY VEGETABLES

Experienced gardeners know that the biggest vegetables are not always the tastiest. In some cases, gourmet baby vegetables are full-sized cultivars harvested young. Others are naturally small. Try some of these.

Aubergine Pick up to 10 cm (4 in) long; any cultivar.

Beans Pick pods when 6 mm (¼ in) wide; any cultivar.

Beetroot Pull when beetroot is about 2.5 cm (1 in) in diameter; try 'Pablo', but any cultivar will do.

Carrot Pull when roots are coloured; 'Mini Finger', 'Mignon'.

Cauliflower Pick when heads are young.

Courgette Pick fruit at any size; 'Bush Champion', 'Crystal Lemon'.

Cucumber Pick when 5–15 cm (2–6 in) long; any cultivar.

Garlic Pick while young before clove development. Serve as you would baby leeks or roast and squeeze onto bruschetta.

Leek Can be picked while very young and cooked whole.

Lettuce Harvest small, young leaves as needed; sow different cultivars together or choose loose-leaf lettuce such as 'Salad Bowl'.

Melon Choose quick-ripening cultivars, such as 'Edonis'.

Onion Pull young for spring onions; pickling onions have small bulbs.

Pea Pick when pods are 5–7.5 cm (2–3 in) long; any cultivar.

Pumpkin Choose small-fruited cultivars; 'Baby Bear'.

Squash Pick at 10 cm (4 in) or longer; 'Patty Pan'.

Sweet pepper Pick small peppers as needed; any cultivar.

Sweet corn Pick tiny ears 2 days after silks appear, or choose small-fruited cultivars; any sweet corn cultivar will do.

Tomato Choose small-fruited cultivars; 'Gardener's Delight', 'Sungold'.

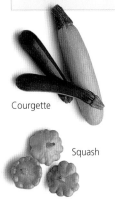

Courgette

Squash

of both will be reduced if you plant them together. Pots of vegetables such as cucumbers or pumpkins, which are usually planted on mounrds, should hold only a few small seedlings. Leafy crops, such as rocket or corn salad, aren't as fussy about spacing; they can be sown, planted and harvested in clumps.

The soil in the seedling pots should be moist, but not soggy. Roots should be well developed, but not so much that they've filled the pot. It's normal for a few threads of root to escape the pot, but avoid transplants with solid masses of tightly woven roots. Also check the seedlings for signs of insect pests or disease symptoms. The presence of beneficial insects, such as ladybirds, might indicate a recent pest problem, but it's better to take home the beneficials rather than the residue of pesticides. Look for webs, insect droppings or signs of damage, such as ragged holes or spotty leaves. Don't buy seedlings with discoloured or wilted leaves. Look for the plant labels, especially if you're unfamiliar with the seedling stages of vegetables. Closely related vegetables, such as broccoli, cauliflower and cabbage, look alike at this stage. If you're interested in a particular cultivar, shop early for the best selection or you might have to settle for unfamiliar cultivars. Most greenhouse

READY FOR ACTION

Keep your gardening kit in a handy carry-all and you won't need to search the house in your muddy boots.

growers have to limit how many cultivars they sow for space reasons. Consult a current seed catalogue if you have to choose an unfamiliar cultivar. A good nursery salesperson should be able to recommend the best for your garden.

Ask how the seedlings were grown. If you're strictly organic, look for growers who use composts, seeds, fertilizers and pest-control practices that conform to organic standards. If you can't find a source for organically grown seedlings and don't want to raise your own, you may have to settle for non-organic seedlings. At this stage, the amount of

CHOOSE STRONG PLANTS

Seedlings should look dark green and healthy. Avoid spindly plants that have not had enough light and those with discoloured leaves. These have been stressed in some way and will not perform as well as they should.

COOK THEM QUICKLY
Steaming, stir-frying and
microwaving do the best job
of preserving the vitamins in
your home-grown vegetables.

synthetic materials imported to your
garden is probably negligible. Also ask if
the seedlings have been hardened off
(gradually acclimatized to outdoor
conditions). If they have been in a warm
greenhouse or an air-conditioned supermarket, you'll have to introduce them
slowly to the outdoors (see page 65).

Once you get your seedlings home,
make sure that you keep them watered
if you are unable to transplant them to
the garden immediately. Place them out
of direct sun, keep a close eye on the
weather and be ready to bring them
indoors if a storm or frost threatens.

BARE-ROOT OR CONTAINER PLANTS?

Depending on when and where you buy,
your fruiting plants may be bare-root or
grown in containers. Bare-root plants are
sold when they're dormant (not actively
growing), without any soil around the
roots. This is the most practical way for
mail-order nurseries to ship plants,
but one disadvantage is that they are
available only at certain times of year
(usually late autumn and early spring).
Bare-root stock must be planted as soon
as possible after arrival.

Local nurseries most often sell their
plants growing in containers. The
disadvantages of container-grown plants
are that they tend to be more expensive

BARE-ROOT PLANTS
Check that the roots and
base of the plant are firm
and healthy looking, with no
unusual swellings (other than
the graft union near the base
of the main stem). Look for
clean, evenly coloured bark,
with no suspicious holes.

than bare-root stock, and you'll have a much more limited selection. On the plus side, though, container-grown plants are available throughout the year and can be planted any time the ground isn't frozen. If you can't plant them right away, you can keep them growing in their pots until you're ready to set them in the ground. Container stock is quite easy to plant, and it tends to have a lower failure rate than bare-root stock.

Don't Buy Problem Plants

Buying disease- and pest-resistant plants is important to the future health of your garden. But it's just as important to avoid buying plants that have problems right now. Otherwise, you might introduce serious problems, such as bacterial and viral diseases, that will affect all your crops. To reduce the risk, where possible, you could look for nurseries that offer certified disease-free plants. This means that the plants have been checked and approved by nursery inspectors.

Fast-Growers

Fast-maturing crops give the best chance for a good harvest in bad summers. They are also useful as "catch crops", to interplant between longer-term crops, as companion plants, or for successive sowing. Here are a few to try: beetroot, chicory (leafy types), Chinese cabbage, corn salad (lamb's lettuce, mâche), cress, kohlrabi, lettuce, mizuna greens, mustard, peas, radish, rocket, spinach.

CHOOSE THE BEST
It may take a few seasons to find the varieties you prefer, but it's well worth the search.

The first thing to check when buying seeds is the date on the packet. Buy fresh seeds and buy only enough for the current year, unless you're able to store seeds under the proper conditions— low moisture and low temperature. Seeds are sold by weight or number of seeds. Check how much you're getting in each packet. Shopping around is time-consuming, but worthwhile. Naturally, look for a reputable dealer because seeds can differ greatly in quality.

If you can find a source, it's even better to buy plants or seeds that are certified virus-free. These come from laboratories that test stock plants and grow only those that are virus-free. The stock plants are then sold to commercial nurseries, which propagate and grow them under controlled conditions that prevent virus infection. Virus-free plants are available for strawberries, as well as onion and shallot sets and seed potatoes.

CONTAINER VEGETABLES

If space is limited, consider using pots. Fill a suitable container with potting compost (not garden soil, which will pack down too tightly after watering). Compact or dwarf cultivars are generally the best choice. Try some of these: aubergine, bean (bush types), carrot (short-rooted cultivars), corn salad (lamb's lettuce, mâche), cucumber (bush cultivars), kale, lettuce, onion, pea (needs a trellis), radish, summer squash (bush cultivars), sweet pepper, Swiss chard (spinach beet), tomato, watercress.

CONTAINER-GROWN PLANTS

Check foliage is a bright, uniformly green colour. Check underneath leaves and at bases of stems for insects or egg clusters hidden there. If you find a problem, send the plant back or don't buy it; you don't want to risk spreading pests or diseases to your other plants.

SOWING SEEDS INDOORS

1. Take a tray with drainage holes and fill with moist, sifted seed compost. Press it firmly into the corners.

2. Level off the surface with a flat piece of wood, so the compost is 12 mm (½ in) below the rim of the container and won't wash over the edge.

3. Mark drills 5 cm (2 in) apart, or sprinkle seeds evenly over surface. Space small seeds 12 mm (½ in) apart, medium seeds 2.5 cm (1 in) apart.

4. Firm surface by pressing seeds lightly with a smooth wooden block. Press gently so seeds are in contact with compost, but not so hard as to bury them.

5. Sieve a light layer of compost over the surface. Do not cover seeds that need light to germinate. Spray with a fine mist of water.

6. Label and cover container with glass or plastic kitchen wrap. Check daily for first seedlings. To prevent disease, remove cover when seedlings appear.

Sowing Seeds

Sowing seeds indoors will get your seedlings off to a good start. Because you can control their environment, you can begin the new season earlier than when you plant outdoors.

Containers

Sow seeds in just about any container that has holes for drainage. Seedlings started in their own pots won't require potting up later. You can even purchase ready-to-use modules with cells for sowing single seeds. If you use biodegradable containers such as coir pots or pellets, you can plant the pot along with the plant. These are a good choice for those vegetables that transplant poorly, such as cucumbers.

Composts

New seedlings need a light, moist seed compost for a quick start. Fill containers with moistened, sifted, seed or sandy multipurpose compost. Once their true leaves have developed (after the first two seed leaves), the seedlings will require extra nutrients. Water them with a liquid organic fertilizer, such as seaweed solution, at half strength. Gradually increase the dose to full strength. Alternatively, transfer the seedlings to a soilless potting compost, or prepare a nourishing substitute by adding a little dry, organic fertilizer to each batch of home-made potting compost. Remember, the longer seedlings remain in pots, the more nutrients they need.

SPECIAL HANDLING

Seedlings in coir pots need special care. Tear a hole in each side of the pot before you plant it, so that the roots can make their way out. Then, tear away the upper collar of the pot, because exposed coir will act like a wick, drawing the moisture up and away from the roots of the seedling. Plant as you would a normal seedling, but plant pot and all.

1. Transplant seedlings in early evening or on cool, overcast days to protect them from sun.

2. Gently slide each seedling out of its container, keeping the soil and root ball intact.

3. Holding gently, plant seedling in a hole slightly wider, but the same depth, as container.

4. Replace soil around roots first, fill hole level with bed, gently firm the surface and water.

HARDENING OFF

At least 2 weeks before transplanting seedlings, begin watering less frequently and withhold fertilizer. A week before transplanting, move the young plants outdoors to a spot protected from strong light and wind. This allows them to adjust slowly to the extremes of temperature, wind and light. Gradually increase the time they spend outdoors. Within a week, they should be outdoors all the time. They'll need more water at this time, since sun and wind quickly dry the compost. Be prepared to bring them back indoors if a frost threatens.

Planting Outdoors

NO WASTE

Plant the seeds of leafy or root vegetables quite thickly and use the thinnings as tender, young additions to salads and stir-fries.

Some plants, such as beans, peas and root crops, do not transplant well. You'll get the best results by sowing these seeds directly into the garden.

Sowing Seed

1. Planting dates vary among species and cultivars, so check your seed packets or a catalogue. Ask local gardeners what is the expected date of the last frost for your area.

2. If you're planting in drills (rows), mark them with canes at both ends before planting. Stretch a length of string down the drill and use it as a guide to keep your drills straight while you plant. Transfer it from row to row as you go.

3. If you have raised beds, divide them into sections by plant cultivar, broadcast the seed over the appropriate section and label them, or simply sow your seed in drills across the raised bed.

4. Follow the spacing guidelines on the seed packet. Some packets indicate what length of drill the package will sow. Most sowing recommendations are higher than necessary, to account for areas that are less than ideal. If conditions are good for germination, you may have to thin your seedlings later.

5. Cover seeds with soil to a depth two to three times the seed diameter, then firm them by pressing the soil lightly with the flat side of a rake or hoe. Don't forget to label the row—it's easy to forget which seeds are sown in what row.

6. The soil should stay moist but not

soggy until your seeds begin to germinate. If you sow in dry weather, you may have to water to ensure good germination. If the soil at the sowing depth is moist when you sow large seeds, they should have sufficient moisture to germinate. Fine seeds may need extra moisture. If necessary, water the drill before you sow the seeds in it.

7. Once seedlings are growing well, thin them to the final plant spacing. Pull or snip off extras, leaving only the best.

8. Keep records of your plantings, and record the location of each vegetable on a rough map of your plot.

ROOM TO GROW

Once your young plants are well established, they may need to be thinned. Pull them out carefully, disturbing the plants next to them as little as possible, or pinch them off at soil level.

Frost Protection and Extending the Season

Season extension means getting a head start in the spring, and prolonging production in autumn, thus squeezing a little more time into each growing season.

Cold Frames

If you build your own cold frames, make the back taller than the front so that the glass light (lid) slants at an angle of about 45 degrees, for the best light. A frame measuring about 90 cm (3 ft) wide by 1.2 m (4 ft) long is a good size. It should be tall enough so your plants can grow in their pots or trays without touching the light. Attach the light at the back with hinges and prop it open with a piece of wood to allow for air circulation. Or the light can simply sit on the frame and you can slide it open when you need to reduce the temperature inside the frame. It's best if the interior is painted white, to reflect light onto your plants.

Keep plants or seedlings in their pots or trays in the frame—you'll find that containers are easier to manage in the small space.

Cloches

These can be made from fabric or transparent plastic, and they provide protection from all but the hardest frosts at night. Lightweight horticultural fleece, made from spun-bonded polyester or polypropylene, allows in water, light and

INDIVIDUAL PROTECTION
Covers such as this one made of corrugated plastic will keep frost off special plants, but glass or plastic bell cloches also work well.

COVER STORY
You can start growing in the garden earlier, and prolong your autumn harvest, if you use tunnel cloches to protect tender plants from frosts.

A COLD FRAME THROUGH THE SEASONS

In autumn, a cold frame will ensure the survival of your late-sown leafy crops, such as lettuce, until well after the first frost.

In winter, use your cold frame to give bulbs, such as golden shallots and garlic, a spell of cold treatment before forcing them on.

In spring, harden off your seedlings in the cold frame before transplanting them out in the garden.

INTERPLANTING

The different growth habits and nutrient needs of lettuce and onions make them ideal candidates for interplanting. This way you get twice the yield from the same space.

HARVEST MANAGEMENT

Successive sowings, about 10–14 days apart, of crops such as dwarf beans will provide you with a continuous harvest. As one planting finishes bearing, the next becomes ready to pick.

air but keeps insects at bay. You can also use open-topped cloches or horticultural fleece as barriers to stop low-flying pests such as carrot root fly.

Plastic cloches will keep plants and soil warmer than fleece. Since heat builds up on sunny days, you'll need to ventilate them during the day. You can also make a tunnel cloche by stretching plastic sheet or horticultural fleece over wire hoops inserted in the soil on opposite sides of the bed or row. You can buy the supports and covering together.

In a smaller garden, protect individual plants (instead of rows) from frost. Many different types of material are used to make cloches.

SUCCESSIVE SOWING

Successive sowing means harvesting two crops from the same space in one season, by planting the second crop after you've harvested the first. Determine the length of your growing season by counting the days between the average date of the last spring frost and the average date of the first autumn frost. Then select two vegetables whose combined days to maturity fit that limit. Sow or transplant the first crop in early spring, then harvest it and replant with the second crop in midsummer. Between crops, prepare the soil as needed but avoid digging.

By midsummer, most weed seeds have germinated, and digging will only bring more seeds to the surface. You can add compost before the second sowing, or after planting, as a mulch. Timing is the challenge. Each crop must get off to a quick start and finish. Good choices for quick crops to grow in spring and autumn are: beetroots, carrots, chicory, endive, kale, kohlrabi, mustard greens, radish, rocket, shallots, spinach and Swiss chard.

GOOD COMPANIONS

Artichokes and plants of the onion family are light feeders, so they will thrive in the same conditions.

Whatever you use, make sure the covering allows enough light and ventilation. Garden centres offer many choices. Or make your own cloches from plastic milk containers. Cut along three sides of the base so the base forms a flap that can be used to anchor it. Leave the top open during the day. Use until danger of frost is past.

Favourite Fruits and Nuts at a Glance

CROP NAME	EXPOSURE	SOIL FERTILITY	HARDINESS	HEIGHT	SPREAD
Almond	Full sun; sheltered spot	Average to fertile soil	Hardy	4.5–9 m (15–30 ft)	4.5–9 m (15–30 ft)
Apple	Full sun	Average soil; well drained	Hardy	2.4–9 m (8–30 ft)	2.4–9 m (8–30 ft)
Apricot	Full sun; against a sheltered wall	Moisture-retentive soil; well drained	Hardy	2.4–7.2 m (8–24 ft)	4.8–7.2 (16–24 ft)
Blackberry	Full sun to light shade	Most soils	Hardy	1.2–2.1 m (4–7 ft)	0.9–1.8 (3–6 ft)
Blueberry	Full sun or partial shade	Light, acid, moist soil	Frost-hardy	0.6–4.5 m (2–15 ft)	0.9–3 m (3–10 ft)
Cherry, acid or sour	Full sun or cool wall	Well drained, fairly deep soil	Frost-hardy	2.4–6 m (8–20 ft)	2.4–6 m (8–20 ft)
Cherry, sweet	Full sun	Well drained, fairly deep soil	Frost-hardy	4.5–9 m (15–30 ft)	4.5–9 m (15–30 ft)
Citrus	Full sun to light shade	Rich, loam-based compost	Tender	3–9 m (10–30 ft)	3–9 m (10–30 ft)
Currants, red or white	Full sun	Well drained, rich soil	Hardy	1.5–1.8 m (5–6 ft)	1–2 m (90–180)
Fig	Full sun; shelter	Average to poor soil	Frost-hardy; needs shelter	3–7.5 m (10–25 ft)	3–7.5 m (10–25 ft)
Gooseberry	Full sun to light shade	Most soils	Hardy	0.9–2.1 m (3–7 ft)	0.9–2.1 (3–7 ft)
Grape	Full sun or greenhouse	Average to rich soil	Hardy, but fruits are not	1.2–1.8 m (4–6 ft)	2.4–4.5 (8–15 ft)
Hazelnut	Full sun to light shade	Average to poor soil	Hardy	5–6 m (15–20 ft)	5 m (15 ft)
Kiwi	Full sun; shelter or greenhouse	Deep, rich soil	Frost-hardy; warm shelter	1.2–1.8 m (4–6 ft)	4.5 m (15 ft)
Mulberry	Full sun	Average soil	Hardy	4.5–9 m (15–30 ft)	3–6 m (10–20 f)
Peach	Full sun; shelter or greenhouse	Well drained but moist soil	Hardy	2.4–4.5 m (8–15 ft)	3–6 m (10–20 f)
Pear	Full sun; shelter	Average soil	Hardy	2.4–6 m (8–20 ft)	2.4–6 m (8–20 ft)
Plum	Full sun; shelter	Best in deep clay soil	Hardy	2.4–6 m (8–20 ft)	2.4–6 m (8–20 ft)
Raspberry	Full sun	Well drained soil; not chalk	Hardy, but fruits are not	1.2–1.8 m (4–6 ft)	0.6–1.2 (2–4 ft)
Strawberry	Full sun	Average to rich soil	Hardy	25 cm (10 in)	30–60 cm (1–2 ft)

A handy reference to 20 of the most popular fruits and nuts for planting in home gardens. Remember that some cultivars may have slightly different needs.

BLOOM TIME	HARVEST TIME	USES AND STORAGE	POLLINATION
Early spring	Midsummer to autumn	Eat fresh; dry for storage	Cross- and self-pollinated
Mid- to late spring	Midsummer to autumn	Eat fresh; keep for several months in cool, dark place or preserve	Cross-pollinated
Late winter to early spring	Early summer	Eat fresh; keep a week or two in refrigerator; dry; or preserve	Self-pollinated
Late spring	Late summer	Eat fresh; keep a week or two in refrigerator; or preserve	Self-pollinated
Mid-spring	Mid- to late summer	Eat fresh; keep a few days in refrigerator; or preserve	Cross- and self-pollinated
Mid-spring	Midsummer	Eat fresh; keep a few days in refrigerator; or preserve	Most are self-pollinated
Mid-spring	Midsummer	Eat fresh; keep a few days in refrigerator; or preserve	Cross-pollinated
Varies	Varies	Eat fresh; keep a week or two in refrigerator; make into marmalade	Self-pollinated
Spring	Early to late summer	Eat fresh; keep a few days in refrigerator; preserve	Self-pollinated
Varies	Varies	Eat fresh; keep a few days in refrigerator; dry; or freeze	Self-pollinated
Mid-spring	Midsummer	Eat fresh; keep a week or two in refrigerator; or preserve	Self-pollinated
Mid-spring	Midsummer to autumn	Eat fresh; keep a week or two in refrigerator; or preserve	Self-pollinated
Early spring	Late summer to autumn	Eat fresh; keep for weeks in refrigerator; or freeze	Cross-pollinated
Mid-spring	Autumn	Eat fresh; keep for several weeks in refrigerator; or preserve	Cross-pollinated
Spring	Mid- to late summer	Eat fresh; freeze; dry; or preserve	Self-pollinated
Late winter to early spring	Midsummer	Eat fresh; keep a week or two in refrigerator; or preserve	Self-pollinated
Early to mid-spring	Late summer to autumn	Eat fresh; keep for several weeks in refrigerator; or preserve	Cross-pollinated
Early to mid-spring	Midsummer	Eat fresh; keep a week or two in refrigerator; or preserve	Cross- and self-pollinated
Midspring	Midsummer to autumn	Eat fresh; keep a few days in refrigerator; or preserve	Self-pollinated
Early summer to autumn	Autumn	Eat fresh; keep a few days in refrigerator; or preserve	Self-pollinated

Planting Your Fruit Garden

It's always exciting when planting day arrives. All the effort you've put into choosing the best cultivars, deciding where to put them and preparing the soil will pay off now as you put in your plants.

Alpine strawberry

When to Plant

Autumn and early winter, when the soil is still warm, are good times to plant most fruit and nut crops. This gives the plants time to develop good root systems before the growing season starts next year. Dormant, bare-root, mail-order plants arrive in early to late autumn; some nurseries also offer root-balled plants. Nurseries and garden centres may also offer container-grown plants, which are best planted from early autumn to spring, although they may be available in summer as well.

If you have light, well-drained soil and winters that aren't severely cold, you can plant crops like apricots, currants, gooseberries, and hardy grapes in autumn, but if you have cold, waterlogged soil in winter, save the rest of your planting for spring.

Otherwise, the planting season extends well into winter. Bare-root gooseberries go in the ground from autumn to late winter and strawberries are best planted in spring, late summer or autumn, according to type.

Planting

Bare-root mail-order plants need to be planted as soon as possible after they arrive, so prepare the planting site in

If you cannot plant a bare-root fruit bush or tree immediately, "heel it in" by placing the roots in a shallow trench and covering them with soil.

STRAWBERRY BEDS

Set out your strawberries in rows that will allow easy access for cultivation and harvesting. Finish the job by applying a thick layer of organic mulch that will gradually break down and enrich the soil.

advance—preferably in autumn—so it will be ready when your plants come. If the plants are put in the ground while they are dormant, they will be well established before the heat of summer.

If you don't have the time to deal with your bare-root plants when they arrive or if the weather in your area is very wet or still dropping well below freezing at night, you may need to keep the plants under cover for a few days. Keep the roots moist and don't let them dry out. Alternatively, heel them in: draw out a shallow trench in a spare patch of ground, place the plants in at an angle and cover over all the roots to keep them moist.

If you buy your plants locally, they'll most likely be growing in containers. While it's ideal to plant them promptly as well, container-grown fruit trees, shrubs or climbers are much more forgiving of delays than bare-root plants, as long as you keep them well watered.

SEASONAL INTEREST
Choose dwarf or semi-dwarf fruit trees instead of purely ornamental trees if your space is limited. You will enjoy the display of spring blossom, followed by an edible harvest.

PLANTING BARE-ROOT PLANTS

If you've never seen a bare-root plant before, you might be surprised when you unpack your box from the nursery. Bare-root plants are just what they sound like—tentacle-like, naked roots topped with bare branches or merely a single stem. They can look rather pathetic, but as long as you bought the plants from a reputable nursery and give them proper care, they will grow beautifully. (If you lose plants right after transplanting, which is not all that uncommon, contact the nursery for a refund or replacement.)

USING VERTICAL SPACE
Choose standard forms, such as this gooseberry, if your garden is small.

To get bare-root plants off to a good start:

1. When you're ready to plant, cut off any sickly, damaged or very long roots. Leave healthy roots alone. Give most fruit and nut plants, except blueberries, a pre-planting booster by

soaking their roots in a bucket of compost tea (see page 34). Soak the roots of strawberries and grapes for 20 minutes; soak bush and tree roots for 2 hours.

2. Dig a hole deep enough to hold the roots without curling them up at the ends. Slice into the walls of the hole with a spade to make them easy for roots to penetrate. Make a mound of soil in the centre of the hole and firm it well.

3. Remove the roots from compost tea. Put the crown of plant (where the roots

FOR A SMALLER GARDEN
Dwarf cultivars, like this peach tree, do well in planters that are at least 60 cm (2 ft) wide and 90 cm (3 ft) deep.

PLANTING BARE-ROOT TREES AND BUSHES

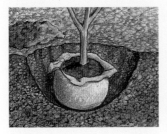

Dig a wide, shallow planting hole and slash the sides with the spade so roots can spread easily.

For bareroot plants, spread the roots over a mound of soil in the centre of your planting hole.

With root-balled plants, set plant in hole so base of stem is level with the soil surface.

Fill hole, gently firm down soil and water to wet the soil thoroughly and settle it around the roots.

come together and shoots emerge) on top of the soil mound in the hole.

4. Check that the crown or graft union is level with the surface of the soil. If your soil tends to sink slightly as it settles, you may want to elevate the plant a little to adjust. If your plant sits too high or too low on the soil mound, lift it out, change the height of the mound and try again.

5. When you have the right crown or graft height, spread out the roots evenly over the soil mound. Holding the plant with one hand, fill in around the roots with the soil you removed from the hole. When the hole is half-filled, add some water so the planting site is thoroughly soaked; then finish filling the hole. Firm the soil gently and add a plant label.

QUARTERING

To loosen a tight root ball, use a knife to make four deep cuts through the base of the ball. Spread the quartered root ball over a cone of good soil, fill the planting hole and water.

SPACE-SAVER

Multi-graft trees can bear many different fruits, saving space and the effort needed to look after several separate trees.

PLANTS IN CONTAINERS

To remove a plant from a pot, squeeze the sides of a plastic pot to loosen, or invert a rigid pot and tap the rim gently, supporting the plant with your hand so that it doesn't fall out and break.

PLANTING PLANTS FROM CONTAINERS

1. Dig a hole the same depth as the pot, leaving the soil in the bottom of the hole undisturbed. If your soil is very heavy (clay) or light (sandy), dig some well-rotted garden compost or other organic matter into the area around the planting hole.

2. Double-check that your plant will sit at the proper level. If you lay a cane across the hole and measure from the cane to the bottom of the hole with a stick, you can judge the right depth without having to lift the heavy plant in and out of the hole.

3. Remove the plant from its pot by putting one hand on the surface of the compost to support the top. Then put your other hand under the container, squeezing the sides gently to separate it from the roots. Turn the pot upside-down and slide the plant out.

4. If the plant has been growing in the pot for a long time, the roots will be matted on the outside of the root ball. Loosen circling roots with your fingers and cut into the root mass a little.

5. Set the plant in the hole, spreading loose roots in different directions so each has its own space. Refill the hole with soil and water thoroughly.

Part Four

MANAGING YOUR GARDEN

GARDEN CARE FOR FOUR SEASONS

PATIO BOUNTY
Container-grown plants on even a tiny, sunny patio can produce a surprising harvest.

Being organized about your garden tasks reduces the work. Follow this simple guide to doing jobs at the right time and your crops will thrive, rewarding your efforts with abundant produce.

WINTER
Winter is as important as any other season. The planning you do on long winter nights will help prevent problems later on. This is the time to decide what you want to grow and how much you are going to plant. As you search through seed catalogues, look for high-yielding cultivars that are insect- or disease-resistant, so you'll have fewer pest problems to cope with. Order seeds and save yourself a trip to the garden centre later on. This is also a good time to plan your planting schedule.

SPRING
The weather's getting warmer and your garden beds and soil are prepared (see page 28). But before you start digging and planting, take a few minutes to review the plans you made during the winter. Check your planting schedule to see what crops should go in first. Get out the seeds you ordered, or take your shopping list to the garden centre and

POTAGER GARDEN
A clump of eschscholzia adds a spot of vivid colour to a mixed vegetable and herb garden.

PLANNING PAYS OFF
Think about where the shade will be so that taller plants don't rob smaller ones of precious sunlight. Mulching reduces the need for water and keeps weeds down.

buy the seeds, seedlings and other supplies you need. Don't be tempted to buy extra plants or plants that aren't on your list. You'll end up either cramming the extras in with the others or digging new beds to accommodate them.

SUMMER

This season is the time that your winter planning and spring planting pay off. As your vegetables and fruits mature in the warm summer weather, a little extra attention can keep yields high and routine maintenance minimal.

Mulches are the cornerstone of good gardening (see page 50). They help keep critical moisture in the soil and moderate temperature extremes for better root growth. They reduce weeding chores by smothering weed seeds and stop soil from splashing onto plants, which reduces the spread of soil-borne diseases and keeps the produce cleaner. And as they break down, organic mulches release a balanced supply of plant nutrients and add organic matter to improve the structure of the soil. Mulches also save water, but not enough that you can forget about watering (see page 94).

AUTUMN

As the lower temperatures arrive, many plants that took a break during the summer heat may make

FRESH FOR THE TABLE
You can pick your vegetables just before the meal.

SUNNY CORNERS
You'll be surprised at what a good supply of fresh vegetables can be produced, with forward planning, in even a tiny space, especially if it is sunny and sheltered.

new growth or set more fruit. Late-summer plantings of crops such as peas and lettuce can yield well into autumn. Once your crops are done for the season, spend a few minutes putting the garden to bed so that it will be ready for spring planting next season. In addition to making it look tidier during the winter, picking up dead plants and dropped vegetable matter eliminates hiding places for insect eggs and disease pathogens.

Check over your garden tools and have any that need sharpening attended to. Wash and dry your tools and apply a light coating of oil before storing them. While you're at it, pull up and clean off any metal or wooden stakes and store them so they don't rust or rot.

MANAGING THE VEGETABLE GARDEN

Carrots and celery

Y ou can stick a few tomato plants in a corner and get a few fruits. But if you want to get the best harvests you've ever had, it's worth preparing the site and maintaining your plants properly.

PREPARING THE SOIL FOR VEGETABLES

In general, vegetables will thrive in normal, healthy garden soil with good drainage. Most grow best in a soil that is slightly acid or neutral (about pH 6.5–7.0). Vegetables that like the nutrient balance in alkaline soil include asparagus, melon, spinach and Swiss chard. If your soil is too acid or alkaline, you may need to adjust the pH by adding lime or sulphur.

Most vegetable crops will thrive in soils with a texture somewhere in the "loam" range: sandy loams, silt loams and even clay loams. Very loose, sandy soils with few rocks are ideal for root crops like carrots, beetroots and parsnips. Celery and members of the cabbage family, such as cauliflower, cabbage and broccoli,

SPECIAL NEEDS

Some vegetables have more specific nutrient needs than just "more of everything". Cucurbits (cucumbers, melons and squashes) require adequate magnesium. Garlic, onions and tomatoes thrive with extra potassium and phosphorus, but don't need much nitrogen. In fact, too much nitrogen will keep tomatoes from bearing fruit. To make sure your plants get just what they need, a soil test (see pages 28 and 29) will be invaluable. That way, you'll know if your soil is deficient or if it is adequately supplied with the necessary nutrients.

can handle wetter soils that are more on the clay side. Of course, working in ample amounts of organic matter can make almost any soil suitable.

If you're starting a new site, strip off the existing turf, spread a 2.5-cm (1-in) layer of compost over the area, and dig or fork over the top 15–20 cm (6–8 in). If you've planted an existing garden with a cover crop or green manure, dig or turn it in at least 2–3 weeks before planting. Or, if you mulched the soil for winter, rake off the mulch or work it in to let the soil warm up. If you're growing root crops, make sure you dig the soil deeply and remove

HEAD START

There's a small extra cost involved in buying plug plants that are ready to be set out, and a more limited selection of cultivars to choose from, but you can save yourself a lot of time.

NATURAL CONTROLS

Growing flowers and herbs in your vegetable garden will help to attract beneficial, pest-eating insects. Few pests do enough damage to reduce your harvest noticeably. If you control pest insects without using poisons, you'll encourage beneficial insects that prey on them and keep their populations in check.

any rocks or clods that could impede good root development. Before planting, rake the soil to remove surface stones and clods.

FEEDING

Many gardeners make a science out of feeding, but it doesn't have to be so complex.

There are two approaches to feeding vegetables (well, three, if you count not feeding at all, which isn't very practical if you want good yields). The easiest way is to treat all your vegetables the same. Feed the vegetable garden each year, before planting, with a balanced material such as well-rotted garden compost or a commercial general-purpose fertilizer. For a mid-season boost, top-dress with a granular fertilizer scratched lightly into the soil near the roots. Or give all of the plants a monthly dose of liquid seaweed

UNFINISHED BUSINESS
If your sweet peppers stop producing in midsummer, don't pull them up. They may set more fruit when the slightly cooler autumn weather arrives.

SPACE SAVERS
If space is limited, look for bush or compact cultivars of squashes and other favourite crops. You'll get high yields from just a few plants in a small garden.

SIMPLIFY THE WORK
Plan your vegetable garden so that plants with similar water and nutrient needs are grouped together.

solution. The other approach is to feed each plant to meet its needs. This customized fertilizing is worth the trouble if you want to get extra-high yields or if you garden intensively (where closely spaced plants need extra nutrients).

GETTING BETTER HARVESTS

Beans To get a steady supply of dwarf beans, plant successive crops at 7- to 10-day intervals. Or try climbing beans—they grow tall, so you must set up a tripod of stakes for them to twine around, but they'll produce for a long season from a single planting and they're easy to pick.

Broccoli Look for cultivars like 'Belstar' and 'Fiesta' that will produce smaller sideshoots after you harvest the main head.

Carrots Sow thickly and harvest the thinnings for eating each week.

Cucumbers If space is limited and you want a high yield of cucumbers, choose bush cultivars to plant.

Lettuce If summer heat makes early sowings bolt and run to seed, try late-summer plantings for harvesting well into autumn.

Peas Peas stop producing as soon as any seed pods ripen, so keep picking the pods to keep the plant producing new ones.

Squash Choose bush cultivars for a high yield from a small space.

Sweet corn Plant successive crops every 7–10 days for a more even yield.

Easy-care Fruit Trees and Soft Fruit

BERRY DELIGHT
Besides their white spring flowers, blueberries often produce outstanding autumn colour, which makes them attractive as ornamentals.

Growing fruit is slightly more complicated than growing vegetables, but the rewards can make it all worthwhile. If you really want low maintenance, stick with the simplest fruit crops.

CANE FRUITS

Cane fruits, such as raspberries and blackberries, are easily grown, and plants can live as long as 10 years, so prepare the site carefully. They need full sun and should be planted far from wild relatives, which might carry disease. Choose a well-drained site or build a raised bed.

To save space and make harvesting easier, train the canes on a trellis. The double-armed T is an easy system. At either end of the bed, set in two vertical posts as tall as the mature plant will be. On each post, attach two horizontal bars, one in the middle and one at the top. Run a wire from the top corner of one crossbar to the top corner of the other. Repeat for the other side and for the lower crossbars. For easy access, remove the wires when it's time to prune.

BLUEBERRY BASICS

Blueberry plants don't bear fruit until they're 3 or 4 years old, but if you're willing to wait, you can enjoy them as ornamentals in the meantime. All species need a moist but loose-textured soil high in organic matter. Most blueberries are not self-fertile, so you'll need to plant at least two, and preferably three, cultivars that can cross-pollinate for good fruit set.

STRAWBERRIES MADE SIMPLE

Summer-fruiting strawberries produce just one big crop. Perpetual strawberries produce smaller crops intermittently until mid-autumn. Both types spread by baby plants, on runners from the parent plant,

LONG-SEASON HARVESTS

Spread your apple harvests by choosing cultivars that flower at the same time (to aid pollination), but mature at different times. 'Sunset' and 'Ashmead's Kernel', for example, will provide you with apples from late summer until well into autumn.

that put down roots. A space-saving planting method is the matted row system. Start with the plants in rows 1.2 m (4 ft) apart. Within the rows, space summer-fruiting cultivars every 45 cm (18 in) and perpetual cultivars every 30 cm (12 in). For easier harvesting, limit the bed to three rows, leaving enough room at the front, back and sides for runners.

Pinch the flowers off summer-fruiting plants the first year, so they put energy into their roots. For perpetuals, pinch off flowers only until the start of summer. Throughout the season, let the runners fill in with new plants wherever they take root. In autumn, keep the plants

PEACH AND NECTARINE
While frosts can spoil the blossom, both these fruit trees need winter chilling if they are to flower properly. Don't plant in soil where a similar tree grew recently, as the decaying roots emit a chemical that can kill the new tree roots.

ESPALIER TRAINING
While this takes patience and careful pruning, the result is beautiful, saving precious space in the garden and allowing unequalled access to the crop, be it apples, peaches, pears or whatever.

watered to increase the next year's crop. Mulch with straw to a depth of 5–7.5 cm (2–3 in) in order to prevent winter damage.

The second summer after planting, rejuvenate the bed right after harvest by setting your lawn mower at 6 cm (2½ in) and mowing over the whole bed. Rake up the debris, then narrow the width of each row to 30 cm (12 in) by digging or turning under the plants on the edges. Spread compost over the bed, and water the plants well to encourage new growth.

Depending on how healthy and productive your cultivar is, you can get 3 years or more of harvest. To ensure an ongoing supply, start a new bed in a different spot every 2–3 years. When you are finished with the first bed, dig it under and plant it with another crop until the new bed is exhausted.

FRESH IS BEST

Fig trees are very productive and generally easy to grow, although they need a long, hot summer for the fruit to ripen. You may have to net your tree to keep the birds off.

SPECIAL NEEDS OF SOME FRUITING CROPS

Blueberries Adjust soil pH levels to fall between 4.5–5.2 for best growth. Blueberries have shallow roots that are easily damaged by cultivation, so mulch deeply instead. Alternatively, if you have alkaline soil, grow them in ericaceous (lime-free) compost in containers, but take care to keep the compost moist.

Cranberries These soft fruits like very moist, acid (lime-free) soil. You can provide this by lining a hollow with black plastic, punctured for drainage, and filling it with ericaceous compost or acid topsoil.

Grapes These are heavy feeders, so mulch well around the vines with plenty of well-rotted compost or manure. Test for potassium regularly and add as needed. Grapes do best in soil that has a pH of between 5.0–6.0.

Peaches and nectarines These heavy feeders don't have extensive roots, so remove all turf from the root zone and keep the trees well mulched. Mix bonemeal into the planting hole.

EFFECTIVE WATERING

When rainfall is lacking, you'll need to provide water to keep your plants growing strongly and producing well. There are many different ways you can supply this water to your garden.

DRIP IRRIGATION SYSTEMS
Be careful if you design this type of system yourself—it's easy to make a mistake. You can eliminate errors by having a professional design the system, based on your garden plan. If the emitters wet only one side of a plant, the roots will grow lopsided.

HAND-WATERING

This is most useful for settling in seedlings and irrigating vegetables in containers or in very small gardens. It's also a handy way to spot-treat wilting plants until you can give a more thorough watering. Hand-watering is not ideal for established plants, since it usually can't supply enough water to soak slowly into the soil.

OVERHEAD WATERING

While sprinklers are common irrigation tools, they're not efficient. Only a small part of the water reaches the crops that need it. Sprinklers also provide an ideal environment for diseases that are spread on wet leaves.

SEEP HOSES

It's much more effective to provide water at ground level. Run a seep hose (which leaks droplets or fine sprays of moisture along its length) next to a single-row planting or between a

Water enough to keep your plants growing, but not so much that roots become oxygen starved. For most soils, one good soaking is better than several shallow sprinkles. While hand-watering is useful to revive wilting plants, there are better long-term options.

Conserving Water

Group vegetables with low, medium and high water needs and water sections individually.

Use a water butt to catch water off your roof and siphon it to your garden with a length of hose.

Cover soil with organic mulch, which holds water like a sponge.

Control weeds that rob your plants of water.

Protect your plants from drying winds.

double-row planting. This will moisten the planting area without benefiting nearby weeds. Weave or loop flexible rubber or plastic seep hoses in and out among clumps of plants. Canvas and rigid rubber hoses work best when run in straight lines.

Drip Irrigation

These have a customized network of hoses or pipes engineered to carry a specific amount of water to any given place in the garden. They use special emitters that let the water seep out to the rooting area of each plant or plant grouping, soaking the soil deeply.

Pruning Basics for Fruit Crops

Pruning is probably the most daunting part of fruit-tree care for novices. It takes practice, and you will probably make a few mistakes, but as plants are very forgiving, these are rarely fatal.

Making the Right Pruning Cuts

Each pruning cut you make affects the plant differently and helps you to direct its growth. With just two different kinds of cuts, you can shape practically any fruiting plant as you wish. Once you understand these two cuts, you're well on your way to pruning success.

Thinning cuts open the tree to sunlight. They are especially valuable for rejuvenating older, overgrown fruit trees,

PRUNING BASICS
A pruning saw, a very sharp budding knife and secateurs are the absolute basics. Substantial gloves will save your hands from accidental damage. The narrow blade of the pruning saw gives good access to tight spaces.

A VERY USEFUL TOOL
Branch loppers have long handles that extend your reach significantly. They can cut branches up to 2.5 cm (1 in) in diameter.

REMOVING LARGE BRANCHES

1. Make a cut half-way through from underneath, about 30 cm (12 in) from the trunk.

2. Make the next cut from above, about 2.5 cm (1 in) farther out; the branch will break off.

3. Finish with a clean, straight cut just outside the branch base (the collar).

CLEAN CUTS

Loppers, shears and secateurs are handy for cutting back climbers and clump-forming weeds. Such plants are effectively weakened by having to use their reserves of nutrients to replace the foliage you have cut off.

A THINNED TREE

Use thinning cuts to shorten overly long branches, clear out crowded growth, remove a branch that crosses or rubs another, or take out dead and diseased wood.

where you want to remove a number of smaller branches and suckers and leave the larger branches. To thin a too-long or poorly placed branch, cut it back to the ground, to a side branch or to a shoot that's growing in an uncrowded or desired direction. If you cut back to the trunk or to another branch, make the cut outside the slanted branch collar that forms a swelling at the base of the branch.

Tip-pruning cuts remove shoot tips, encouraging buds farther back on the stem to break. You can choose the best new shoots to become main branches on a young tree or to provide productive new growth on older trees (especially peaches and nectarines). In most cases, it's best when tip-pruning to cut just above a bud to avoid leaving a stub.

CHOOSING PRUNING TOOLS

A few good tools will make your pruning sessions easier. Here's the basic tool collection you'll need to maintain your fruiting trees, shrubs and climbers, along with some tips on how to use them.

THE KINDEST CUT

If you prune and train your young fruit trees carefully, you can eliminate the need to take out large branches later on. This is a big help, since removing big branches leaves wounds that are easy marks for pests and diseases. But if disease, damage or some other dilemma requires you to remove a large branch, see the three-step approach on page 97, or hire a professional tree surgeon to do the job— for your safety and the health of your tree.

Secateurs are used for cutting shoots less than 13 mm (½ in) in diameter.

Loppers (basically secateurs with very long handles) are useful for cutting stems up to about 2.5 cm (1 in) in diameter, depending on the model you buy. The long handles make pruning thorny-stemmed plants much more pleasant, since your hands will be farther away from the thorns.

Pruning saws are perfect for cutting branches larger than 2.5 cm (1 in) in diameter, especially in tight spaces.

Extendable pruners are handy if you need to prune branches farther than your normal reach. They have either shear-type blades or a saw blade (or sometimes both) on a pole 1.2–1.8 m (4–6 ft) long.

SECATEURS

Choose the "bypass" kind, with two curved blades that cut like scissors; they cut more cleanly than the straight-edged blade-and-anvil types. If you are cutting back thorny blackberries, raspberries or gooseberries, look for cut-and-hold bypass shears that grip the trimmings so they're easy to pull out.

DEALING WITH PESTS AND DISEASES

The best pest controls are specific, safe, easy and effective. If your garden plants are bothered by pests, choose control methods that target the pests and not other organisms.

PROPER IDENTIFICATION

This is the first step toward successful pest control. Consult a book on how to identify garden pests, or submit insect or disease samples to advisory bodies such as the Royal Horticultural Society (RHS). Then select controls that are environmentally safe.

SAFE CONTROLS

Larvae of the cabbage white butterfly (top) and aphids (bottom) can be knocked off your plants with a forceful jet of water. Or pick off these and other pests by hand early on cool mornings, when they are sluggish.

RESISTANCE

One of the easiest ways to avoid problems is to choose cultivars that are designed to resist the pests that plague your vegetables. Plant breeders have developed an array of new cultivars that are able to defend themselves against specific diseases and insect pests. Find out which conditions could be a problem and look for resistant cultivars in catalogues and garden centres.

WEEKLY INSPECTION

Check leaves, flowers and stems for signs of insects or pathogens at least once a week. In large stands, examine three to five plants at three different locations. Become familiar with insect life cycles so you'll recognize resting (egg and cocoon) and active (larva and adult) stages.

COMMON VEGETABLE PESTS AND DISEASES

PEST	DAMAGE	PREVENTION AND CONTROL
Snails and slugs	Seedlings eaten, irregular holes in leaves.	Place shallow containers of beer in garden, or trap pests under boards.
Aphids	Foliage wilted or curled, deformed buds and flowers.	A short, sharp spray of water from the hose will dislodge them. Spray with fatty acids.
Cabbage whitefly	Leaves yellow and sticky.	Use horticultural fleece or spray with fatty acids or pyrethrum.
Carrot root fly	Carrot roots eaten.	Rotate carrot plantings. Use cloches or horticultural fleece. Plant crops in late spring to minimize the damage.
Cutworms	Plant stem chewed at soil surface.	Place cardboard or plastic cutworm collars around the stems of the plants. Control weeds around the crop to reduce the population. Add parasitic nematodes to the soil at least a week before planting.
Leaf miners	Winding or large, blotchy lines on leaves, especially those of beetroots, spinach and tomatoes.	Use tunnel cloches. Pick off and destroy infected leaves. Control adults with yellow sticky traps.
Frit fly	Tunnels in sweet corn stalks and ears.	Raise seedlings under cover and plant out after egg-laying season ie. after early summer.
Flea beetle	Chewed foliage.	Eliminate weeds. Use tunnel cloches or horticultural fleece. Spray with bifenthrin.
Red spider mite	Discolouration and bronzing of the foliage.	Use a fatty acid spray or a biological control (predatory mite *Phytoseiulus persimilis*) on crops under cover.
DISEASE	**DAMAGE**	**PREVENTION AND CONTROL**
Powdery mildew	Downy patches on foliage.	Provide good air circulation. Control weeds. Spray foliage with compost tea.
Damping off	Seedlings weaken and collapse because of rot at soil line.	Sow seeds in well-drained compost. Avoid overwatering, crowding and poor air circulation. Disinfect re-used pots and seed trays.
Rust	Rust-coloured powder on the leaves.	Plant resistant cultivars. Provide good air circulation. Remove infected leaves.
Wilt (Fusarium and Verticillium)	Leaves yellow, plant gradually wilts.	Rotate crops. Plant resistant cultivars. Destroy infected plants.

Dealing with Weeds

A weed is any plant growing where you don't want it. What plant it is doesn't matter, but where it is does. Although any plant can be a weed, some plants are considered weeds more often than others.

Plan a Weed-control Strategy

To control your lawn and garden weeds effectively and efficiently, you need to use the right technique at the right time. This requires an essential piece of knowledge: how long do your particular weeds live?

Annual Weeds Are Spread by Seed

Annual weeds, such as fat hen (*Chenopodium album*), live an entire life within a year; they germinate from seed, grow, flower, set seed and die. Most annuals start this cycle in the spring and finish by autumn. Some annuals, such as common chickweed (*Stellaria media*), groundsel (*Senecio vulgaris*) and thale cress (*Arabidopsis thaliana*), continue germinating, flowering and setting seed through the winter whenever conditions are favourable. They have short lifecycles and produce several generations in one year.

One part of controlling annuals is never to let them set seed. If the original plants die without making more seed, they won't be back the following year. Unfortunately, seeds from previous years' weeds can survive in the soil for many years, and new weed seeds may drift

TIMING IS CRUCIAL

The annual and biennial weeds in this field reproduce by setting abundant seeds. Preventing them from flowering is one key to controlling them.

in on the wind or be carried in on clothing or fur. For these reasons, the other half of controlling annual weeds involves mulching and other techniques to prevent those seeds from germinating.

LET'S GET PHYSICAL

Pulling up annual weeds is very effective if the soil is damp enough to release the roots. Dispose carefully of any that re-root easily, such as chickweed, so that you get maximum return from your crop.

BIENNIALS TAKE TWO YEARS

For biennial weeds, such as ragwort (*Senecio jacobaea*), the seed-to-seed cycle spreads over 2 years. These weeds germinate from seed in the spring or summer, then usually grow into a ground-hugging circle of leaves called a rosette. The leaves produce sugars that

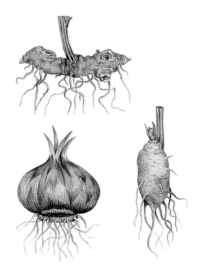

STORAGE SYSTEMS
Plants have many ways
to store the products of
photosynthesis. Clockwise
from top: a rhizome; a tuber;
and a bulb.

DIG IN THE DARK

If you're determined
to dig, but also want
to keep weeds to a
minimum, consider
digging your garden
after dark. It sounds
crazy, but researchers
have had remarkable
success with this
technique, reducing
weed cover by 70 to
80 per cent. It seems
that exposure to just
a few seconds of light
is all some weeds
need to germinate.
If you dig only when
it's dark, many of
the seeds will be
re-buried without
being triggered to
germinate. Dig any
time between 1 hour
after sunset to 1 hour
before sunrise.

move down to the roots and are stored
as starch. Next spring, the plant uses
the stored food energy to send up a
flowering stalk, which may or may not
have leaves. The plant flowers, sets
seed, then dies.

You have two main options with
biennial weeds: dig out the rosette—root
and all—in the first year; or, if the weed
isn't too visible or crowding other plants,
wait until the second year and cut the
plant down to the ground. If you wait
until the weed is just about to flower, the
plant will have used up most of its stored
energy and will be unlikely to return.

PERENNIALS ARE PERSISTENT

Wild garlic (*Allium vineale*), greater
plantain (*Plantago major*) and other
perennial weeds live for 3 years or
more. Like biennials, perennials store
carbohydrates to fuel early growth the next
spring. That food energy may be stored
in a taproot, in spreading underground
stems called rhizomes or in spreading

COLD FRAMES
While generally used to give
seedlings a head start, cold
frames are also effective in
keeping weeds from sharing
the water and nutrients you
have provided for the benefit
of your salad greens.

EFFECTIVE HOEING

If you have a standard pull or draw hoe, where the neck of the hoe curls back toward you, place your hands with your thumbs pointing up and pull the hoe toward you with a sweeping motion. If you use a push hoe, with the blade pointing away from you, hold the handle with your thumbs pointing down. Push it in front of you as you walk, running the blade just under the soil surface.

above-ground stems called runners or stolons. Or it may be stored in a tuber (like a potato) or a bulb (like an onion).

Some perennials, such as dandelions (*Taraxacum officinale*), reproduce only sexually—by setting seed from fertilized flowers. But some also reproduce non-sexually, by a process called vegetative reproduction. New plants can sprout from rhizomes and stolons. Tubers have "eyes" that produce new plants. And bulbs multiply, giving rise to new bulbs (offsets) that can each become a plant. You can think of this vegetative reproduction as a type of self-cloning for plants.

Perennial weeds are generally the most difficult to control. Carbohydrates stored in their taproots, rhizomes, tubers or bulbs give them a strong start each spring, as well as the power to grow again if their leaves are lost or damaged. Just preventing seed formation on perennials is not enough to get rid of

them; you must either dig up all of the underground structures or force them to use up their food reserves by repeatedly removing their top-growth.

Each time you remove the stems and leaves, the plant must draw on stored carbohydrates to send up new growth. Because the new growth soon starts to photosynthesize more food for the plant, frequent weeding—every 7 to 14 days— is best. If you can't weed that often through the spring and summer, weed before flowering and again later in the season. Perennials build up their food reserves in late summer and autumn to prepare for the next year's early growth. Cut them down until they are too weak to survive winter.

SUSTAINED ATTACK
Mowing an area repeatedly until the new shoots stop appearing can help control both biennial and perennial weeds. The roots may be too depleted to survive winter.

INVASIVE PLANTS
Weeds can be a big problem at the edges of the vegetable garden, where grasses and a variety of weeds may creep in. A mowing strip will help, but the best way to deal with these weeds is by hand, giving them regular attention before they can take over.

Controlling Weeds in the Vegetable Garden

While prevention can go a long way toward reducing weeds, a few are sure to pop up during the season. When they do sneak past your defences, you have several ways to get rid of them.

Hand–pulling and Hoeing

When it comes to killing weeds among your crops, the tried-and-true methods are pulling them out by hand or cutting them down with some type of blade (usually a hoe). You can also try flaming them, if you take care not to damage the vegetable plants nearby, but don't be fooled into thinking that one weeding will get you through the season.

The secret to control is persistence. Take a little time each week and pull up weeds as they emerge. Weaken perennial weeds by forcing them to use up food stores to re-grow. And no weed should ever get the chance to set seed. Best of all, you'll use less time and energy weeding a little each week than you would if you waited until the weeds were a tall, menacing, seed-filled mess.

Smothering Weeds

Weeds like the same things as your vegetables: light, water and nutrients. If you're willing to leave part of the garden unplanted for a season, you can deprive

COMPETITION

A green manure is a plant that grows well when crowded. By growing close together, green manures choke out weeds. If you have a really bad weed infestation, you may have to take the vegetable garden out of production for a year to let the green manure do its job.

the weeds of all three with a green manure which smothers weeds, but also adds nutrients because it is dug in before it flowers. Such a crop must do its work before or after the vegetable season.

A green manure sown in winter, such as field beans (*Vicia faba*), will cover the soil up to early spring, but you can turn it under early enough for it to break down (2–4 weeks before you plan to plant). Other effective green manures include Hungarian grazing rye (*Secale cereale*), as well as some broad-leaved plants, such as buckwheat (*Fagopyrum esculentum*). Plant buckwheat in spring, turn it under before it goes to seed, then follow it with another buckwheat crop in summer and in autumn.

If your vegetable garden backs onto a fence, don't plant right against the fence. Use a mulch along the fence or create a barrier with black plastic or cardboard and check regularly for invasive weeds.

CONTROLLING WEEDS IN THE FRUIT GARDEN

Unlike a vegetable garden, which you replant each year, fruit plantings are relatively permanent, so make sure the area is as free of weeds and weed seeds as possible before you start planting.

STRAWBERRIES

Strawberries send out runners to produce new plants, so any mulch you use must be sparse enough to let the runners reach the soil. Straw is a popular choice. Spread the mulch about 2.5 cm (1 in) thick. Pull out any weeds as they emerge through the mulch. Add another 2.5–5 cm (1–2 in) of mulch in the autumn to protect the plants during the winter.

SOFT FRUITS

A hoe and about 10 cm (4 in) of mulch are your best tools for keeping down weeds around soft fruit bushes and fruit canes (such as raspberries and blackberries). You'll especially appreciate the long handle on your hoe if you grow raspberry cultivars with thorns. Training raspberry canes to a post-and-wire trellis will make weed control easier.

FRUIT TREES

Your fruit trees are probably already surrounded by one of the best weed-control materials: grass. Even commercial orchards have returned to growing grass between the rows of trees because it stops the soil from washing or blowing

AUTUMN SWEETNESS
Mulch under grape vines to control weeds. Once the vines are well established, reduce the water supply and keep the soil dryish.

If fruit canes are supported
on wires, it is much easier
to keep the weeds down
among them. Once the area
around the plants is cleared,
apply a layer of mulch to
discourage regrowth and
to conserve moisture.

away and competes well against weeds.
Remove the grass in a 60-cm (2-ft) ring
around the base of each tree to make
mowing simpler and reduce the chance
of damaging the trunk with the mower.
Mulch the bare area with a good layer
of straw, compost, chipped bark or some
other organic mulch. Keep it away from
the trunk and rake it away in autumn to
keep rodents from nesting in it.

CLEAN FRUIT
Besides keeping the weeds
down, a good layer of mulch
around your strawberries will
keep the fruit from coming in
contact with the soil.

Part Five

PLANT DIRECTORY VEGETABLES

Abelmoschus esculentus

HARDINESS
Half-hardy.

DAYS TO MATURITY
56–85 frost-free
days.

COMMENTS
Cultivars include
'Annie Oakley' and
'Clemson Spineless'.
Will not bear as
prolifically as in
warmer climates.

OKRA

A POPULAR INGREDIENT IN CURRIES, OKRA IS
ALSO ADMIRED FOR ITS LOVELY, HOLLYHOCK-
LIKE FLOWERS. IT THRIVES IN HOT WEATHER.

Position Plant in full sun in fertile
and well-drained soil; pH 6.5–7.5.

Cultivation Sow seed when frost
danger is past and the soil is warm.
Pre-warming the soil with black
plastic mulch will speed up
germination. For best results, start
seed indoors in individual pots
2–4 weeks before the last frost and
set out under cloches when the
weather is settled. Plant out or thin
to 30–37.5 cm (12–15 in) apart.
Needs warm weather and both food
and water; irrigate in dry spells and
give it compost tea or seaweed
solution once a month.

Pests and diseases Aphids are a
problem under cover. Fruits may
rot in cool, wet summers; pick off
promptly to avoid it spreading.
Red-podded cultivars, such as 'Red
Burgundy', are often the most
prolific producers.

Harvesting and storage Cut or pinch
off young pods when they are
2.5–10 cm (1–4 in) long and still
soft. Larger pods will be woody.
Harvest daily in warm weather.
Okra freezes well.

Special tips Blossoms are edible.

Allium spp.

HARDINESS
Spring onions,
hardy; bulb onions,
frost hardy, but
choose cultivars for
either spring or
autumn planting.

DAYS TO MATURITY
Spring onions can be
harvested from seed
in about 56 days.
126–168 days for
spring seed or sets;
252–294 days for
autumn seed or sets.

COMMENTS
More mature plants
can withstand
severe frost.

ONION

A STAPLE FOR MANY CENTURIES, THE BULB
OF THE VERSATILE ONION PROVIDES PLENTY
OF GOOD EATING IN LITTLE GARDEN SPACE.

Position Plant in full sun in well-
drained soil that is rich in humus;
pH 6.0–7.5.

Cultivation For summer harvest, sow
indoors from midwinter to mid-
spring and set out 7.5–10 cm (3–4 in)
apart a month before last frost. For
onions to overwinter, sow thickly a
month before the last frost and thin
to 7.5–10 cm (3–4 in) apart. For
quicker crops, grow onions from
small bulbs called "sets", available
at garden centres or by mail order.
Plant sets 2.5 cm (1 in) deep and
5 cm (2 in) apart, pulling every
second one when ready for use as
spring onions. Grow onions in beds
or small patches to maximize yield
in small spaces. Keep well weeded
because they are easily shaded out.
Irrigate and feed with seaweed
solution or compost tea to encourage
good early growth, which will
determine eventual bulb size.

Pests and diseases Garden-grown
onions are prone to several pests
and diseases. Where onion fly is
troublesome, use horticultural fleece
supported by hoops to prevent
egg-laying. Rotate onions and their
relatives with other crops to avoid
soil-borne diseases such as onion
white rot and onion neck rot

Onion continued

Bulb onion cultivars can be pulled before the bulbs have begun to form and used as spring onions.

(which most often affects stored bulbs). Cold weather may prevent bulb formation, but damp weather may encourage downy mildew. Onion thrips cause mottled leaves. In hot weather, onions may bolt.

Harvesting and storage Pull spring onions and onions for fresh use as needed. For storage onions, wait until most tops have fallen over, then knock over any upright stalks with a rake. Pull the onions 1–2 days later and let them dry on the ground. (In wet weather, dry them on open mesh or shallow trays in a well-ventilated place.) Use onions with thick, green stems immediately; they will not store. When onions are thoroughly dry, plait the tops and hang in a cool, dry place or cut off the tops and store bulbs in mesh bags or slat-sided boxes.

Special tips For space-saving spring onions, sow several seeds in one pot and transplant later as a clump.

Related plants

Pickling onion *A. cepa* Also called pearl onion. Cultivars produce lots of small bulbs that are cooked or pickled whole. Try 'Brown Pickling' and 'Paris Silver Skin'.

Red (Spanish) onion *A. cepa* Cultivars include 'Electric', 'Cipolla Rossa di Toscana' and 'Long Red Florence' (elongated shape).

Red onions are also called Spanish onions. These red-skinned cultivars are often sweeter than types with white or yellow skins.

Slicing onion *A. cepa* Refers to mild-flavoured onions grown for fresh use. Most store poorly.

Bulb onion *A. cepa* Large bulbs with mild flavour, usually with yellow or white skin. In favourable conditions, bulbs can weigh up to 2.5 kg (5 lbs).

Egyptian onion *A. cepa* **Proliferum Group** Also called tree onion. Edible, but strongly flavoured. Instead of flowers, it produces a curious-looking head of small onion bulbs, some of which can be planted in spring or autumn to produce the next year's crop.

Welsh onion *A. fistulosum* Also called ciboule, Japanese bunching onion. Does not form a bulb, but rather a slender, white stalk.

Spring onion *A. cepa* An immature bulb onion, pulled when it still has white stems and not much bulb. Most popular is the Lisbon type.

Allium cepa Aggregatum Group

HARDINESS
Hardy.

DAYS TO MATURITY
140–168 days; or
pull earlier to eat
as spring onions.

COMMENTS
Will withstand
moderate frost.

SHALLOT

A RELATIVE OF THE ONION, THE SHALLOT
PRODUCES SMALL, FIRM BULBS THAT KEEP
LIKE GARLIC BUT ARE MUCH SWEETER AND
MILDER IN FLAVOUR.

Position Plant in full sun in well-
drained soil that is rich in humus.
Shallots will tolerate all but the most
acid soil.

Cultivation Shallots are most often
grown from bulblets or "sets". Plant
from late winter to early spring,
2.5 cm (1 in) deep and 10–15 cm
(4–6 in) apart. Keep weeded or
mulch and water regularly to
encourage strong early growth. Each
set will divide and produce 8 to 10
shallots. Where conditions permit,
autumn planting will produce larger

shallots the following summer.

Pests and diseases Shallots suffer
from much the same problems as
bulb onions, especially bolting and
downy mildew. Do not plant where
shallots or their relatives, such as
onions or leeks, have grown the
previous year. Dry conditions or
poor soil produce scrawny shallots.
Work in plenty of compost or well-
rotted manure and water regularly.

Harvesting and storage When the
tops are nearly dry, pull out the
plants and dry the bulbs in a
well-ventilated, sunny area. Store
by hanging in a cool, dry place,
or cut off the stems and store the
bulbs in mesh bags.

Allium porrum

ALLIACEAE

HARDINESS
Hardy; can be grown as a winter vegetable.

DAYS TO MATURITY
112–140 days in the garden.

COMMENTS
'King Richard' and 'Titan' are early leeks; 'Longbow' and 'Toledo' are good for overwintering. "Baby" leeks can be harvested earlier.

LEEK

THIS ONION RELATIVE IS GROWN FOR ITS STOUT, FLAVOURFUL STEM. IT HOLDS WELL IN THE GROUND FOR LATE HARVESTING.

Position Plant in full sun in loose, very rich, well-drained soil; pH 6.0–7.5.

Cultivation Start seed indoors up to 12 weeks before last spring frost. Transplant from seed trays to small, individual pots when large enough to handle. This produces larger transplants and better leeks. Plant out after frost, 15 cm (6 in) apart, in a trench 15 cm (6 in) deep or in holes made with a hoe handle or dibber, covering all but 2.5 cm (1 in) or so of the leaves. Keep well weeded. As leeks grow, fill in the trench gradually or, if planted on level soil, "earth" them up by drawing soil up around the stems. This produces a longer white stem, which is the edible part. You can also use a deep mulch to blanch the stems. Keep the soil moist, especially early in the season.

Pests and diseases To avoid damage by onion fly, do not plant leeks where other members of the onion family have been grown the previous year. Short, tough stems indicate either a lack of moisture or soil fertility or inadequate earthing up.

Harvesting and storage Dig up or pull out leeks when they are large enough for use. Before a hard frost,

Leek continued

Feed your leeks regularly to ensure that their growth is unchecked and that they will have plump, tender stems.

mulch the bed heavily to keep it diggable through winter. Harvest overwintered leeks before spring growth begins. Pack leeks in damp sand or soilless compost and store in a cool place. Harvested leeks stored in this way will keep for 6–8 weeks.

Special tips Young plants will tolerate light frost; mature ones, severe frost. Cultivars include 'Musselburgh' (large, thick stem, matures from autumn to spring, very cold-tolerant); 'Bandit' (uniform stems, produces high yields); 'Titan' (long, thick stem, grows quickly).

Related plants

Chinese chives *A. tuberosum* Also called garlic chives. A hardy perennial grown for its mildly garlic-flavoured leaves, which are used in stir-fries and soups. The spring flowers are also edible. Named cultivars are not generally available.

Chives *A. schoenoprasum* A popular herb that can be grown in a pot or as an edging for the vegetable garden. The long, cylindrical leaves are usually cut and used as a flavouring or garnish. The mauve flowers are also edible and make a pretty garnish.

Allium sativum

HARDINESS
Hardy; must be
pre-chilled before
planting to form
good bulbs.

DAYS TO MATURITY
112–252 days,
depending on
whether it is
planted in spring
or autumn.

COMMENTS
Garlic was crushed
and soaked to
make a garden
spray for insects
in past times.

GARLIC

GARLIC IS AN EASY-TO-GROW AND
REWARDING CROP. PLANT IT IN AUTUMN
TO HARVEST THE FOLLOWING SUMMER.

Position Plant in full sun or partial
shade, but bulbs will be smaller in
partial shade. Likes well-drained,
fertile soil that is rich in humus;
pH 6.0–7.0.

Cultivation Best planted in autumn,
2–4 weeks before first frost. Plant
individual cloves, pointed end up,
2.5–5 cm (1–2 in) deep and 10–15 cm
(4–6 in) apart. Deeper planting is
best where frequent freezing and
thawing may cause heaving (when
the soil lifts due to temperature
changes and plants are dislodged
from their roots). Apply seaweed

solution or compost tea in spring to
encourage vigorous growth. Keep
the bed cultivated or mulched.
Irrigate until tops begin to brown,
then withhold water to let the plant
dry naturally.

Pests and diseases Little troubled
by pests, but reduce threat of onion
fly by not planting where garlic or
its relatives, such as onions and
shallots, have been planted the
previous year. Humid conditions at
harvest may induce neck rot. Use
these heads immediately or freeze,
as they do not keep well.

Harvesting and storage Use spring
shoots and flower stems chopped
in salads and dips, as you would

Garlic continued

The soft drying stems of garlic plants are easy to plait in the traditional way. The plaited bunches are then hung up to finish drying out.

chives. Pull mature garlic plants when about 75 per cent of the foliage is brown; tie in bundles and dry in a dark, well-ventilated place. Plait for storage or cut stems and store in mesh bags in a dry, cool area. Freeze peeled cloves; thaw slowly before using.

Special tips Pot garlic heads or cloves and grow indoors for winter use as greens.

Related plants

Elephant garlic *A. ampeloprasum* Elephant garlic is more closely related to leeks. It is milder and has larger heads (up to 500g [1 lb]) than true garlic. Plant deeper than garlic, up to 10 cm (4 in) deep.

Soft-neck garlic *A. sativum* The standard garlic and most commonly grown. Cloves form in an overlapping pattern, like the scales of an artichoke. Cultivars include 'Purple Wight' and 'Solent Wight'.

Hard-neck garlic *A. sativum*, var. *ophioscorodon* Also called rocambole. Prized in oriental cuisine, it produces a coiled flower stem. Remove the stem to direct growth to the roots. Cloves are large and form in a single ring around a central, woody stem. Cultivars include 'Russian Red'.

Amaranthus tricolor

HARDINESS
Half-hardy, but
needs some
protection in
colder areas.

DAYS TO MATURITY
Requires 70–84
frost-free days,
although thinnings
can be harvested
earlier.

COMMENTS
Other common
names include
African or Indian
spinach, leaf
amaranth and
vegetable amaranth.

AMARANTH

GROW AMARANTH FOR ITS NUTRITIOUS
LEAVES, WHICH CAN BE EATEN BOTH RAW
IN SALADS AND COOKED AS GREENS.

Position Prefers heat and full sun.
Not fussy, but prefers soil rich in
humus; pH 6.0–7.0.

Cultivation Sow seed after frost,
when soil has warmed; use a plastic
mulch if necessary to warm the soil.
Barely cover and keep moist until
germinated. For earlier crops, sow
amaranth indoors 4 weeks before
last frost date. Water freely and thin
to 45 cm (18 in) apart.

Pests and diseases Protect plants from
flea beetles with tunnel cloches
or horticultural fleece. Rotate
plantings to avoid stem rot from
soil-borne diseases.

Harvesting and storage Harvest whole
plants as thinnings; pick the young,
tender leaves from mature plants.
Harvest frequently to encourage
new growth. Can be frozen in the
same way as spinach.

Special tips Plant away from
brassicas (cabbage-family plants) or
cucumbers to reduce pest damage;
or plant adjacent to those crops to
serve as a "sacrificial crop". Seed
companies often carry natural
variants with light green, dark green
or red-striped leaves; try 'Kahulu' or
'Red Amaranth'.

Apium graveolens var. *dulce*

CELERY

IT ISN'T EASY TO GROW, BUT WITH A LITTLE
ATTENTION TO ITS NEEDS, CELERY DOES
BEAUTIFULLY IN THE GARDEN.

Position Plant in full sun in
moisture-retentive, rich soil, with
adequate calcium and plenty of
well-rotted manure or compost
worked in; pH 5.5–7.5.

Cultivation Start seed indoors
4–6 weeks before the last spring
frost. Germination and seedling
growth are slow. Keep seedlings
watered and do not expose to
temperatures below 13°C (55°F),
which can cause plants to bolt to
seed. Set plants out when the
weather is well settled (about a
month after the last frost),

25–30 cm (10–12 in) apart. Because
the roots are relatively shallow,
do not allow the soil to dry out;
feed the plants with compost tea
or seaweed solution at least once a
month. If desired, you can blanch
trenching celery before harvest by
slipping a bottomless paper bag
over the plant and tying it in place,
or by putting wide boards on edge
on both sides of the celery row and
holding the boards in place with
stakes. The idea is to keep the sun
off the stems. This whitens them and
keeps them from becoming tough,
although self-blanching cultivars are
available. Excessive heat, lack of
moisture or low soil fertility will
also result in tough, stringy celery.

The stems of trenching celery need to be blanched by keeping light off them; many methods are used, including using drainpipe sections (above) and newspaper.

Pests and diseases Rotate plantings with other crops to avoid root rots. Hand-pick off slugs and snails or leaf-miner maggots. Protect against carrot fly by covering in early spring.

Harvesting and storage Cut celery for immediate use just below soil level. Harvesting can be extended if plants are protected by an insulating mulch of straw and covered with opaque white plastic or horticultural fleece. However, before a hard frost, pull up the entire plant and roots, and store, packed in dry leaves or straw, in a cool shed or garage.

Special tips Plant celery in well-manured beds, three or four plants abreast and 25–30 cm (10–12 in) apart. Dense growth will shade out weeds and automatically blanch the celery. Cultivars include 'Loretta' and 'Tango', both green, self-blanching cultivars. 'Giant Red' has stalks tinged with red, while 'Lathom Self-Blanching' has been bred to resist bolting to seed.

Apium graveolens var. *rapaceum*

HARDINESS
Frost hardy. Use
as an autumn and
winter alternative
to celery.

DAYS TO MATURITY
182 days; can
withstand
increasingly severe
frost for the last
30–45 days.

COMMENTS
Cultivars include
'Giant Prague',
which is a
traditional or
heirloom celeriac,
and the early 'Prinz'.

CELERIAC

IN SALADS, SOUPS AND STEWS OR AS A
COOKED VEGETABLE, THE ROOT OF CELERIAC
HAS ALL THE FLAVOUR OF CELERY.

Position Plant in full sun in rich,
moisture-retentive soil, with
adequate calcium and plenty of
well-rotted manure or compost
worked in; pH 5.5–7.5.

Cultivation Start seed indoors
6–8 weeks before last spring frost
and plant out, 25–30 cm (10–12 in)
apart, when the threat of frost is
past. Celeriac can be direct-sown,
but it germinates slowly and can be
overtaken by weeds. Keep bed well
weeded and watered. Apply compost
tea or seaweed solution at least
once a month.

Pests and diseases Rotate plantings
of celeriac and celery with other
crops to avoid the root rots to
which they are both vulnerable.
Hand-pick off slugs and snails.
Inadequate moisture will yield small,
tough, fibrous roots.

Harvesting and storage Harvest the
turnip-like root when large enough
for your needs. Harvest all plants
before the ground freezes; cut stems
close to the roots and store like
turnips (see page 155) in damp
soilless compost or sand in a
cool place.

Special tips Other common names
include celery root, turnip celery.

Arachis hypogaea   FABACEAE

HARDINESS
Tender, but may
produce light crops.

DAYS TO MATURITY
112–140 frost-free
days.

COMMENTS
Another common
name is groundnut.
Cultivars are either
of Spanish-Valencia
type, with more
upright habit, or
the more prostrate
Virginia type.

PEANUT

NOT A NUT BUT A PROTEIN-RICH MEMBER OF
THE LEGUME FAMILY, THE PEANUT CAN BE
ROASTED, BOILED OR MADE INTO A SAUCE.

Position Plant in full sun in loose,
well-drained soil rich in humus and
with adequate calcium; pH 5.8–6.2.

Cultivation In spring, sow seed in
warm temperatures in individual pots
4–6 weeks before last frost. Harden
off and plant out, 30 cm (1 ft) apart,
in soil that has been pre-warmed
with black plastic mulch or grow on
in a greenhouse soil bed. Plant
whole shells, or remove shell first,
taking care not to damage the
papery skin. Keep weeded. Do not
mulch; if plastic mulch is used to
warm soil, it must be removed

when the peanuts flower. Stems
bearing fertilized flowers dive into
soil around the plant, and a peanut
forms at the end of each stem.

Pests and diseases Greenhouse pests
such as red spider mite and
whiteflies.

Harvesting and storage Dig up
plants when frost has killed the
foliage. Hang by the roots in a
well-ventilated place until the pods
have completely dried. Roast shelled
nuts, or roast them in the shell by
soaking clean pods in salted water
for several hours, then heating in a
150°C (300°F) oven until completely
dry and crisp (about 1 hour).

Arctium lappa

HARDINESS
Hardy, although
the eventual length
of the root will
depend on the
length of the
growing season.

DAYS TO MATURITY
120 days or more.

GREATER BURDOCK

MILDLY BITTER AND AN EXCELLENT ADDITION
TO SOUPS AND STEWS, GREATER BURDOCK
GROWS WILD, BUT CAN BE GROWN AS A
NUTRITIOUS ROOT VEGETABLE.

Position Plant in full sun or light
shade. Requires deep, well-prepared
soil, as the roots can grow to 60 cm
(2 ft) or more in length; pH 6.0–7.3.

Cultivation Sow seed in spring
for an autumn harvest, or in late
summer for overwintering. Thin
the plants to 60–90 cm (2–3 ft)
apart. Greater burdock looks much
like its relative, the lesser burdock
(*A. minus*), with large, heart-shaped
leaves, but it can grow to 2.4 m (8 ft)
tall. Hoe shallowly until the plant is
large enough to shade out weeds.

Pests and diseases Burdock is rarely
troubled by pests. In rocky or heavy
soil, roots may fork or become
deformed, making harvesting
difficult. Planting in raised beds
will help to avoid this problem.

Harvesting and storage Harvest after
autumn frosts, or leave roots in the
ground for spring harvest. Burdock
stores well in a cool cellar if you
treat it in the same way as you
would turnips or carrots (see
pages 155 and 181 respectively).

Armoracia rusticana

HARDINESS
Hardy.

DAYS TO MATURITY
150–180 days in
first year where the
season permits;
otherwise, first
harvest is in the
second year.

COMMENTS
Severe frost will
kill horseradish
leaves, but will not
damage the roots.
Young leaves of
horseradish can be
added to salads.

HORSERADISH

HORSERADISH IS A HARDY PERENNIAL
GROWN FOR ITS ROOTS, WHICH ARE GRATED
FOR USE AS A TANGY CONDIMENT.

Position Plant in sun or partial
shade in well-drained, deep and
preferably rich soil; pH 6.0–7.0.

Cultivation Plant this invasive
vegetable in a bottomless bucket
sunk into the soil. Plant root cuttings
in spring, 5 cm (2 in) deep and
30–45 cm (12–18 in) apart. Weed
or mulch after the leaves appear
above the ground. Even soil
moisture encourages rapid growth
and large roots.

Pests and diseases Flea beetles
sometimes attack, but rarely do
more than cosmetic damage. Avoid

growing in heavy, shallow or stony
soil. May be difficult to eradicate or
move once established—new plants
grow from root bits left in the soil.

Harvesting and storage Dig up roots
when 30–37.5 cm (12–15 in) long,
up to 5 cm (2 in) thick and fairly
smooth, in autumn while still
tender. Older roots get woody and
tough. Store whole roots in damp
sand in a cool place.

Special tips Pack smaller roots in
damp sand and save for planting
next year. Cut tops flat and bottoms
at an angle, so you put them in the
ground the right way up, thereby
producing straighter and more
uniform roots.

Asparagus officinalis

ASPARAGUS

THIS CLASSIC SPRING VEGETABLE REQUIRES WELL-PREPARED SOIL WITH HIGH FERTILITY. A WELL-MAINTAINED PATCH CAN YIELD ABUNDANTLY FOR TWO DECADES.

Position Avoid wet, heavy soils and frost pockets, to reduce the possibility of violet root rot and frost damage to spears, respectively. Prefers full sun, but will tolerate some shade. Likes fertile, well-drained soil; pH (6.5–6.8), but will tolerate slightly alkaline and saline soils.

Cultivation Grow from seed sown indoors or in an outdoor seedbed; or hasten the first harvest by using year-old crowns. Dig a trench 20 cm (8 in) deep and 30 cm (12 in) wide in enriched and, if needed, limed soil. Make a mounded ridge of soil along the centre of the trench, about 10 cm (4 in) tall. Place the crowns on the ridge 37.5 cm (15 in) apart, fanning the roots in all directions. Fill in with soil so the buds at the tops of the crowns are just visible. As the foliage grows, keep filling in the trench, always leaving the tops clear. Mulch well to keep the soil moist and irrigate during dry spells. Keeping the foliage healthy and lush after harvest is critical to the next year's crop. Each autumn, cut back the dead, ferny foliage and mulch heavily with well-rotted compost or straw-rich manure. Early each spring, rake off all but 2.5–5 cm (1–2 in) of

HARDINESS
Hardy, but late
frosts can damage
the young spears.

DAYS TO MATURITY
Gardeners used to
wait until the third
year to take a first
small harvest of
asparagus; newer
hybrid cultivars can
be picked sparingly
for 1–2 weeks in
the second year.
A mature patch can
be harvested for as
long as 8 weeks.

A dense stand of ferny fronds (see opposite) grows up after you stop harvesting the spears. The foliage helps the plants to build up nutrients needed for the next crop.

mulch to let the spears emerge.

Pests and diseases Violet root rot can be a problem in wet, acid soils. Lift and destroy affected plants; don't replant with asparagus. Reduce damage from asparagus beetles, which overwinter in garden debris and emerge in spring to feed on the young spears, by burning the old asparagus foliage and hand-picking adults and larvae from late spring. Perennial weeds and grasses can be troublesome in the asparagus patch. Be sure the area is free of perennial weeds before planting, and mulch or cultivate to keep them at bay.

Harvesting and storage Carefully cut the spears just below ground level, when they are about 15 cm (6 in) tall. Harvest while the tips of the spears are still tightly closed; in warm spring spells, this may mean daily harvesting. Freeze excess spears. A mature patch, say 5 years old, can yield 500 g (1 lb) or more of asparagus per 30 cm (1 ft) of row.

Special tips Cultivars include 'Backlim', a high-yielding hybrid; 'Connover's Colossal', a dependable, purple-tipped old favourite; and 'Purple Pacific', which is very tender.

Atriplex hortensis

HARDINESS
Hardy.

DAYS TO MATURITY
40–50 days;
thinnings can be
harvested sooner.
Will withstand
moderate frost.

COMMENTS
Also known as
mountain spinach.

ORACH

THE VIVID FOLIAGE OF RED ORACH MAKES
IT AN ATTRACTIVE ADDITION TO BOTH
ORNAMENTAL AND VEGETABLE GARDENS.

Position Plant in full sun. Not fussy,
but prefers fertile, well-drained soil;
pH 7.3–8.0. Good for coastal areas.

Cultivation Sow seed 4–6 weeks
before the last spring frost; thin to
20 cm (8 in) apart, using the
thinnings in salads. Like spinach,
orach bolts, or runs to seed, quickly
in hot weather; unlike spinach, it
will germinate and grow in warm
weather. For an extended harvest,
keep the flowerheads pinched out.
Sow frequent small batches to
assure plenty of young, tender leaves
in spring, summer and autumn.

Pests and diseases Little troubled by
pests. Pull bolting plants, as they
can grow to 1.8 m (6 ft) or taller
when in flower and may self-sow,
becoming a weed problem.

Harvesting and storage Pick the
succulent, young leaves as needed.

Special tips Red orach *A. hortensis*
var. *rubra* (shown above) holds its
colour during cooking and is
striking in salads and as a garnish.
Named cultivars are not generally
available, but seed companies offer
variants based on leaf colour, usually
dark green, light green or red.

Basella alba

HARDINESS
Tender.

DAYS TO MATURITY
70–84 frost-free
days.

COMMENTS
Cultivars include
'Rubra', which has
red-veined leaves
and red stems.
Other common
names include
Ceylon spinach,
Indian spinach and
vine spinach.

SPINACH, MALABAR

A CLIMBING PLANT NATIVE TO TROPICAL AFRICA AND ASIA, MALABAR SPINACH HAS GLOSSY LEAVES THAT ARE USED IN THE SAME WAYS AS SPINACH.

Position Plant in full sun, on netting supports or near a fence or trellis, in moist soil that is rich in humus; pH 6.0–7.5.

Cultivation Malabar spinach grows quickly and is treated as an annual climber in the UK climate. Sow seed indoors up to 8 weeks before the last frost and harden off and plant out after frost danger is well past. This plant likes heat and grows slowly, if at all, until the temperature is to its liking. It grows best in temperatures over 25°C (77°F),

so you may want to try growing it under cover in a greenhouse or conservatory. Space plants 90 cm (3 ft) apart and provide a fence or trellis to support them. Water well in dry weather. Malabar spinach usually achieves a spread of 1.8–3 m (6–10 ft) in the UK climate.

Pests and diseases Little troubled by pests.

Harvesting and storage Pick the fresh leaves as needed; regular picking encourages it to re-grow rapidly.

Special tips Try growing it as an ornamental cover over a trellis, arch or pergola, using the leaves as required.

Beta vulgaris subsp. *cicla*

CHENOPODIACEAE

HARDINESS
Hardy; can be grown as a winter vegetable.

DAYS TO MATURITY
56–84 days; thinnings can be harvested sooner.

COMMENTS
Other common names include seakale beet, spinach beet. Cultivars include 'Bright Lights' with multi-coloured stems, 'Fordhook Giant', 'Rhubarb Chard' (red-stemmed).

SWISS CHARD

VIGOROUS AND EASY TO GROW, A SINGLE PLANTING OF SWISS CHARD CAN PROVIDE A FULL SEASON OF FRESH LEAVES. USE IT AS YOU WOULD SPINACH, OR PLANT IT IN THE FLOWER GARDEN FOR ITS VIVID COLOUR.

Position Plant in full sun. Not fussy, but prefers rich, well-drained, moisture-retentive soil; pH 6.0–6.8.

Cultivation Sow in spring and early summer, or in mid- to late summer for overwintering and spring crops. Sow 12 mm (½ in) deep and thin to 20–30 cm (8–12 in) apart, using the thinnings in salads or transplanting them to new beds. Weed and water regularly to keep your plants growing strongly.

Pests and diseases Little troubled by pests. Horticultural fleece will deter flea beetles. Swiss chard is fairly drought tolerant, but water stress results in tough stems.

Harvesting and storage Pick the large outer leaves by pulling stems from the base with a slight twist. Leave the centre to sprout new leaves. Leaves are usually cooked separately from the wide inner rib, which is often steamed and eaten like asparagus. You can freeze the leaves as you would spinach.

Special tips Swiss chard makes a good cut-and-come-again crop for young salad leaves. Interplant it with flowers for an ornamental and edible border.

Beta vulgaris subsp. *vulgaris*

HARDINESS
Hardy.

DAYS TO MATURITY
70–91 days in the garden, or sooner if you grow quick-maturing cultivars such as 'Pronto' after starting seedlings indoors.

BEETROOT

DON'T WASTE BEETROOT LEAVES—THEY ARE DELICIOUS. STEAM OR LIGHTLY FRY IN OIL AS YOU WOULD SPINACH, OR USE THE YOUNG LEAVES RAW IN SALADS.

Position Plant in full sun in well-drained, rich, neutral soil, free of stones. If soil is heavy or shallow, grow only round cultivars; long-rooted ones may be deformed or tough at maturity; pH 6.0–7.5.

Cultivation Beetroot seeds are compound—each "seed" actually contains as many as a half-dozen seeds. For this reason, many gardeners sow beetroots sparingly to reduce the need for thinning. But because beetroots are known for spotty germination, other gardeners sow them heavily to assure a full crop. The middle course is a moderately heavy seeding—after first soaking the seeds in tepid water for several hours to encourage germination. Early sowings tend to bolt: sow indoors in modules in spring and transplant after the last frost; use bolt-resistant cultivars, such as 'Boltardy'; or protect outdoor sowings with tunnel cloches. Sow 2.5 cm (1 in) deep and 5–10 cm (2–4 in) apart, about 1 month before the last spring frost. Firm the seedbed well with your feet or the back of a hoe. Thin the young plants when they are 5–7.5 cm (2–3 in) tall. Beetroots are among the few root vegetables

Beetroot continued

All types of beetroot can be served raw or cooked. Start harvesting when the beetroots are about 2.5 cm (1 in) in diameter.

that can be transplanted, so you can move any surplus seedlings to another spot, taking care not to double over the taproot when transplanting. The thinnings can also be used as salad greens. Beetroots tend to become woody and tasteless when left in the ground too long; small monthly sowings will give you a continuous supply of tender, sweet beetroots for the table. The exceptions are cultivars such as 'Boston'. Sow these in midsummer, at least 2 months before the first autumn frost (or in the spring if your growing season is short), and leave in the ground until a hard frost threatens. Beetroots need regular watering to keep them tender and to prevent interior discolouring that results from uneven soil moisture.

Pests and diseases Tunnel cloches will thwart flea beetles and leaf miners. Discourage the disease leaf spot by not growing beets where they or their relatives, such as spinach and chard, have been grown in the previous year.

Harvesting and storage Harvest greens as soon as they are large enough for use. Harvest baby beetroots when they are 2.5 cm (1 in) or more in diameter; check by gently probing the soil at the plant's base. When removing the tops, leave 2.5 cm (1 in) of stem

'Burpee's Golden', with its golden orange flesh, adds a gourmet touch to salad. Grate or julienne the flesh; like that of all beetroots, it is rich in folic acid and vitamin C.

attached to the roots to prevent bleeding. Cook with stems attached and cut away the stems before serving. Pull beetroots for storage before a hard frost, cut tops close to the roots, and store in damp sand in a cool place. Beetroots can also be bottled or pickled.

Special tips Grow small-rooted cultivars, such as those bred as special "baby beetroots", in a cluster without thinning. Plant two or three seeds together, each cluster 15 cm (6 in) apart, and harvest when the beets reach eating size.

Related plants

Cylindrical beetroot *B. vulgaris* **subsp.** *vulgaris* Tapered roots, up to 17.5 cm (7 in) long and 5 cm (2 in) in diameter. Earth up the crowns to keep the topmost part of the root from being exposed and toughened. 'Cylindra' and 'Alto' are popular cultivars. They are easy to peel and slice into uniform pieces for pickling or bottling.

Golden beetroot *B. vulgaris* **subsp.** *vulgaris* Sweet and tender-fleshed, and prized for its unusual golden orange colour, which does not "bleed" when cooked as red beetroots do. Plant more thickly than other types because they tend to germinate poorly. Cultivars include 'Burpee's Golden'.

Brassica napus Napobrassica Group

HARDINESS
Hardy.

DAYS TO MATURITY
140–182 days. Will
withstand severe
frost.

COMMENTS
Although a root
crop, swede is a
member of the
cabbage family and
has similar needs.

SWEDE

THIS LONG-SEASON CROP IS A RUGGED
GARDEN VEGETABLE THAT SHRUGS OFF THE
COLD AND OTHER ADVERSE CONDITIONS.

Position Plant seed in full sun
in fertile, well-drained soil. Will
tolerate heavy soil better than most
other root vegetables, as long as it
is well-drained; pH 5.5–6.8.

Cultivation Sow from late winter
indoors, or in late spring and early
summer outdoors. Thin to 10–15 cm
(4–6 in) apart. Weed early on; the
large leaves will quickly grow to
shade out weeds.

Pests and diseases Rotate swedes
and other root crops to avoid
clubroot and mildew. Protect young
plants from flea beetles and

cabbage root fly with tunnel cloches
or horticultural fleece; larger plants
may suffer cosmetic damage, but
that will not affect the yield.

Harvesting and storage Pull swedes
when they are large enough for use.
The greens are also edible. Harvest
all roots in autumn and early winter
before the worst of the cold
weather and store in damp sand
in a cool place.

Special tips Cultivars include
'Magnes' and 'Marian'.

Brassica oleracea Acephala Group　　　BRASSICACEAE

KALE

A CABBAGE RELATIVE, KALE IS AMONG THE
MOST NUTRITIOUS OF GARDEN GREENS.

Position Plant in full sun in fertile,
moist but well-drained soil with
adequate lime; pH 6.5–6.8.

Cultivation Sow seed in mid- to late
spring and thin to 45 cm (1½ ft),
or transplant as you would cabbage
(see pages 144-6). Spring-sown kale,
if well cared for, will keep producing
past the first frost, but you can also
sow in midsummer for an autumn
and winter crop. Tolerates summer
heat, but prefers cool weather, so
mulch to keep the soil cool. Keep
moist and apply seaweed solution
or compost tea once a month for
lush growth of summer crops; don't
overfeed or water winter kale—lush
growth is less hardy—but feed in
autumn if it starts to yellow.

Pests and diseases Protect young
plants from flea beetles and
cabbage root fly with horticultural
fleece or tunnel cloches. Rotate kale
and other cabbage-family members
to avoid soil-borne diseases. Sowing
too thickly may result in crowded
and spindly plants. Thin gradually.

Harvesting and storage Harvest leaves
as needed from the base of plant,
leaving the crown to sprout new
leaves. Harvest crown before winter
for tender leaves. Freeze for winter use.

Special tips Kale can tolerate heat,
but is tastier after frost.

Brassica oleracea Acephala Group

HARDINESS
Hardy.

DAYS TO MATURITY
55–65 days, but
thinnings can be
harvested sooner.

COMMENTS
Cultivars include
'Red Russian', a
non-curly cultivar
with purplish stems
and leaves, 'Dwarf
Green Curled'
and 'Winterbor'.
Common names
include borecole.

KALE, CURLY

HARDY AND NUTRITIOUS, CURLY KALE
PROVIDES TASTY GREENS LATE IN THE
SEASON, EVEN UNDER A BLANKET OF SNOW.

Position Plant in full sun in fertile,
moisture-retentive and well-drained
soil, with adequate lime; pH 6.5–6.8.

Cultivation Direct-sow 4–6 weeks
before the last spring frost, about
12 mm (½ in) deep. Thin to
30–37.5 cm (12-15 in) apart; use the
thinnings in salads. Hoe or mulch to
control weeds. Tolerates heat, but
prefers cool soil. Sow autumn and
winter crops 6–8 weeks before first
frost, or later to overwinter. Give
seaweed solution or compost tea
liberally once a month to encourage
lush leaf growth on summer crops;

water late crops more sparingly, but
feed in autumn if the leaves begin to
yellow. Leaves toughen with age. Keep
the plant well picked; sow an autumn
crop for a second harvest of tender
leaves. Kale is sweeter after frost.

Pests and diseases Use tunnel cloches
or horticultural fleece to protect
young plants from flea beetles and
cabbage root fly. Rotate kale and
other cabbage-family plants to avoid
soil-borne diseases, such as clubroot.

Harvesting and storage Pick leaves
as needed from base of the plant;
new ones will sprout from the top.

Special tips Young plants will take a
light frost; mature ones, severe frost.

Brassica oleracea Botrytis Group

HARDINESS
Hardy, but heads
vulnerable to frost.

DAYS TO MATURITY
56–112 days,
summer and
autumn cultivars;
210–280 days,
winter types;
300–360 days,
spring cultivars.

COMMENTS
New cultivars with
purple (left),
yellow or green
curds are now
being introduced.

CAULIFLOWER

CAULIFLOWERS ARE HEAVY FEEDERS THAT
REQUIRE PLENTY OF WATER. THE HEADS OF
WHITE VARIETIES MUST BE PROTECTED FROM
THE SUN (BLANCHED) TO KEEP THEM WHITE.

Position Plant in full sun in rich,
well-drained soil with ample amounts
of well-rotted manure or compost
worked in; pH 6.0–7.0. A light
dressing with lime will be necessary
if the soil is too acidic. This will
also reduce the likelihood of club
root infection. Leave the soil to settle
several months before planting.

Cultivation There are cultivars for
all seasons, but cauliflowers occupy
the ground for a long time and are
not easy to grow. Erratic watering
affects crops, so early-maturing

types are easier. Sow most crops
indoors and do not plant out too
early; severe frost can cause the
plant to form a "button" instead
of a full-sized head. It's easier to
start plants in modules indoors,
to avoid frosts and using up lots of
space. Sow early-summer cultivars
indoors in mid-autumn and plant
out in early spring; summer types
indoors in mid-spring and plant out
in early summer. Sow autumn
cauliflowers indoors in late spring
for transplanting in early summer;
and winter and spring cultivars in a
seedbed in late spring for planting
out in late summer. Space plants
45–90 cm (18–36 in) apart, and
mulch to keep the soil cool.

Cauliflower continued

Try planting aromatic herbs, such as pennyroyal, peppermint, sage and thyme, near your cauliflowers. It may help to deter insect pests.

Any check in watering will result in small heads, so keep cauliflowers growing steadily with plenty of water and one or more applications of seaweed solution or compost tea. When heads appear, use a clothes peg to clip several large leaves together over the head to shade it and keep it white, or remove a large lower leaf and lay it over the developing head. "Self-blanching" cultivars grow their own "shading" leaves, but may still need help from you if warm weather wilts the protective leaves.

Pests and diseases Control cabbage root fly with tunnel cloches or horticultural fleece. Do this early,

as it is difficult to control the larvae when they have become established inside the developing head. Tunnel cloches will also deter caterpillars, especially of cabbage white butterfly, as well as flea beetles on young plants; older, vigorous plants can withstand flea beetle attack. Rotate brassica plantings to avoid soil-borne diseases such as clubroot and mildews. In damp areas, heads may discolour during blanching due to excess moisture. Clip or tie the leaves together loosely to keep sunlight off the head, but do not cut off the circulation of air. Cauliflowers are also prone to nutrient deficiencies, such as whiptail or boron deficiency.

As an interesting change, try growing some of the cauliflowers with colourful, more open heads that do not need to go through the blanching process.

Harvesting and storage Cut heads before the curds begin to coarsen and separate. Cool weather may slow head development. When harvesting, leave a few leaves around the head to avoid breaking it. Cauliflower keeps, refrigerated, for up to 2 weeks. It can also be broken up into segments before being plunged into boiling water, refreshed in cold water and then frozen or used for making pickles.

Special tips Young plants will withstand a light frost; mature ones, moderate frost. 'Jerome' and 'Igloo' are early cultivars; late-season cultivars include 'Snowball' and 'Aalsmeer'.

Related plants

Green cauliflower *B. oleracea* Botrytis Group This has yellow-green, rather than white, curds. Like purple cauliflower, it is easier to grow than the white cultivars, since it does not require blanching. Try 'Romanesco'.

Mini cauliflower *B. oleracea* Botrytis Group Grow minis if space is limited. They have smaller curds, measuring 10 cm (4 in) across. Up to 5 can be grown in the space taken by one cauliflower of the usual size.

Brassica oleracea Capitata Group

CABBAGE

VALUED FOR THOUSANDS OF YEARS BECAUSE
OF ITS HARDINESS AND LONG STORAGE LIFE,
CABBAGE CAN BE GROWN ALMOST ANYWHERE,
ALTHOUGH IT IS SUBJECT TO ATTACK BY
SEVERAL PESTS AND DISEASES.

Position Plant in full sun. Any soil
texture, provided it is well drained,
not acid, and fertile; pH 6.0–6.8.
Lime if necessary to avoid clubroot.

Cultivation There are cultivars
available for sowing in every season,
so you could pick cabbages all year
round. Sow either in modules or a
seedbed in successive batches. Sow
spring cabbages in late summer and
plant out in early autumn; early-
summer types in late winter or early
spring for transplanting in mid-spring.

Sow summer cultivars in early spring
to plant out in late spring to early
summer; autumn types in late spring
for transplanting in summer; winter
cabbages in late spring to plant out
in early or midsummer. Give seedlings
plenty of light and withhold fertilizer
to discourage spindly growth. Set
plants 30–45 cm (12–18 in) apart,
depending on expected head size.
A good mulch will help to retain
moisture. Cabbage prefers rich soil;
add well-rotted compost or manure
before planting and allow the soil
to settle for a couple of months.
Apply seaweed solution or compost
tea a month after planting.

Pests and diseases Use tunnel
cloches or horticultural fleece to

Cabbage continued

HARDINESS
Hardy; young
cabbage plants will
withstand light
frost; mature ones
more severe frost.

DAYS TO MATURITY
60–120 days.

COMMENTS
Cabbage is an
excellent source of
calcium in the diet.

Standard cabbage types (above) form a tighter head than Savoy cabbage (opposite), which has puckered or crinkled leaves. Savoy cabbage is also milder and sweeter.

control cabbage root fly, cabbage-white-butterfly caterpillars, flea beetles, and birds such as pigeons. Another method of stopping root fly laying eggs is to place cardboard or felt discs around the stems of young plants. Aphids cause distorted leaves; hose them off with a strong water spray or spray with fatty acids. Rotate brassica plantings to avoid soil-borne diseases such as clubroot and mildews.

Harvesting and storage Harvest early cultivars as needed, as they do not store well. Harvest red cabbage before a hard freeze and store, roots and all, in dry leaves in a cold shed or garage. Can be pickled or made into sauerkraut. Hardier winter cabbages can be left in the ground until you need them.

Special tips Cut early and mid-season cabbage high on the plant, leaving as many loose lower leaves as possible. As many as six small cabbages, called spring greens, will form on the stem, providing a delicious second harvest. Grow cabbages with plants that won't compete for calcium.

Related plants

**Ornamental cabbage *B. oleracea*
Acephala Group** This is actually a kale, rather than a cabbage. The flowering cabbage forms a loose head or rosette of colourful green and red, white or magenta leaves.

Red cabbage makes excellent coleslaw and soup, and is pretty enough to grow in the flower garden. Marigolds and aromatic herbs planted nearby may help to deter pests.

Ornamental cabbages are edible but are grown chiefly as ornamentals for autumn and winter colour (cool temperatures are needed for the striking colours to develop fully). Seed suppliers often offer a mix of colours.

Pointed-headed cabbage *B. oleracea* Capitata Group Forms a cone-shaped head. It is quick-maturing, and has been popular for centuries. Cultivars include 'Hispi', 'Greyhound' and 'Kalibos'.

Red cabbage *B. oleracea* Capitata Group Attractive blue-purple leaves and red-purple heads with white veining. Cultivars include 'Ruby Perfection Hybrid', 'Red Acre' and 'Red Rookie'.

Round-headed cabbage *B. oleracea* Capitata Group Globe-shaped or flattened round heads. Early cultivars include 'Spring' and 'Durham Early'. Mid-season cultivars include 'Stonehead' and 'Primo'. Late or storage cultivars include 'Red Jewel' and 'Tarvoy'.

Savoy cabbage *B. oleracea* Capitata Group Puckered, crinkly, light green or blue-green leaves. Heads are often less tight than smooth-leaved cabbage, but the flavour is superior. Cultivars include 'Savoy January King' and 'Savoy Melissa'.

Brassica oleracea Gemmifera Group

HARDINESS
Hardy winter
vegetable.

DAYS TO MATURITY
90–252 days.
Mature plants
withstand heavy
frost, but grow
only slowly.

COMMENTS
Harvested sprouts
are a late-season
treat, when a light
frost has sweetened
their flavour. They
freeze well.

BRUSSELS SPROUTS

INDIVIDUAL BRUSSELS SPROUTS LOOK LIKE
TIGHTLY WRAPPED, MINIATURE CABBAGES.

Position Plant in full sun in well-drained, firm, and fertile soil, with adequate lime levels; pH 6.0–6.8.

Cultivation Require a long growing season and are best when matured in cold weather. Sow early cultivars indoors and transplant when you sow other spring crops. Sow late cultivars for cropping through winter in early and mid-spring outdoors and plant out in early to midsummer. Space plants about 60 cm (2 ft) apart and keep weeded or mulched. Pinch off top leaves to encourage side growth.

Pests and diseases Rotate with non-brassica crops to avoid soil-borne diseases such as clubroot. Use tunnel cloches or horticultural fleece to deter caterpillars, flea beetles and cabbage root fly, or use collars around the stems to stop cabbage root fly. Whitefly can be difficult to wash out of sprouts. Water well and grow in fertile soil to reduce vulnerability to aphids.

Harvesting and storage Harvest the lower sprouts first, once they reach about 2.5 cm (1 in) in diameter, by breaking off the leaf below and snapping off the sprout. Sprouts higher up will continue to grow. Entire stalks can also be harvested.

Special tips Sprouts keep for several weeks on the stalk if you pull up the whole plant and keep it cold.

Brassica oleracea Gongylodes Group

HARDINESS
Hardy. Purple cultivars are usually grown as an autumn and winter vegetable, and green types are grown for harvest in spring and summer.

DAYS TO MATURITY
38–84 days.

COMMENTS
Cultivars include 'Early Purple Vienna' (purple-skinned cultivar), and 'Kolibri Hybrid'.

KOHLRABI

BOTH THE SWOLLEN, TURNIP-LIKE STEM AND THE LEAVES OF KOHLRABI ARE EDIBLE, AND THEY ARE OFTEN COOKED TOGETHER.

Position Plant in full sun in fertile, firm and well-drained soil with adequate lime; pH 6.0–7.0.

Cultivation Direct-sow 2–4 weeks before the last spring frost or start indoors 6–8 weeks before last frost and plant out 15 cm (6 in) apart. Use thinnings of direct-sown crops as salad greens. Mulch or hoe to control weeds. Plant out autumn crops from transplants, or direct-sow 2 months before autumn frost.

Pests and diseases Suffers same pests and diseases as other brassicas (see pages 144–5), but leaf damage is not as serious because they are not the main crop. Keep watered or mulched and avoid leaving in summer crops too long in hot weather, which produces tough, woody stems.

Harvesting and storage Harvest the entire plant when swollen stem is about 5 cm (2 in) in diameter. Overgrown kohlrabi can be woody. Best eaten fresh, but will keep for 2 weeks in the refrigerator.

Special tips Will withstand a light frost. Thin raw slices make a good low-calorie nibble, with a crunch like stir-fried water chestnuts.

Brassica oleracea Italica Group

HARDINESS
Purple and white
sprouting broccoli
are hardy and are
grown as winter
and early crops;
green sprouting
broccoli is less
hardy and grown
for autumn harvest.

DAYS TO MATURITY
Purple and white
sprouting broccoli,
8–12 months; green
sprouting broccoli,
77–98 days.

BROCCOLI

VIRTUALLY UNKNOWN IN HOME GARDENS
50 YEARS AGO, SPROUTING BROCCOLI AND
CALABRESE ARE NOW COOL-WEATHER
FAVOURITES.

Position Full sun. Well-drained, firm
and rich soil with plenty of lime;
pH 6.7–7.2.

Cultivation All types of broccoli may
be sown in spring, for harvest in
autumn (calabrese), autumn to early
spring (Romanesco), late winter
(sprouting broccoli), early summer
(Chinese broccoli and broccoli raab).
Purple and white sprouting broccoli
are also sown in late winter for
summer and autumn crops; Chinese
broccoli through the summer for
harvest until mid-autumn; and

broccoli raab is sown in summer for
autumn crops or in autumn for a
spring harvest. Start spring seedlings
indoors, about 2 months before the
last spring frost. Set out hardened-
off transplants in the garden a month
before the last frost. Space plants
30–60 cm (1–2 ft) apart; wider spacing
will yield larger heads. Hoe or mulch
and keep the soil evenly moist. Lack
of water will stress the plant, which
may fail to head or may become
vulnerable to insect pests. Sow
autumn crops directly about 90 days
before the first autumn frost, or
transplant about 60 days before frost.

Pests and diseases Use cardboard
"collars" to deter cutworms. Cloches

Broccoli continued

Broccoli is now known to be a valuable addition to the diet, and is thought to provide protection against a number of ills, including some cancers.

and horticultural fleece will thwart flea beetles, cabbage root fly and other root maggots. To avoid soil-borne diseases, don't plant broccoli and other brassicas in the same spot more than once every 3 years.

Harvesting and storage Harvest broccoli heads when they have reached maximum size, but before the tight, green flower buds begin to loosen and show yellow. Spring crops are best harvested once, with as much of the edible stem as possible. Cut later broccoli heads with less stem attached, leaving as much of the plant intact as possible so that it will produce smaller sideshoots or "florets", which you can harvest until there is a hard frost. After picking, broccoli freezes well.

Special tips A small planting of Chinese cabbage nearby will draw flea beetles away from broccoli.

Related plants

Chinese broccoli *B. oleracea* Alboglabra Group   Also called Chinese kale or kai laan. Similar to sprouting broccoli, but the buds and leaves are lighter green and sweeter. The stems and young leaves are also eaten steamed or stir-fried. More heat-tolerant than standard broccoli.

Purple and white sprouting broccoli *B. oleracea* Italica Group   The sprouting broccolis form lots of shoots with loose, small heads.

Purple sprouting broccoli is striking even in the flower garden but, unfortunately, the colour fades during cooking.

They are the hardier types of broccoli and very useful as a late or an overwintering crop, for harvest from autumn through to early spring. The purple broccoli loses its colour when cooked.

Romanesco broccoli *B. oleracea* **Italica Group** Unusual conical heads of pale green, peaked florets that resemble little rocket ships. The crunchy texture is more like cauliflower than broccoli. Requires wider spacing—up to 90 cm (3 ft)—and a longer growing season than most standard broccoli. In most areas it is planted in late spring for autumn harvest.

Calabrese *B. oleracea* **Italica Group** Also called Italian broccoli, American broccoli, or green sprouting broccoli. Forms green heads that are larger and denser than the purple and white sprouting broccolis. It is grown as an annual crop to harvest in spring. Cut the central head, with surrounding small leaves, before its flowers open. The plant will produce a few more new, smaller sideshoots.

Broccoli raab *B. rapa* **Ruvo Group** Also called rapini or rapine; this vegetable is prized in Italy. It is usually blanched, then chopped and fried in olive oil with garlic. The glossy, dark green leaves are harvested along with the flower buds and stems. Spring crops may bolt to seed quickly; autumn plantings usually produce three or more harvests of flower shoots and leaves.

Brassica rapa var. *chinensis*

HARDINESS
Half hardy. Will stand light frost, but early sowings outdoors tend to bolt. Sow in warmth indoors in spring, outdoors through summer or under cover in early autumn.

DAYS TO MATURITY
14 days, cut-and-come-again; 50–70 days, mature plants.

COMMENTS
Leafy relative of Chinese cabbage.

PAK CHOI

USE THIS VERSATILE AND NUTRITIOUS ORIENTAL BRASSICA AS A CUT-AND-COME-AGAIN CROP FOR SALAD LEAVES OR ADD THE MATURE LEAVES TO STIR-FRIES.

Position Likes a sheltered, sunny site, in well-drained but moisture-retentive, rich soil; pH 6.5–7.0.

Cultivation Use bolt-resistant cultivars for spring sowings in modules; transplant when large enough to handle. Sow direct in summer. Space 15–30 cm (6–12 in) apart, depending on the cultivar; broadcast sow outdoors or in a grow-bag for a cut-and-come-again crop.

Pests and diseases Use cloches to protect from flea beetles. Protect against slugs and snails and rotate sowings to avoid clubroot.

Harvesting and storage Pick leaves from seedling stage onwards; they wilt quickly if stored, so use fresh.

Related plants

Pak choi *B. rapa* var. *chinensis* Also called celery mustard. Spoon-shaped, light to blue-green leaves and thick, crisp, white, green or purple stems. Cultivars include 'Mei Qing Choi' and 'Joi Choi'.

Choy sum *B. campestris* subsp. *chinensis* var. *utilis* Similar to pak choi, but the leaves are thick, glossy and dark green. Cultivars include 'Hong Kong' and 'Hon Tsai Tai'.

Brassica rapa var. *nipposinica*

HARDINESS
Hardy; will withstand a moderate frost or grow over winter under cover.

DAYS TO MATURITY
40 days; the thinnings can be harvested earlier.

COMMENTS
Cultivars include 'Green Spray', 'Mizuna'. Other common names include Japanese greens.

MIZUNA GREENS

MILDER THAN MOST MUSTARDS AND EASY TO GROW, MIZUNA GREENS ADD DASH TO SALADS AND STIR-FRIES, OR CAN BE COOKED IN THE SAME WAY AS OTHER GREENS.

Position Plant in full sun. Not fussy, but best in fertile soil that does not dry out; pH 5.8–6.2.

Cultivation Sow in spring indoors in modules and transplant after the frosts. Sow in summer outdoors until autumn, then sow under cover for winter crops. Thin to 10–15 cm (4–6 in) apart, using thinnings in salad. Irrigate to promote rapid growth.

Pests and diseases Affected by the usual problems of brassicas (see cabbages, pages 144–5). Cloches or fleece will protect young plants, especially spring crops, from flea beetles, cabbage root fly, whitefly and birds. Mizuna greens can become strong-flavoured in hot weather; use them as cooked greens.

Harvesting and storage Leaves will grow to 30–35 cm (12–14 in); cut when 10–15 cm (4–6 in) long for best salad greens. Cut about 2.5 cm (1 in) above the crown; new leaves will sprout. Four or five harvests are possible. Or harvest whole plants for cooking.

Special tips Seeds packaged as "cut-and-come-again mix" contain mizuna greens with lettuce and spicy salads. Eat as mixed baby leaves.

Brassica rapa var. *pekinensis*

HARDINESS
Frost hardy. Sow
through spring and
summer for harvest
from midsummer
to late autumn.
Quickly goes to
seed (bolts) in
warm weather
or if seedlings
are exposed to
severe frost.

DAYS TO MATURITY
63–70 days. Mature
plants will tolerate
moderate frost.

CABBAGE, CHINESE

NUTRITIOUS AND FAST-GROWING, CHINESE CABBAGE CAN BE ADDED TO STIR-FRIES, OR EVEN EATEN FRESH IN SALADS. IT IS A GOOD SOURCE OF DIETARY CALCIUM.

Position Likes to be planted in a sheltered site in full sun, in well-drained but moisture-retentive soil that is rich in humus; pH 6.0–6.8.

Cultivation Sow quick-maturing cultivars for early crops. Transplants poorly in spring, unless sown in biodegradable pots. Direct-sow after the last frost; thin to 30 cm (1 ft) apart. Protect outdoor sowings from late frosts with cloches or horticultural fleece.

Pests and diseases As for pak choi (see page 152).

Harvesting and storage Harvest when heads feel solid; they may re-sprout to provide salad leaves. Also cut leaves from bolted plants. Keeps for 6 weeks in a refrigerator.

Related plants

Chinese cabbage **B. rapa** var. **pekinensis** Also called Chinese leaves. Forming large, barrel-shaped heads, this type grows up to about 4.5 kg (10 lb). Cultivars include 'Blues' (early), 'Kasumi' (late), 'Wong Bok' and 'Yuki'.

Michihi cabbage **B. rapa** var. **pekinensis** Tall-growing, smaller-headed type, cylindrical in shape. Cultivars include 'Jade Pagoda'.

Brassica rapa Rapifera Group

TURNIP

GROWN BOTH FOR ITS TENDER LEAVES AND
FOR ITS CRISP ROOT, TURNIP HAS THE BEST
FLAVOUR AND TEXTURE IN COOL WEATHER.

Position Plant in moist, loose, deep
soil that is rich in humus; can stand
light shade; pH 5.5–7.5.

Cultivation Sow 13 mm (½ in) deep
from late winter to autumn; protect
early sowings from frost. Thin to
7.5 cm (3 in) apart; use thinnings
as fresh or cooked greens. Water
regularly for fast growth in spring,
because turnips bolt (run to seed)
in hot weather.

Pests and diseases Use cloches or
fleece to protect from flea beetles
and cabbage root fly. Reduce
damage from turnip gall weevil
and cutworms, especially in spring
crops, by not planting where
other root crops have grown the
preceding year. Turnips that mature
in hot weather may be fibrous or
strong-flavoured.

Harvesting and storage Pull turnips
as needed, as 2.5-cm (1-in) wide
"babies" up to 8–10-cm (3–4-in)
roots. Larger turnips can be woody.
Turnips will store in the ground
until early winter, but are damaged
by hard frost. Store roots in damp
sand in a cool place; freeze leaves
as you would spinach.

Special tips Avoid overhead
watering to prevent mildew.

Brassica rapa var. *perviridis*

HARDINESS
Frost hardy; mature
plants will tolerate
-12°C (10°F).

DAYS TO MATURITY
28–84 days, for
mature plants,
depending on time
of year; earlier if
picking as cut-and-
come-again crop.

KOMATSUNA

ALSO KNOWN AS MUSTARD SPINACH,
THIS ORIENTAL BRASSICA HAS GLOSSY GREEN
LEAVES THAT MAY BE PICKED YOUNG FOR
SALADS OR WHEN MATURE FOR COOKING.

Position Grows well in open site in
full sun, or light shade in the height
of summer, and well-drained but
moisture-retentive soil that is rich
in humus; pH 6.0–6.8.

Cultivation Sow from early spring
to autumn outdoors; shield early
and late sowings from frosts with
cloches or horticultural fleece.
Thin to 10 cm (4 in) apart for small
plants or up to 30 cm (1 ft) apart
for large plants. Broadcast sow
for cut-and-come-again crops.

Late sowings may be lifted and taken
under cover to provide winter greens.

Pests and diseases Suffers the usual
brassica problems (see cabbage,
pages 144–5). Slugs and snails are
attracted most to the seedling plants.

Harvesting and storage Harvest the
leaves at any stage from seedling
to mature plants. New growth will
appear, for an extended harvest.

Brassica spp.

HARDINESS
Mostly hardy; can
be grown as a
winter vegetable.
Will withstand
moderate frost.

DAYS TO MATURITY
40–90 days;
thinnings can be
harvested earlier.

COMMENTS
As the weather
gets hotter, so do
the leaves of
mustard plants.

MUSTARDS, ORIENTAL

MUSTARD IS GROWN MAINLY FOR ITS SPICY
SEEDS, WHICH ARE GROUND OR LEFT WHOLE
TO PRODUCE A POPULAR CONDIMENT. THE
LEAVES OF SOME TYPES ADD A DELICIOUS
ZING TO SALADS.

Position Plant in full sun. Not fussy,
but prefers light, well-drained and
fertile soil; pH 5.8–6.2.

Cultivation Sow bolt-resistant cultivars
in spring and early summer in
modules in warmth, for transplanting
as soon as large enough. Direct-sow
in summer outdoors. Thin to
10–15 cm (4–6 in) apart, adding the
thinnings to salads or soups. Can be
broadcast-sown for cut-and-come-
again crops. Irrigate, especially during
dry spells, to promote rapid growth.

Pests and diseases Rarely troubled
by pests. Good air circulation
prevents mildew. Bolts (runs to
seed) quickly in hot weather.

Harvesting and storage Pick leaves
as needed from the outside of the
plant, allowing new leaves to sprout
from the centre. Tender leaves do
not store well in the refrigerator.

Special tips Cut off the flower stalk
as soon as it appears in the centre
of the plant. This will prolong your
harvest of leaves, which can be
mixed with cress in the traditional
"mustard and cress" combination
salad. However, if you are growing
this crop for its black seeds, leave the
flowers undisturbed until the seeds

Mustard continued

The striking purple-red leaves of red mustard (*B. juncea* var. *foliosa*) add colour to salads, but use sparingly, as the bite can be startling to diners unfamiliar with mustard leaves.

are set and ripened. Always harvest your seed crops in dry weather.

Related plants

Black mustard *B. nigra* Grown chiefly for its seed, which is used to produce a traditional spicy condiment, in warm climates. In the UK's temperate climate, seeds rarely ripen in the cooler summers, so the plants are grown for their leaves.

Brown mustard *B. juncea* Large, curly or frilled green leaves, usually grown for greens. Cultivars include 'Green in Snow' and 'Southern Giant'.

Oilseed rape *B. napus* Grown mainly as an oilseed crop. Oilseed rape is also grown by organically minded gardeners, who make use of the

way its strong taproots break up heavy clay soils; they also grow it to dig in as a green manure crop to help in the control of nematodes.

Red mustard *B. juncea* var. *foliosa* Broad, flat leaves with red or purple colouring, very spicy. Cultivars include 'Osaka Purple' and 'Red Giant'.

White mustard *B. hirta* The seeds are ground for a condiment; less pungent than black mustard.

Capsicum annuum

HARDINESS
Frost tender; in all
but the mildest
areas, best grown
in the greenhouse
or conservatory.

DAYS TO MATURITY
80–140 days for
green peppers;
20–50 days more
for mature, fully
coloured peppers.

COMMENTS
Scientific studies
show that planting
marigolds nearby
reduces the
number of aphids
on sweet peppers.

PEPPERS, SWEET AND CHILLI

SWEET PEPPERS ARE CRISP AND JUICY WHEN
GREEN, BUT SWEETER WHEN ALLOWED TO RIPEN
TO RED, YELLOW OR ORANGE. CHILLI PEPPERS
INCREASE IN PUNGENCY AS THEY RIPEN.

Position Plant in a sheltered site in
full sun in light, well-drained soil, not
overly rich, or in a grow-bag or
soilless potting compost; pH 6.0–7.0.

Cultivation Sow seeds indoors
6–8 weeks before last spring frost.
Do not overwater pepper seedlings,
as they are vulnerable to root rot.
Harden off and plant out 25–37.5 cm
(10–15 in) apart when frost danger
is well past and the soil has warmed.
It helps to pre-warm the soil with
black plastic mulch. Protect young
peppers under cloches until warmer
weather arrives. Hoe shallowly;
do not mulch until the soil is
thoroughly warm. Too much
nitrogen will produce lush foliage
and few peppers, but an application
of compost tea when the plants are
in flower can help to increase the
yield. Alternatively, plant into
grow-bags or containers in the
greenhouse and feed regularly with
tomato fertilizer, once the first
flowers appear. Peppers, particularly
thick-fleshed sweet peppers, are
prone to blossom-end rot if they
become drought-stressed. Plants
with ripening fruits, especially those
in grow-bags, may need support.
Don't pinch out the growing tips;
it delays fruiting.

Peppers, sweet and chilli continued

Essential to many Asian and Mexican dishes, chilli peppers come in many sizes, shapes and degrees of "heat". Wear gloves when cutting up and avoid contact with eyes.

Pests and diseases Do not plant where pepper or related plants, such as tomatoes and aubergines, have been grown in the preceding 2 years. Protect young plants from cutworms with cardboard collars. Under cover, aphids, red spider mites and whitefly can be a problem, but biological controls are effective. Rot (*Botrytis*) afflicts plants in cool, damp conditions.

Harvesting and storage Pick immature or green peppers when they are large enough for use to encourage further fruiting. Leave some fruit on the plant to mature. Fully ripe sweet peppers will be yellow, orange or red, depending on the cultivar. Ripe chillis come in a range of colours, from yellow and red to purple and black. Pick mature peppers when 50–75 per cent coloured; they will finish ripening in 1–2 days at room temperature. When frost threatens, harvest all the remaining fruit. Fresh peppers will keep for 2 weeks or more if stored at around 13°C (55°F), or freeze them for winter cooking. Freeze or pickle thick-fleshed chilli peppers, such as jalapeño and hot cherry; dry thin-fleshed ones, such as Thai chillis. Chillis may be dried on the plant—cut the main stem and hang upside-down in the greenhouse or another warm, sunny, well-ventilated space.

Less juicy than sweet peppers, cone peppers retain their shape and flavour well during cooking. They may drop their flowers in the heat, so provide shade during hot spells.

Special tips Chilli peppers and sweet peppers may cross-pollinate. Plant them well away from each other, especially if you intend to save the seed. Handle chilli peppers with care—the capsaicin they contain will burn sensitive tissues, such as the eyes and mouth.

Related plants

Chilli peppers *C. annuum* **Longum Group** Chilli peppers come in a wide variety of shapes, sizes and degrees of "heat". The milder cultivars include 'Ancho', a large, mildly hot pepper that is often served stuffed. Medium-hot chillis include 'Jalapeño' and 'Hungarian Wax'. Fiery chillis include cayenne and Thai peppers. Hot weather intensifies the flavour and heat.

Pickling peppers *C. annuum* **Conoides Group** Usually small, thin-fleshed peppers with a cone shape, borne upright on the plant. The long and thin 'Peperoncini' is an Italian favourite, usually picked when green, but turning red at maturity.

Sweet peppers (bell) *C. annuum* **Grossum Group** Blocky in shape and thick-fleshed, these peppers are most often used fresh in salads and as crudités or for stuffing. Most cultivars turn red or yellow when fully ripe; purple and "chocolate" peppers are coloured at their immature stage and turn red when fully ripe. Popular cultivars include

Peppers, sweet and chilli continued

These small pickling peppers, which ripen to red, yellow and orange, also provide a lovely contrast in colour in the salad bowl.

'Ace' (red at maturity), 'Gourmet' (yellow), 'Jupiter' (red), and 'Orange Bell' (orange).

Sweet peppers (other) *C. annuum* **Grossum Group** Long sweet peppers, also called Italian or cone peppers, have elongated fruit up to 30 cm (1 ft) long. They are generally thinner-fleshed than bell peppers and hold their shape and flavour better in cooked dishes. Cultivars range from dark green to light yellow when immature and ripen to red, orange or yellow; they include 'Biscayne' (pale green, ripens red), 'Sweet Banana' (yellow, ripens red) and 'Gypsy' (yellow, ripens red).

Chrysanthemum coronarium var. *spatiosum*

ASTERACEAE

HARDINESS
Hardy; use as a winter vegetable in mild areas. Tolerates light to moderate frost.

DAYS TO MATURITY
45 days, but thinnings can be harvested earlier.

COMMENTS
Cultivars include 'Shungiku'.

CHOP-SUEY GREENS

THE AROMATIC, EDIBLE LEAVES OF CHOP-SUEY GREENS ARE POPULAR IN ORIENTAL CUISINES, EITHER STIR-FRIED OR DROPPED INTO SOME OF THE CLASSIC SOUPS.

Position Avoid hot, dry areas. Not fussy, but prefers fertile, moist soil; pH 6.0–6.7.

Cultivation Direct-sow about 13 mm (½ in) deep from mid-spring to autumn and thin to 10–15 cm (4–6 in). Use the thinnings in stir-fries, soups or salads.

Pests and diseases Little troubled by pests, but to avoid leaf diseases, don't plant where ornamental chrysanthemums (now more correctly called dendranthemas)

have been grown. Hot weather and inadequate moisture can cause premature bolting. The flowers, however, are attractive.

Harvesting and storage Harvest whole plants or side leaves as needed before flowering, but avoid planting in hot weather, as the leaves become disagreeably bitter. Can also be cut as a cut-and-come-again crop. Chop-suey greens "cook down" in the pot, so several plants may be needed for a soup.

Special tips Remove flower buds to prolong the harvest of leaves. Other common names include chrysanthemum greens.

Cichorium endivia

HARDINESS
Half-hardy.

DAYS TO MATURITY
70–90 days; earlier
for cut-and-come-
again crops.

COMMENTS
Sow broad-leaved
cultivars such as
'Batavian Full Heart'
in midsummer to
early autumn. Sow
curly-leaved
cultivars such as
'Salad King',
'Pancalieri'
and 'Green Curled'
in spring and
summer.

ENDIVE

WITH A STRONGER FLAVOUR THAN LETTUCE,
ENDIVE HAS EITHER CURLY LEAVES (FRISÉE
TYPE) OR BROAD LEAVES (BATAVIAN TYPE
OR ESCAROLE).

Position Full sun or, in midsummer,
partial shade. Prefers fertile, well-
limed, well-drained soil; pH 5.5–7.0.

Cultivation Sow in modules indoors
8 weeks before last frost and harden
off and transplant a month before
last frost, 25–30 cm (10–12 in) apart.
Cover plants if a hard frost threatens.
Sow direct outdoors from early
summer to early winter, depending
on type. Protect late sowings of
hardier, broad-leaved endives for
winter crops under cloches. They
can be blanched by inverting a pot
or box over the plant, or by tying

the outer leaves together at the top.

Pests and diseases Control slugs and
snails with beer traps set in the soil.
Aphids, lettuce root aphids and
caterpillars may also attack the
foliage and roots. Early plantings
may bolt in cold conditions.

Harvesting and storage Harvest
curly-leaved endive in spring and
summer; broad-leaved types in
autumn and winter. Both types may
be used as cut-and-come-again crops
from spring to autumn. Cut entire
head at base in the morning while
dew is still on plant. Rinse; wrap in
paper towels, then in a plastic bag.
Keeps up to 2 weeks refrigerated.

Cichorium intybus

HARDINESS
Frost hardy; can be
grown as a winter
vegetable, but some
cultivars may bolt
in cold springs.
Some cultivars
can be planted in
autumn for spring
harvest.

DAYS TO MATURITY
40–130 days,
depending on type.
Leaf chicory (left)
grows quickly.

CHICORY

THE LEAVES OF CHICORY IMPART
A TANGY FLAVOUR TO GREEN SALADS.
FORCING (BLANCHING) CHICORY
CREATES A MILDER FLAVOUR.

Position Full sun. Well-drained,
moderately fertile soil; pH 6.0–6.5.

Cultivation Sow Witloof cultivars in
late spring and early summer, for
forcing in autumn. Sow radicchio,
sugarloaf and leaf types from
mid-spring to late summer; you can
also sow them indoors as cut-and-
come-again salads in late winter,
spring and autumn. To avoid bolting
of early sowings, choose bolt-resistant
cultivars and sow in modules indoors,
then harden off and transplant
under the protection of a cloche or
horticultural fleece. Space plants
20–30 cm (8–12 ins) apart. Keep
radicchio, leaf and sugarloaf chicories
well watered in hot weather.

Pests and diseases Chicory is little
troubled by pests, except possibly
aphids and slugs. Keep the soil
moist to avoid interior browning of
head-forming types. Hearting types
are inconsistent; some plants will
produce only leaves or loose rosettes,
despite the best conditions.

Harvesting and storage Harvest
leaves as needed. Cut hearting
types as needed when the heads
are firm (plants will last in the
garden for several weeks). Harvest
chicons (chicories grown for their
roots) 3–4 weeks after being
covered for forcing.

Chicory continued

Hearting chicory, which is popular broiled, roasted or served in salads, grows faster than loose-leaved chicory, but more slowly than endive.

Related plants

Witloof chicory *C. intybus* Also called Belgian endive. Cut off the first heart in autumn, then dig up roots, trim to 20 cm (8 in), and bury upright in moist sand or coir compost. Kept in complete darkness at 10–15°C (50–60°F), the roots will produce small pale sprouts or "chicons" in about 3 weeks. Cultivars include 'Zoom' and 'Witloof'.

Radicchio *C. intybus* Also called red chicory. Red-tinged leaves surround a small, red heart with white veining, resembling red cabbage. Older cultivars, such as 'Rossa di Treviso', may require cutting back to 2.5 cm (1 in) in midsummer to form hearts in autumn. Modern cultivars form hearts without cutting back. Cultivars include 'Rossa di Verona'.

Sugarloaf chicory *C. intybus* This chicory makes large hearts similar to romaine (cos) lettuces. Mature plants withstand drought well. Cultivars include 'Pain du Sucre' and 'Sugar Loaf'.

Leaf chicory *C. intybus* Also called catalogna or Italian dandelion. It is grown for its leaves, which vary in shape from dandelion-like to smooth or rosette-like, and in colour from light to dark green and also red-tinged. Some can be cut and left to re-sprout for continued harvest. Cultivars include 'Variegata de Castelfranco' and 'Spadano', but not many are available.

Crambe maritima

HARDINESS
Hardy.

DAYS TO MATURITY
Grown from seed,
sea kale will not
provide a harvest
until the third year.
After that, harvest
annually in spring.

COMMENTS
Tolerates salty
environments
very well.

SEA KALE

GROW SEA KALE FOR THE TENDER SHOOTS
THAT EMERGE IN SPRING. YOU CAN BLANCH
AND EAT THESE LIKE ASPARAGUS.

Position Plant in full sun or partial
shade in rich, well-drained, slightly
alkaline soil; pH 6.0–7.0.

Cultivation Best started from root
cuttings, called thongs, either
taken from a three-year-old plant,
or obtained from specialist suppliers.
Alternatively, sow about six seeds
in mounds 60–90 cm (2–3 ft) apart,
2–4 weeks before last spring frost.
Thin to three or four plants per
mound. Mulch over winter. Top-
dress with compost or well-rotted
manure each spring.

Pests and diseases Rarely troubled
by pests, except sometimes flea
beetle. Sea kale roots tend to rise
to the surface. Cover exposed roots
with soil each autumn to prevent
cold damage and to increase shoot
production the following year.
Rotate crops to avoid clubroot.

Harvesting and storage In late
winter, before first shoots appear,
invert a large clay pot over the
mound. To speed shoot emergence,
mulch around the pot with straw or
dry leaves. Check periodically for
shoots, and cut them below the soil
surface when they are 15–20 cm
(6–8 in) long. Cut third-year plants
for 1–2 weeks; harvest older plants
for 3–4 weeks. Remove the pot
when the harvest is finished.

Cucumis sativus

CUCUMBER

HOME-GROWN CUCUMBERS HAVE A FAR
BETTER FLAVOUR THAN SHOP-BOUGHT ONES.
THEY ARE COOL AND REFRESHING IN SALADS,
BUT CAN ALSO BE PICKLED.

Position Grow greenhouse cucumbers
in grow-bags, in a warm but well-
ventilated site, or in a greenhouse
bed with fertile, light, free-draining
soil, to avoid rot. Plant outdoor
cucumbers in full sun, in a site with
good air circulation, in light soil
with well-rotted manure or compost
worked in; pH 6.0–7.0.

Cultivation Cucumbers dislike cold
soil, so wait for 3–4 weeks after the
last frost to direct-sow or transplant
them into the garden. Indoors,
sow seed in biodegradable pots

2–3 weeks before you plan to
harden them off and plant them
out, or germinate the seeds on a
moist kitchen towel and plant into
soil that has been warmed by
covering it for 4 weeks with a sheet
of black or clear plastic mulch.
Thin plants to stand 30–37.5 cm
(1–1¼ ft) apart in rows. If the soil
is heavy, grow cucumbers in a
raised bed, or on a ridge of soil—
each with four or five plants, about
1.2 m (4 ft) apart. Mulch, or keep
cultivated until plants begin to climb.
Cucumbers, like most climbing plants,
need support. Outdoors, train them
over a trellis or up a fence. In the
greenhouse, use wires or lengths of
garden twine hung from the roof.

Cucurbita spp.

PUMPKIN

AS FAMILIAR AS FALLING LEAVES IN AUTUMN, THE HANDSOME PUMPKIN MAKES FINE PIES AND BAKED DISHES, AS WELL AS LANTERNS FOR HALLOWE'EN.

Position Plant in full sun. Not fussy about soil texture, but likes a fertile, well-drained soil; pH 6.0–7.0.

Cultivation Pumpkins are hungry plants and need a long season to ripen fully. Give them a good start by filling a trench with half-rotted vegetable scraps or manure, then fill in with soil to a slight mound and sow on top. Thin to 1.2 m (4 ft) apart. Protect the seedlings from frost with a cloche or horticultural fleece. Trailing cultivars can be trained up supports, such as an arch or trellis. Thin the fruits to 3 per plant for larger fruits. As the pumpkins swell, place them on a tile to stop soil spoiling the skin, or support trailing ones in nets. The broad leaves will shade out most weeds. If space is limited, try growing some of the space-saving, extra small, bush-type pumpkins.

Pests and diseases Pumpkins are relatively trouble-free. Prevent the main disease, powdery mildew, by providing good air circulation. Slugs and snails may attack young plants, especially in cold, wet conditions— try beer traps or a barrier mulch, such as cocoa shells.

Pumpkin continued

Pumpkins come in a huge variety of sizes and colours. The flowers, like those of other kinds of squash, can be stuffed, lightly fried and eaten.

Harvesting and storage Harvest pumpkins when they are fully coloured and their shells are hard, or after light frost has killed the top-growth. Ripe pumpkins ring hollow when tapped. Leave them to "cure" and harden their skins, in a dry, warm, sunny place. Store in a cool, dry area. Pumpkins keep for several months, but lose flavour in long storage. The cooked flesh freezes well, however. Cultivars meant for cooking, such as 'Small Sugar', taste better than large field pumpkins.

Special tips If you want to win the big-pumpkin contest, cultivate plants such as borage and lemon balm near your pumpkin patch to attract bees. Research shows that pumpkins pollinated by numerous bees form larger fruits. A crop of beans, peas or clover in the pumpkin patch will enrich the soil for next year's crop. Cultivars that produce giant pumpkins include 'Atlantic Giant' and 'Mammoth'.

Cucurbita spp.

HARDINESS
Half-hardy.

DAYS TO MATURITY
85–140 frost-free
days after planting.

COMMENTS
The flesh of the
fast-growing 'Gold
Nugget' (left) is
rich in flavour.

SQUASH, WINTER

WINTER SQUASH MAY NOT ALWAYS GROW
WELL OR RIPEN FULLY IN COOL, SHORT UK
SUMMERS, BUT THEY ARE WORTH A TRY.

Position Plant in full sun, in an area
with good air circulation. Prefers
rich, well-composted, well-drained
soil; pH 6.0–6.5.

Cultivation Winter squashes are best
grown like pumpkins on top of a
mounded trench, with half-rotted
vegetable scraps or manure at the
bottom. Space them 45–60 cm
(18–24 in) apart. Protect the
seedlings from frost with a cloche
or horticultural fleece. Trailing
cultivars can be trained up supports,
such as a wigwam of canes. Thin the
fruits to 3 per plant for larger fruits.

As they swell, place the squashes
on tiles to stop soil spoiling the skin,
or support trailing ones in nets.

Pests and diseases Like pumpkins,
winter squashes are fairly easy to
grow and are not much troubled by
pests. To deter insects, interplant
with radishes or basil. Provide good
air circulation to avoid powdery
mildew. Do not plant where squash
or its relatives, such as cucumbers
and melons, have been grown in
the preceding year. Mildew can be
a problem in late-summer damp
spells. Plants may be weakened too
much to ripen fruit. Pick off affected
leaves and avoid watering from
overhead and splashing the leaves.

Squash, winter continued

'Sweet Dumpling' is a small and attractive squash that requires no curing before storage. Squash flowers can be stuffed, fried lightly and served as an entrée.

Slugs and snails and cucumber mosaic virus might also pose a problem.

Harvesting and storage Harvest when the shell is hard enough that it cannot be dented with a fingernail. Harvest all fruit as soon as light frost has killed the top-growth; any more than a light frost will shorten storage life. Leave on the ground, or bring indoors and leave in a warm, bright spot, to "cure" in the sun for 10–14 days, but cover the fruit if frost threatens. This curing sweetens the flesh and toughens the skin for storage. Wipe the skin with a cloth dipped in a weak bleach solution to prevent rot. Store in a cool, well-ventilated place such as an unheated bedroom or frost-free garage.

Related plants

Acorn squash *C. pepo* var. *pepo*
Acorn-shaped, usually dark green to near black. Sweet, moist, orange flesh. High-yielding, usually five to seven fruits per plant. Try 'Ebony Acorn', 'Celebration' and 'Cream of the Crop' (white-skinned with off-white flesh).

Delicata squash *C. pepo* Oblong fruits striped green and ivory, 20 cm (8 in) long and 7.5 cm (3 in) in diameter. Orange flesh. Doesn't need curing. Cultivars include 'Delicata'.

Spaghetti squash *C. pepo* Also called vegetable spaghetti. Oval-shaped, with buff or light yellow skin and pale orange-yellow flesh. Bake, then scrape out the flesh with a fork

Butternut squashes are very good for baking because of their dense, buttery flesh; simply half lengthways, de-seed and bake in their skins.

(it separates into pasta-like strands). Serve topped with tomato sauce. Cultivars include 'Vegetable Spaghetti'.

'Sweet Dumpling' squash *C. pepo* Flattened, round fruit, 7.5–10 cm (3–4 in) in diameter, with pale orange flesh and striped skin.

Buttercup squash *C. maxima* Dark green and blocky, with a "turban" or small cap at the blossom end. Orange-fleshed fruits that keep well. The Japanese kabocha squashes are similar. Cultivars include 'Queensland Blue' and 'Turk's Turban', a colourfully orange and green striped squash.

'Gold Nugget' squash *C. maxima* A quick-maturing winter squash with round, orange fruits. A bush-type plant good for small gardens.

Hubbard squash *C. maxima* Large, sometimes warty fruits, usually one or two to a vine, with hard rind. An excellent keeper. Non-stringy flesh can be cooked, puréed and frozen. Cultivars include 'New England Blue Hubbard' and 'Uchiki Kuri'.

Butternut squash *C. moschata* Small seed cavity with a thick neck of solid, orange flesh. An excellent keeper. Cultivars include 'Waltham Butternut' and 'Hunter'.

Cynara cardunculus

HARDINESS
Half-hardy; may
not survive severe
winters.

DAYS TO MATURITY
220–240 days
for first harvest;
in areas where
cardoon is
perennial, spring
shoots can be
blanched and eaten
like mature stalks.

COMMENTS
Cultivars include
'Gigante de
Romanga' and
'Thornless White'.

CARDOON

THIS THISTLE-LIKE PLANT, A RELATIVE OF THE
GLOBE ARTICHOKE, IS GROWN CHIEFLY FOR
ITS STALKS, WHICH ARE BLANCHED AND USED
MUCH LIKE CELERY.

Position Plant in full sun in deep,
well-drained, fertile soil with ample
moisture; pH 6.0–7.0.

Cultivation Sow seeds indoors in
early to mid-spring. Harden off and
plant out from late spring, when
about 25 cm (10 in) tall. Plant about
60 cm (2 ft) apart. A month before
autumn frost, or earlier if the plant
is large enough, tie the leaf stalks
together and wrap the plant with
sacking or cardboard to exclude
sunlight and whiten the stalks. Stalks
will be fully blanched in 3–4 weeks.

Pests and diseases Slugs and snails,
as well as black bean and root
aphids, attack the plants. Provide
good drainage to prevent crown rot.

Harvesting and storage Harvest
blanched stalks as needed until a
hard frost threatens, then bank the
plant with earth or straw to protect
the crown over winter. You can also
dig up and eat the main roots.

Special tips Cardoon plants may not
reach their full height, but will still
supply usable stalks. Will withstand
light frost. Plants usually need
replacing after 3 years or so.

Cynara scolymus

HARDINESS
Half-hardy; avoid
frost pockets or
exposed sites.

DAYS TO MATURITY
May produce edible
buds in the first
year, but the first
harvest is more
likely to be in the
second year. Buds
appear in summer.

COMMENTS
'Green Globe' is
widely available.

ARTICHOKE, GLOBE

THIS PLANT IS GROWN CHIEFLY FOR ITS
LARGE, EDIBLE FLOWERHEADS, WHICH MAKE
IT A FAVOURITE FOR ORNAMENTAL VEGETABLE
GARDENS AND POTAGERS.

Position Plant in full sun in a
sheltered spot. Prefers rich, well-
drained soil; near-neutral pH.

Cultivation Usually grown from
high-yielding offsets available from
garden centres, or you can take
them off existing plants: cut rooted,
healthy shoots from the base in
spring. Plant offsets in rows and
cover with cloches or fleece to
protect them from frosts and drying
winds. Remove all the flower buds
in the first year to allow the plant
to establish.

Pests and diseases Little troubled
by insect pests, but is susceptible
to crown rot. Well-drained soil is
essential. Do not allow mulch to
smother the crown. Cut the plant
back in late autumn and protect over
winter by inverting a basket or box
over the crown and mulching deeply.

Harvesting and storage Cut the
buds before the scales have begun
to open, with 2.5 cm (1 in) of stem
still attached.

Special tips Top-dress with dried
blood or another high-nitrogen
fertilizer in early spring.

Daucus carota subsp. *sativus*

CARROT

THE NUTRITIOUS CARROT IS A POTENT ALLY IN YOUR BODY'S FIGHT AGAINST ILLNESS.

Position Plant in full sun in deep, light soil without stones or other obstructions. In heavier or shallow soil, plant round or short-rooted cultivars. Improve clay soil with organic matter; pH 5.5–6.8.

Cultivation Sow the first crop in late winter under cloches, after threat of severe frost is past. Seed is very small; mix half-and-half with fine sand to help avoid oversowing. Sow a scant 12 mm (½ in) deep and firm the seedbed gently with the back of a hoe. Mark the row well; carrots are slow and erratic germinators and may not appear for 3–4 weeks.

Or drop a radish seed every 5 cm (2 in) into the row with your carrot seeds to help mark it. Radishes germinate quickly and will also help break up any soil-crusting that could smother the more delicate carrot seedlings, which look like fine blades of grass. Keep the soil evenly moist until the carrots are up. Thin to 5–7.5 cm (2–3 in) apart. Plant successive crops every few weeks until midsummer. Weed carrots carefully during their growing period. Do not overwater as continually wet soil causes rot.

Pests and diseases Use cloches or horticultural fleece to deter carrot root flies, which lay eggs at the

HARDINESS
Hardy to half-hardy. Plant early-maturing types in cold areas.

DAYS TO MATURITY
60 days, early cultivars; 140 days, maincrop cultivars. Will tolerate light frosts.

COMMENTS
Early-maturing 'Parmex' and 'Oxheart' suit heavy soils. 'Autumn King 2' and 'Berjo' store well. 'Flyaway' is resistant to carrot root fly.

Short carrot cultivars (above), do well in containers. The longer Nantes or Amsterdam-type cultivars (facing page) are grown in deeper soils.

bases of carrot plants. The larvae feed on the roots. Crops sown after late spring and harvested before late summer often escape damage without protection. Rotate carrot plantings to avoid bacterial diseases. Twisted roots point to inadequate thinning. Forked roots often mean that the seedbed was not fine enough. Hairy roots indicate excessive fertility. Do not use fresh manure or high-nitrogen fertilizer on carrot beds. Splitting occurs when heavy rain follows a dry period.

Harvesting and storage Carrots are ready to eat when fully coloured. Pull when the ground is moist to avoid breaking roots, or dig with a garden fork. Harvest autumn crops before the ground freezes, or earlier if shoulders (root tops) appear above the ground. Dry in the sun and store, packed in compost or moist sand, in a cool place. To spread the harvest, pull "baby" carrots. Carrots can be left in the ground in winter, if protected with straw or a mulch, but are more vulnerable to carrot root fly.

Special tips Cover newly seeded carrot rows with boards or black plastic for 3 weeks, then remove. This preserves soil moisture and prevents weeds appearing before the slower-germinating carrots. Never step on the carrot seedbed. If space is limited, grow carrots in the ornamental garden. Their feathery tops are pretty in a border.

Eruca vesicaria subsp. *sativa*

BRASSICACEAE

HARDINESS
Hardy.

DAYS TO MATURITY
20–40 days,
although thinnings
can be harvested
earlier.

COMMENTS
Other common
names include
rucola and arugula.

ROCKET

THE TENDER LEAVES OF THIS GARDEN
FAVOURITE ADD A NUTTY, PEPPERY BITE TO
SALADS AND SANDWICHES.

Position Sow in full sun, as well as
partial shade. Avoid hot, dry positions.
With suitable protection in autumn
and winter, rocket can be grown
nearly all year round. Not fussy, but
prefers fertile, moist soil; pH 6.0–7.0.

Cultivation Rocket bolts very readily,
especially in hot weather. To avoid
this and get an extended crop, sow
successive batches frequently from
mid-spring to early autumn. Sow
direct outdoors (it transplants poorly)
and protect early and late sowings
under cloches or fleece. Thin to
about 15 cm (6 in) apart and use
thinnings in salads. Sow more
thickly in grow-bags for a cut-and-
come-again crop. Water well in dry
conditions to avoid bolting.

Pests and diseases Slugs and snails
and flea beetle may eat the leaves.
Rotate with other brassicas to
avoid clubroot.

Harvesting and storage Pick large
leaves from the base of the plant.
New leaves will sprout from the
crown centre. Weekly picking should
yield 8 to 12 large leaves per plant.
Use fresh; do not freeze.

Special tips Add the flowers of
bolting plants to salads.

Foeniculum vulgare var. *azoricum*

HARDINESS
Half-hardy; tolerates
light frosts.

DAYS TO MATURITY
65–105 days.

COMMENTS
Cultivars include
'Zefa Fino' and
'Sweet Florence'.
Fennel is not an
easy vegetable to
grow well.

FENNEL, FLORENCE OR SWEET

FLORENCE FENNEL IS GROWN CHIEFLY FOR
ITS ENLARGED LEAF BASES, WHICH HAVE AN
INTRIGUING FLAVOUR OF LIQUORICE.

Position Plant in full sun in fertile,
well-drained, sandy soil; pH 6.5–7.0.

Cultivation Plant small, successive
crops to prolong your harvest and
use bolt-resistant cultivars before
midsummer. Sow indoors in early
to mid-spring; transplants poorly
so do not let roots outgrow the
pots before planting in mid- to late
spring. Then sow direct until late
summer; thin to 20–25 cm (8–10 in).
Protect early and late sowings
under cloches or fleece. Mulch
and water well to keep soil moist.
When bulbs begin to swell, earth

up halfway to blanch them.

Pests and diseases A basal rot may
affect the bulbs; avoid soil in which
lettuces and radishes have grown.
Slugs and snails are alos partial to
fennel. Florence fennel becomes
woody when over-mature; if bulbs
begin to elongate, cut them before
they become tough.

Harvesting and storage Cut the
entire plant below the base of the
bulb. Use fronds as seasoning for
fish. Fennel does not freeze well.

Special tips Use the ripe seed of
bolted plants in salads.

Glycine max

HARDINESS
Tender.

DAYS TO MATURITY
65–120 frost-free
days.

COMMENTS
Not many cultivars
are available to suit
the UK climate; try
'Elena' or 'Ustie'.

SOYA BEAN

ONE OF THE OLDEST FOOD CROPS,
THE NUTRITIOUS SOYA BEAN IS WIDELY USED
IN ORIENTAL CUISINES, EITHER FRESH OR
PREPARED AS TOFU, SOY SAUCE OR MISO.

Position Sow in full sun in light,
well-drained soil; pH 6.0–7.0.

Cultivation These beans need a long
season to ripen, so start them off in
early spring indoors. Sow them into
deep pots. Then transplant after
frost danger is past, 5 cm (2 in)
apart. Mulch or hoe until the plants
grow large enough to shade out
weeds. Sufficient watering is critical
when plants are in flower.

Pests and diseases Less troubled by
pests than other beans. Rotate
plantings of soya bean and its legume
relatives, such as beans and peas.
The small pods at the top of the
plant ripen after the leaves fall off
in autumn. In cool summers, they
may not mature for use as a dried
bean, but some cultivars can be
grown for use as fresh beans.

Harvesting and storage Harvest for
fresh use when beans are plump
and tender. Freeze fresh beans.
For dry soya beans, pull the plants
when most of the foliage has died
and hang them to finish drying in a
warm, sunny, well-ventilated place.
Shell and store as you would any
dried bean. Soya beans should
always be boiled before eating,
to avoid digestive problems.

Helianthus tuberosus

HARDINESS
Hardy.

DAYS TO MATURITY
110–140 days for
a first-year crop.

COMMENTS
'Fuseau' is a
smooth-skinned
yam type and the
most popular;
older, knobbly
types are not easy
to get hold of.

JERUSALEM ARTICHOKE

THE JERUSALEM ARTICHOKE IS A TALL, HARDY PERENNIAL VEGETABLE. IT PRODUCES TASTY POTATO-LIKE TUBERS.

Position Plant in full sun or partial shade. Plant away from other garden beds, as many cultivars are invasive. Not fussy and will stand heavy soils, but prefers loose, fertile soil; pH 6.0–6.5.

Cultivation Plant egg-sized pieces of tuber 6–8 weeks before the last spring frost. Plant in the same way as potatoes, each piece with one or more "eyes", 7.5 cm (3 in) deep and 30–45 cm (12–18 in) apart in rows or beds. Mulch or weed early; plants will grow quickly and shade out weeds.

Pests and diseases Rarely troubled by pests and diseases. Difficult to eradicate once it is established, but diligent harvesting each year will keep the bed under control.

Harvesting and storage Mulch the bed to keep the ground diggable after a hard frost. Jerusalem artichokes do not store well, so dig them up as needed. Cook them as you would potatoes.

Special tips Plants can withstand moderate frost; frost does not damage tubers. The plants make useful windbreaks at the edge of a plot and will also break up heavy soil.

Ipomoea aquatica

HARDINESS
Tender perennial
grown as an annual.

DAYS TO MATURITY
100–120 days.
It grows poorly in
temperate climates
and will not
withstand frost.

COMMENTS
Named cultivars
are not generally
available. Treat this
plant as an annual
greenhouse crop
for the best chance
of success.

SPINACH, WATER

A MEMBER OF THE MORNING GLORY FAMILY,
WATER SPINACH IS A PERENNIAL WHEN
GROWN IN ITS NATIVE SUBTROPICS.

Position Plant in full sun or partial
shade in rich, constantly moist soil;
pH 5.5–6.5.

Cultivation Sow the seed indoors
in a deep greenhouse bed prepared
with plenty of well-rotted organic
matter. Allow plenty of space as this
plant sends out runners and roots
at the leaf nodes, quickly growing
into a clump. Keep the soil quite
moist, as water spinach is really
a semi-aquatic plant.

Pests and diseases Greenhouse pests
such as aphids, red spider mite and
whitefly may appear—biological

controls are available, if so. Slugs and
snails may be attracted by the moist
soil; hand-pick them. Water spinach
needs day temperatures higher than
22°C (72°F) to grow quickly so you
might want to try creating an inner
greenhouse, with sheet plastic, to
keep the temperature at a suitable
level. Do not plant too early.

Harvesting and storage Pick young
leaves and shoots for use in salads,
stir-fries or cooked dishes.

Special tips You can eat both the
young leaves and the shoots. Other
common names include entsai.

Ipomoea batatas

HARDINESS
Tender perennial
grown as an annual.

DAYS TO MATURITY
120 frost-free days.

COMMENTS
Grow these
sub-tropical plants
in a warm, sheltered
spot in mild areas,
or under cover in
colder regions.

SWEET POTATO

SWEET POTATOES ARE A WARM-WEATHER
CROP THAT PRODUCE TASTY AND NUTRITIOUS
TUBEROUS ROOTS. THEY CAN BE COOKED IN
THE SAME WAY AS POTATOES.

Position Plant in full sun in sandy,
well-drained soil that is very fertile;
pH 5.5–6.5.

Cultivation Plant from cuttings or
"slips", which are available by mail
order. Plant after frost danger is well
past. With a rake, make a ridge of
soil 15–25 cm (6–10 in) high and
15–20 cm (6–8 in) wide. Plant the
slips into the ridge about 30 cm
(12 in) apart. Mound the soil onto
the ridge at least once before the
trailing plants make further cultivation
impossible. Keep the newly set slips

watered until they begin to grow.
After that, irrigate sweet potatoes
only during extended dry spells.
The stems sprawl across the garden
bed and tend to grow roots at leaf
nodes, many producing more tubers,
so don't be tempted to train your
plants up a trellis or keep the stems
off the ground. Allow plenty of space
for a bountiful crop. Alternatively,
grow the plants in a grow-bag or
large, deep pot in the greenhouse,
but expect a smaller crop.

Pests and diseases Use certified
disease-free slips. Rotate plantings
and keep soil organic matter high
to reduce nematode damage. Deer
love the tender leaves and shoots;

Sweet potato continued

The leaves of sweet potato look very similar to those of its close relative, morning glory *Ipomoea purpurea*.

if they are a problem in your area, you may need to fence off your sweet potatoes. In the greenhouse, aphids, red spider mite and whitefly may attack the leaves; biological controls are a good option.

Harvesting and storage Dig up sweet potatoes before the first frost or as soon as the top-growth has been killed by a light frost. Left in the ground, they will spoil. The tuberous roots are very tender, so dig and handle them carefully. Cure them for 10–14 days in a warm, fairly humid area, and store where the temperature does not fall below 13°C (55°F). With proper storage, they will keep for 6 months or more.

Special tips Cultivars that suit the UK climate include 'T65', with pale orange flesh; 'Beauregard Improved', a smaller tuber with bright orange flesh; or 'O'Henry', with compact clusters of long, cream-fleshed tubers.

Lactuca sativa

HARDINESS
Hardy; lettuce can be grown almost all year, depending on the cultivar.

DAYS TO MATURITY
28–100 days depending on the time of year and cultivar. The young leaves and thinnings can be harvested earlier. Loose-leaf lettuces mature most quickly, followed by butterhead and cos.

COMMENTS
The iceberg lettuce (left) forms a crisp, cabbage-like head.

LETTUCE

HEARTING LETTUCES REQUIRE A LONGER SEASON THAN SOME OTHERS. THE YOUNG PLANTS WILL WITHSTAND LIGHT FROST OR MODERATE FROST WITH PROTECTION.

Position Plant in full sun, or in midsummer, partial shade. Prefers fertile, well-drained but moisture-retentive soil; pH 6.0–6.8.

Cultivation Begin sowing directly in the ground in late winter, using hardy cultivars. Protect with cloches or fleece until risk of frost is past. Barely cover the seeds and firm the soil with the back of a hoe. Alternatively, sow early batches indoors into modules (lettuces don't like root disturbance), harden off and plant out 20–25 cm (8–10 in) apart, 1–2 weeks before last frost. Leave loose-leaf lettuces unthinned for cut-and-come-again salad greens and pick at about 21 days, or thin for large-leaved plants. Sow or transplant successively until a month before the first frost, ending with a cold-tolerant cultivar such as 'Winter Density'. Grow summer-maturing crops in partial shade. Sow seeds in summer in late afternoon so they germinate in the cool of the evening. Hoe shallowly or mulch; water frequently, especially during hot spells, as the stress of a water shortage can cause them to bolt, running to seed prematurely. Water at ground level, rather than spraying with a garden hose, because damp foliage encourages various rots.

Lettuce continued

The cultivar 'Little Gem' forms a neat little heart. These and other similar attractive varieties can be planted as an edible border around your flower beds.

For best results when growing these quick-to-mature vegetables, provide a regular, light application of a high-nitrogen fertilizer, compost tea or seaweed solution to ensure that growth is not checked in any way. Protect late crops under cloches, fleece or in the greenhouse.

Pests and diseases Lettuce are prone to various troubles. Cutworms, wireworms and leatherjackets may eat the roots; aphids attack roots or the leaves. In wet or cold weather, mildews and rots may set in; cut out affected outer leaves. Slugs and snails and pigeons also love lettuce. Rotate crops to avoid soil-borne diseases. Control slugs by trapping them in shallow pans of beer. Bitter leaves

suggest heat and water stress, or simply over-mature lettuce.

Harvesting and storage Harvest as needed for fresh use. Cut cut-and-come-again loose-leaf lettuce 2.5 cm (1 in) above roots, leaving the plants to re-sprout for a second harvest. Cut larger whole plants at soil level. Harvest lettuce in the morning, when juicy and crisp.

Special tips Many varieties that can be cut leaf by leaf for the salad bowl make attractive additions to the flower or vegetable border and are decorative enough to grow in containers on a sunny patio or balcony. If your needs are limited, look for packets of seeds with a

Many of the crinkly, red-leaved cultivars of lettuce make a welcome addition of both colour and texture to a bowl of mixed salad greens.

mixture of lettuce and other salad leaves. Lettuce germinates poorly at temperatures above 27°C (80°F). Pre-chill seed before sowing, or start summer crops in a cool place.

Related plants

Butterhead lettuce *L. sativa* Forms loose heads of soft, folded leaves and is often grown in summer as it tolerates hot, dry conditions better. Cultivars include 'Buttercrunch', 'Sangria' (red-tinged leaves) and 'Tom Thumb' (miniature).

Crisphead lettuce *L. sativa* Iceberg lettuces are crispheads that form very solid hearts and take longer to mature. Forms a tight head of crisp-textured leaves. More demanding than other lettuces, needing more feeding and watering. Cultivars include 'Robinson' and 'Webb's Wonderful'.

Loose-leaf lettuce *L. sativa* This is the quickest and easiest-to-grow lettuce. It can double as an ornamental garden edging. Also called salad bowl lettuce. Instead of heads, it forms loose leaves that can be harvested while quite small and are also grown as cut-and-come-again crops. Cultivars include 'Lollo Rossa', 'Red Sails', 'Salad Bowl' and 'Oak Leaf'.

Cos lettuce *L. sativa* Also called romaine lettuce. Forms an upright, elongated, loose heart of crisp, ribbed leaves. Cos are hardier than other lettuces, so are often used for winter crops under cover. Cultivars include 'Paris Island' and 'Valmaine'.

Lactuca sativa var. *augustana*

ASTERACEAE

HARDINESS
Half-hardy. In colder areas, harvest only the leaves if the stalk takes too long to develop.

DAYS TO MATURITY
45 days for leaves (thinnings can be harvested earlier); 90 days for stalks. Tolerates light frost.

COMMENTS
Named cultivars are not generally available.

CELTUCE

CELTUCE HAS LETTUCE-LIKE LEAVES AND CELERY-LIKE STALKS. WHEN COOKED, IT TASTES LIKE A CROSS BETWEEN SUMMER SQUASH AND ARTICHOKE.

Position Plant in full sun in fertile, well-drained soil; pH 6.0–6.7. Otherwise not fussy.

Cultivation Sow in spring, either indoors or outdoors under protection. Best if matured in cool weather. Seeds are small; sow thinly and cover lightly. Thin to 30 cm (1 ft) apart, using the thinnings with other salad greens. Keep well-watered, especially in early stages.

Pests and diseases Prone to the same problems as lettuce (see page 190). Water frequently to delay the leaves becoming bitter and to help to keep the central stalk tender. Warm weather induces the plants to bolt, which also toughens the stalk.

Harvesting and storage Pick the leaves as needed. Use young leaves in salads and cook older ones. Cut the stalk at its base and peel for use as a raw or boiled vegetable, or in stir-fries and soups.

Special tips Other common names include asparagus lettuce.

Lagenaria siceraria

HARDINESS
Tender.

DAYS TO MATURITY
90 frost-free days
for mature gourds;
a shorter period for
immature, edible-
sized fruits.

COMMENTS
Other common
names are cucuzzi
and Italian edible
gourd. Other types
of *L. siceraria*
include calabash
gourd; some are
classed as poisonous
so check when you
buy seeds that they
are edible.

GOURD, BOTTLE

ALTHOUGH EDIBLE, BOTTLE GOURDS ARE
COMMONLY GROWN AS ORNAMENTALS.

Position Plant in full sun in well-
drained, rich soil; pH 6.0–6.5.
Provide good air circulation.

Cultivation Plant after frost danger
is past. Sow 2 or 3 seeds to a mound
and site mounds 1.8 m (6 ft) apart,
or sow more closely if you can train
the stems up a trellis or fence.
Mulch or keep weeded. If allowed
to sprawl, the trailing plant will
eventually shade out weeds. It is
drought-tolerant, but irrigate for
larger and more numerous fruits.

Pests and diseases Train the plant
up supports, such as a wigwam of
canes or a trellis, to improve air
circulation and reduce mildew
problems. Rotate plantings of gourds
and their relatives, such as courgettes
and squashes. Pinch off flowers
after the plant has set several fruits
to ensure maturity before frost.

Harvesting and storage Pick young
fruits and cook as you would
summer squash. For use as a bird-
box, dry the mature gourd until the
seeds inside rattle. Wax the gourd
to preserve it.

Special tips Hang up dried gourds
for bird-boxes. Cut an entrance for
the birds by drilling many small
holes close together, then scrape out
the centre and dry out the gourd.

Lepidium sativum   BRASSICACEAE

HARDINESS
Hardy; grow as a
winter vegetable
indoors or under
cover.

DAYS TO MATURITY
10–14 days.
Will withstand
severe frost.

COMMENTS
It is easiest to grow
in containers or
grow-bags to avoid
soil splash. Named
cultivars are not
generally available.

CRESS

QUICK AND EASY TO GROW, CRESS ADDS A
SPARK TO SALADS OR IS A PRETTY GARNISH.

Position Plant in bright light or
partial shade in soil that is moist
and rich in humus; pH 6.0–7.0.

Cultivation Sow outdoors between
late spring and late summer, thickly
in rows. Barely cover and firm the
soil with the back of a hoe. Sow
indoors anytime, in soilless compost.
Cress can also be germinated and
grown for a single crop on damp
kitchen paper. Sow successive small
batches every 7 days. Later plantings
may bolt in summer heat.

Pests and diseases Do not grow
where members of the brassica family

have been grown in the preceding
year. Cloches and horticultural fleece
will help to deter flea beetles. Hot
weather and inadequate supplies of
water will cause cress to bolt.

Harvesting and storage Cut with
scissors just above the crown and
let the plants re-sprout for two or
three more cuttings.

Special tips Land cress (*Barbarea
verna*) has a spicy flavour like
watercress (see page 202). It forms
a small rosette of dark green,
rounded leaves, which can be
harvested whole or leaf by leaf.
Sow outdoors as above and thin
to 15 cm (6 in).

Lotus tetragonolobus

HARDINESS
Half hardy; grown
as annual crop.

DAYS TO MATURITY
55–70 frost-free
days for edible
pods.

COMMENTS
Other common
name is winged
pea. Will grow
happily in drier
soils than do peas.

ASPARAGUS PEA

ITS UNIQUE FLAVOUR AND HIGH PROTEIN
CONTENT MAKE THE ASPARAGUS PEA POPULAR
IN ASIAN STIR-FRIES AND OTHER DISHES.

Position Plant in full sun near
a trellis or fence in sandy, well-
drained soil; pH 7.3–8.0.

Cultivation Plant after frost danger
is past, 2.5 cm (1 in) deep and
5–10 cm (2–4 in) apart. The climbers
grow to a height of 1.8–2.4 m
(6–8 ft), so support with sturdy
canes or fence. Hoe shallowly or
mulch to control weeds. The
purplish red flowers form in loose
clusters. The pods are four-sided,
rather than round, with distinct
flanges or "wings" at each corner.

Pests and diseases Suffers the same
problems as peas (see page 216).
Do not grow where legumes, such
as peas and beans, have grown the
preceding year. Keep the plants
growing strongly with regular
watering to deter aphids. Requires
a long, warm growing season.
Where the weather is not to its liking,
it may die without flowering.

Harvesting and storage Harvest the
immature pods at 2.5–5 cm (1–2 in)
long and eat steamed or stir-fried.
Pick frequently, as pods can quickly
become over-sized.

Special tips Named cultivars are not
generally available.

Luffa acutangula and *L. cylindrica*

HARDINESS
Frost-tender.

DAYS TO MATURITY
80 days for
immature, edible
fruits. Up to
150 days for fully
mature fruits.

COMMENTS
Common names
include sponge
gourd and
dishcloth gourd.

LOOFAH

LOOFAH PRODUCES SQUASH-LIKE FRUITS THAT
ARE EDIBLE WHEN YOUNG. ITS MATURE
FRUITS ARE DRIED AND USED AS SPONGES.

Position Plant in full sun, near a
fence, trellis or other support, in rich,
sandy, well-drained soil; pH 6.0–6.5.

Cultivation Sow in spring in warmth
indoors, then harden off and plant
out in mounds about 1.8 m (6 ft)
apart, or closer, when frost danger is
past. Train to a fence, canes or trellis;
loofahs grow to 4.5 m (15 ft) or more.

Pests and diseases Greenhouse pests
such as red spider mite, whitefly
and aphids may be a problem
under cover; use biological controls
if necessary. Also provide good air
circulation. Pinch off flowers after

several large fruits have set, to ensure
maturity before the first frost.

Harvesting and storage Pick fruits
when 10–15 cm (4–6 in) long and
cook them as you would a summer
squash. For sponges, leave fruits on
until they turn yellow, then hang up
and dry in an airy place. Soak to
loosen the skin from the fibrous
interior, remove skin, and let dry
again. Shake out the seeds.

Special tips Named cultivars are not
generally available. *L. acutangula*
produces 37.5-cm (15-in), dark green,
smooth-skinned fruit; *L. cylindrica*
produces 52.5-cm (21-in), light
green, ridged fruit.

Lycopersicon esculentum   SOLANACEAE

HARDINESS
Half hardy.

DAYS TO MATURITY
70–90 frost-free
days from
transplanting.
Small-fruited
cultivars mature
fastest.

COMMENTS
Low-acid tomatoes
are milder and
sweeter than some
other cultivars.

TOMATO

PURCHASED TOMATOES CAN'T COMPARE
WITH AN OLD-FASHIONED TOMATO GROWN
IN YOUR OWN GARDEN. TRY TO FIND SOME
OF THE "HEIRLOOM" CULTIVARS FOR
FLAVOUR YOU WON'T BELIEVE.

Position Plant in full sun in fertile,
deep, well-drained soil, in soil-based
compost in deep containers, or in
grow-bags; pH 6.0–7.0.

Cultivation Tomatoes are usually
started indoors from late winter to
late spring. Grow on and repot the
seedlings and feed regularly. Once
they are showing the first flower
truss and all risk of frost is past,
harden off and plant out 60–90 cm
(2–3 ft) apart for bush tomatoes, or
as close as 37.5 cm (15 in) if they

are to be grown as cordons. Use
black plastic mulch to pre-warm the
soil. Alternatively, plant in grow-bags,
either indoors or outdoors, in deep
pots, or in greenhouse soil beds.
You could try planting tomatoes by
burying the stem horizontally, right
up to the top-most leaves. New roots
will emerge from the buried stem,
making a sturdier plant. To grow
tomatoes as cordons, that is, with
a tall central stem, prune them by
pinching out all leafy shoots that
emerge from leaf axils. Support the
growing central stem by tying it into
a cane or by trailing a length of
twine from the greenhouse roof and
gently twining it around the stem.
Water tomatoes regularly, but do

Tomato continued

Cherry tomatoes produce generous quantities of fruit in a variety of colours. They are perfect for salads and lunch boxes.

not fertilize until the plant is well established and has set the first truss. Then give weak compost tea or tomato fertilizer. Too much nitrogen will result in lots of foliage but few fruits. Mulch will help retain soil moisture but will also cool the soil, so do not mulch tomatoes until the soil is well warmed.

Pests and diseases Outdoor tomatoes may suffer from moulds and rots in cold, wet conditions, as well as soil-borne pests such as potato cyst eelworm, which eats the roots. To avoid soil-borne diseases, do not plant where tomatoes or their relatives, such as aubergines and potatoes, have been grown in the preceding 2 years. If that is not

possible, grow disease-resistant cultivars if you suspect your soil harbours diseases such as blight or verticillium wilt. Blossom-end rot indicates that the plant is not taking up enough calcium from the soil. If soil calcium levels are adequate, the problem is probably a lack of soil moisture. Keep the soil moist, but not soggy. Dark brown, circular spots on tomato leaves suggest fungal disease or blight. The latter can be a serious problem in prolonged humid weather. Once blight infects a plant, it spreads rapidly, blackening the stems and fruits, and can kill the plant within a week. It is possible to save fruits by promptly removing any leaves or sideshoots that show

Plum tomatoes have fewer seeds and less juice than standard tomatoes, which makes them the best choice for soups and sauces.

early signs of blight, but if it gets a hold, dig up and burn the plant to stop the fungal spores infecting other plants, or the soil. Blight can also affect potatoes. Provide good air circulation and do not disturb plants when they are wet.

Harvesting and storage Pick the fruit when it is evenly coloured, but still firm. Chutney, freeze or dry surplus tomatoes. Cover tomato plants to protect them through a light, early frost, but harvest all fruit when more severe frost threatens. Completely green tomatoes will not ripen; pickle them or make into chutney. Blemish-free fruit that has begun to change colour will continue to ripen. Wrap each tomato in tissue or newspaper and keep in a spot that stays above 13°C (55°F); check often and discard any fruit that develops bad spots. Placing a banana among the tomatoes speeds ripening—the banana gives off ethylene gas.

Special tips Tomato cultivars are usually described as "indeterminate" or "determinate". Indeterminates, also called cordon or vine tomatoes, continue to grow and set fruit all season, and usually require a sturdy support or stake. Determinates, or bush tomatoes, have a more compact, sprawling habit and stop growing and flowering when they reach a certain height. They are often earlier to mature and may not require support, but they produce fruit for

Tomato continued

The tiny fruits of currant tomatoes are produced in abundance. They look most attractive left in sprays in salads, and as garnishes.

shorter periods than indeterminates. Where space is limited, plant cordon tomatoes at the back of the flower garden or train them on a wire fence.

Related plants

Beefsteak tomato *L. esculentum* Large, fleshy fruit, up to 1 kg (2 lb) and more, with meaty flesh and often a thick central core. Most are indeterminate. Cultivars include 'Legend', 'Beefmaster' and many "heirloom" cultivars such as 'Supermarmande' and 'Brandywine Pink'.

Cherry tomato *L. esculentum* var. *cerasiforme* Prolific bearers of fruits that are usually about 2.5 cm (1 in) in diameter, often borne in grape-like clusters. Cultivars include the classic favourite 'Gardener's Delight' (red, indeterminate), 'Gold Nugget' (yellow-orange, determinate) and 'Sungold' (golden-yellow, indeterminate).

Low-acid tomato *L. esculentum* Reduced acidity usually means milder flavour, with sweet undertones. Yellow-skinned cultivars are often, but not always, low in acid. Try 'Pink Girl' (pink skin, indeterminate) and 'Lemon Boy' (yellow skin, indeterminate).

Plum tomato *L. esculentum* Meatier than other tomatoes, with fewer seeds and less juice. Most cultivars are determinate, and many have concentrated fruit-set, with up to

The large, meaty beefsteak tomato was the classic garden tomato in mainland Europe and in the USA. Because the fruits are so heavy, most cultivars need sturdy supports.

90 per cent of the fruit ripening at once. Cultivars include 'Roma' (small, pear-shaped), 'Olivade' (large, juicy plum-shaped) and 'Golden Sweet' (small, yellow, plum-shaped).

Trailing tomato *L. esculentum* Determinate cultivars bred for growing in containers such as hanging baskets, but also good for small gardens. Cultivars include 'Tumbling Tom Red'.

Pear tomato *L. esculentum* var. ***pyriforme*** The fruits look like tiny pears. Red and yellow variants are available. The vigorous, indeterminate vines will need supports.

Standard tomato *L. esculentum* Grown primarily for fresh use. Scores of cultivars are available in a wide range of colours, growth habits, maturity dates and disease resistance. Among the most popular are 'Alicante' (firm fruit, early-ripening), 'Big Boy' (large, red fruit), 'Celebrity' (large, red fruit, very disease-resistant) and 'Ailsa Craig' (versatile, fairly acidic, deep red fruit).

Currant tomato *L. pimpinellifolium* Has tiny, currant-sized fruit. Both red and yellow variants are available such as 'Matt's Wild Cherry' (red). The vigorous, indeterminate vines will need cages or stakes for support.

Nasturtium officinale

HARDINESS
Hardy; naturally grows in shallow, flowing water, but easy to grow indoors in pots.

DAYS TO MATURITY
120–150 days. A newly established watercress bed may not produce a harvest in the first year.

COMMENTS
Named cultivars are not generally available.

WATERCRESS

AT ITS BEST IN AUTUMN AND EARLY SPRING, WATERCRESS IS A TASTY AND HEALTHY ADDITION TO SALADS AND SANDWICHES.

Position Plant in full sun or partial shade in wet, well-limed soil that is rich in humus, preferably at the edge of a stream or stream-fed pond; pH 6.0–7.0.

Cultivation Sow indoors 4–8 weeks before the last spring frost and stand the pots in water, or sprinkle seeds as thinly as possible where they are to grow, about a month before the last frost, pressing them into the soil. Fill gaps in the planting by breaking off pieces of stem and pressing them into the soil, where they will root easily. Gardeners without access to constantly moist soil can grow watercress in pots, indoors or out. Set pots in pans of water and change the water daily to avoid the soil becoming stagnant. Another way is to transplant seedlings into grow-bags that have no drainage holes.

Pests and diseases Little troubled by pests and diseases.

Harvesting and storage Harvest the leaves as needed, as soon as they are large enough. If you grow watercress under cover, you may be able to use it as a winter salad.

Special tips The flavour of the leaves deteriorates during the period the plants are flowering.

Pastinaca sativa

HARDINESS
Hardy.

DAYS TO MATURITY
126–140 days.

COMMENTS
Steam or bake
parsnips as you
would potatoes.
Popular cultivars
include the long
'Tender and True'
which resists canker
and 'Hollow Crown'.

PARSNIP

THE PARSNIP'S DISTINCTIVE FLAVOUR MAKES
THIS ROOT A CLASSIC WINTER VEGETABLE.

Position Plant in full sun in friable,
open, well-drained soil; pH 6.0–7.0.

Cultivation Sow after spring frosts
have finished. Sow seeds directly
where they are going to grow in a
drill 6 cm (2½ in) deep and keep
moist until germinated. Parsnip
seeds take 21–28 days to germinate.
Thin seedlings to 5–7.5 cm (2–3 in)
apart and control weeds by hand-
weeding and hoeing. Do not overfeed with high-nitrogen fertilizers.

Pests and diseases Carrot root fly
may attack parsnips, if not protected
early in the season. Shallow, heavy
soil or fresh manure in the soil may
result in misshapen roots. Parsnip
canker can damage the skins—use
resistant cultivars.

Harvesting and storage Start pulling
early to spread the harvest. Those
left keep well in the soil. In winter
cover crowns with a thick layer of
straw mulch and mark the bed. Dig
through mulch layer all winter for a
continuous, fresh harvest. Roots
store for up to 2 weeks on a shelf
and a little longer in the refrigerator.

Special tips If parsnips are grown on
a well-prepared and fertilized bed,
extra fertilizer is rarely needed, but
liquid feeds applied in mid-season
promote faster growth and a
sweeter flavour.

Persicaria odorata

HARDINESS
Tender.

DAYS TO MATURITY
Leaves can be picked as soon as the plant is established.

COMMENTS
This plant grows 30–60 cm (1–2 ft) tall. Its other common names include Vietnamese mint.

VIETNAMESE CORIANDER

THE SPICY LEAVES OF THIS ATTRACTIVE PLANT HAVE RED MARKINGS TOWARDS THE STEM, BUT THESE OFTEN DISAPPEAR IN WINTER OR WHEN THE PLANT IS GROWN IN SHADE.

Position Plant in a well-drained, moist position in partial shade to full sun; pH 6.0–7.0.

Cultivation Space plants about 40 cm (16 in) apart. Given ideal conditions, Vietnamese coriander can be invasive as the stems root wherever they touch the ground. However, it is best grown as an annual outdoors or overwintered in a container as it does not tolerate frost. Do not let it dry out between waterings. Pot-bound plants will stop producing leaves.

Pests and diseases Little troubled by pests and diseases.

Harvesting and storage Cut the stems as needed. The older leaves are hotter, spicier and more flavoursome than younger ones; the strongly flavoured stems can be removed before serving.

Special tips Cuttings are easily grown. Stems will quickly sprout roots if they are placed in water, or you can simply snip off the new plants where the stems have touched the soil and rooted.

Petroselinum crispum var. *tuberosum*   UMBELLIFERAE

HARDINESS
Hardy.

DAYS TO MATURITY
210 days. Will
withstand severe
frost (frost actually
sweetens the
flavour).

COMMENTS
This plant is also
commonly known
as turnip-rooted
parsley. 'Berliner'
is a commonly
available cultivar.

PARSLEY, HAMBURG

GROWN FOR ITS THICK, WHITE PARSNIP-LIKE
TAPROOT AND PARSLEY-LIKE LEAVES,
HAMBURG PARSLEY IS ATTRACTIVE IN THE
GARDEN AS WELL AS TASTY.

Position Plant in full sun in sandy,
deep, well-drained soil, free of stones;
tolerates heavy soils; pH 6.0–7.0.

Cultivation Sow 4–6 weeks before
the last spring frost, keep moist and
cover with cloches or fleece to speed
germination, which can take several
weeks. Thin to stand 15–20 cm
(6–8 in) apart. Hoe or mulch to
keep free of weeds. Water regularly
in dry spells to produce large, more
tender roots. Raised beds help.

Pests and diseases Shallow, stony or
heavy soil can result in misshapen
roots. Break up clods, remove stones
and don't step on the seedbed.
Carrot root fly may attack the roots
if not protected early in the season.
Canker may spoil the skins.

Harvesting and storage Dig up roots
when large enough for you. The
roots keep well in the ground (mulch
to keep soil workable), or dig up
before a hard frost and store in a
cool place in damp sand.

Special tips Dig up overwintered
plants before they begin to grow in
spring. Roots shrink and toughen as
the plants draw nutrients from them
to set seed.

Phascolus, Lablab spp.

HARDINESS
Tender to half-hardy.

DAYS TO MATURITY
90–150 frost-free days. The most popular quick-maturing garden cultivars are ready to harvest in 100 days or less.

COMMENTS
Native to India, the lablab bean (left) produces delicious pods and seeds.

BEANS, DRIED

MANY OF THE BEAN TYPES THAT DRY AND STORE WELL ARE PANTRY STAPLES IN THE WORLD'S VARIED CUISINES. WHILE YOU MAY NOT HAVE SPACE TO GROW EVERY BEAN YOU WILL USE EACH YEAR, EVEN A SMALL CROP GOES A LONG WAY AND IS FUN TO TRY.

Position Plant in full sun, in a sheltered, warm site with good air circulation. Well-drained garden soil is acceptable; pH 6.0–7.0.

Cultivation To extend the growing season and allow the beans to dry, pre-warm the soil by covering it for a few weeks in spring before sowing. Sow seed after the last frost and when soil has warmed, 2.5 cm (1 in) deep and 7.5 cm (3 in) apart in single or double rows. Hoe shallowly until the plants are large enough to shade out weeds. Mulch between rows to help prevent pods from rotting if they touch the ground. Moisture is critical when the plants are in flower; when pods begin to mature, withhold water to hasten drying. Plants in the greenhouse or under fleece should be ventilated once in flower, to allow pollination.

Pests and diseases Provide good air circulation to help prevent blights, foot and root rots and anthracnose; to avoid spreading rust, do not disturb plants when foliage is wet. Dig in all plant debris in autumn to destroy any disease organisms, and do not plant beans or other legumes in the same place more than once

If you grow a selection of beans for drying, for example kidney, pinto and borlotti beans, you can enjoy your own, nutritious produce right through the winter months.

every 3 years. The most common pests are slugs and snails and black bean aphid, but root aphid eats the roots, mice steal the seeds and bean seed fly larvae eat the seeds. Whitefly or red spider mite may attack beans under cover. Damp weather late in the season, when the pods are maturing, can encourage beans to sprout in the pod. Pull plants when most of the foliage has died and hang by the roots in a well-ventilated warm place to complete drying.

Harvesting and storage Harvest when pods rattle and are completely dry and when the beans can barely be dented when bitten. Shell pods individually or thresh by placing in an old pillowcase and walking on it until pods are thoroughly crushed. Remove the resulting chaff by pouring the beans back and forth between two bowls in a breezy area or in front of a fan. Store in airtight jars or bags in a dry, cool place.

Special tips To avoid potential problems with your crop being eaten by weevils, freeze the well-dried beans for several hours before storing. And remember that they will need to be soaked before cooking. One very good reason to grow beans is that they belong to the plant family that produces soil nitrogen, in nodules on their roots, by using ("fixing") the nitrogen in the atmosphere in co-operation with various soil bacteria. Grow a crop

Beans, dried continued

Pinto beans *Phaseolus vulgaris* are often used in Mexican cooking. You can either use them fresh, or dry the seeds.

of beans in rotation with roots and leafy green brassicas to ensure that your garden soil remains as healthy and productive as possible.

Related plants

Haricot bean *P. vulgaris* These are the dried seeds of the French bean; haricots are also known as kidney beans. Historically the term "kidney bean" was used for all common beans, green and shelled as well as dry. But today it is usually used to refer to large, dry beans with the characteristic kidney shape—not just the dark, red-brown ones familiar from the supermarket shelf, but white, brown, yellow, black and mottled beans as well. French beans are half-hardy and grown as annuals.

Most are dwarf plants, but climbing cultivars are available. Among firm favourite haricot bean cultivars are 'Cannellino', a dwarf white-seeded bean, and 'Borlotto Linguadi Fuoco', an "heirloom" bean that has large beans and pods splashed with red.

Pinto bean *P. vulgaris* The pinto bean is a medium-sized, oval bean, usually mottled on a buff background. Its resistance to heat and drought makes it a favourite in arid areas. It is the standard bean in Mexican cooking.

Lablab bean *Lablab purpureus* Also known as hyacinth bean. This is a fast-growing, climbing plant that is grown in its native tropics for both its pods and seeds. It is a tender perennial, but can be grown in

The tender lablab bean must be grown indoors or on a warm patio, but its fragrant, white or pink flowers and purple pods make it a splendidly handsome plant.

temperate climates as a greenhouse annual. Grow the plants in grow-bags or pots of soil-based compost and ventilate when the plants are in flower to aid pollination. The wisteria-like blossoms are ornamental, the young pods are purple and edible 6 to 9 weeks after sowing, and the seeds can be dried 10 to 14 weeks after sowing and eaten like beans. They also freeze well.

Lima bean *P. lunatus* Also known as butter bean. Climbing cultivars of this bean require sturdy supports, but are considered superior to the bush types in flavour. They are tender perennials grown as annual crops and need a sheltered, warm site and at least 85 frost-free days for the first beans to mature. A full harvest takes at least 100 days' favourable weather. The crop may still be unreliable after cool or wet summers. The seed, rather than the pod, is eaten, either immature as a fresh vegetable or mature as a dried bean. The dried beans are ready to pick once the pods have fattened, then browned and dried out.

Phaseolus, Vicia, Vigna spp.

HARDINESS
Tender to hardy, depending on species/cultivar.

DAYS TO MATURITY
50–90 days, French beans including purple and waxy types; 60–100 days, flageolets; 195–250 days, autumn-sown broad beans; 84–112 days, all other types.

COMMENTS
The scarlet runner (left) has edible flowers, pods and large seeds, used as fresh beans.

BEANS, FRESH

EVERY GARDEN CAN ACCOMMODATE SOME FRESH BEANS, BE IT A FEW SMALL BUSH PLANTS OR A FULL CROP ON A TRELLIS.

Position Plant in full sun. Likes soil that is rich in humus but not excessively fertile; pH 6.0–7.5.

Cultivation Sow seed outdoors after frost danger is past or start them indoors, sowing 2–3 seeds in deep modules or root-trainers. Sow about 2.5 cm (1 in) deep and 7.5 cm (3 in) apart in single or double rows. Keep well weeded or mulched. Regular watering will increase yield; thorough watering is critical when beans are in flower. French and broad beans bear heavily but only for a few weeks. To assure a steady supply, make successive small sowings 2–3 weeks apart, ending in mid-autumn; protect later sowings under cloches or fleece.

Pests and diseases Possible pests include slugs and snails, aphids, bean seed fly, mice and birds. Plants under cover may suffer from red spider mite or whitefly. Avoid the bean patch when the plants are wet to avoid spreading anthracnose, halo blight and bean rust. Sown too early in cold, wet soil, bean seeds may rot before germinating. Cold conditions encourage soil-borne foot and root rots; avoid by rotating the sowing each year.

Plant butter beans (*Phaseolus lunatus*) grown for their pods successively for a regular supply. Water frequently when flowers appear for a heavy yield.

Harvesting and storage Pick at any size, but before seeds have begun to swell noticeably inside the pod. Tiny, fresh beans are a tender treat, but larger pods have a more characteristic "beany" flavour. Freeze or pickle young pods, or leave pods on the plant a while longer to collect the young seeds; if they get too stringy, dry the beans and use as you would other dried beans.

Related plants

Scarlet runner bean *P. coccineus*
Climbing bean and tender perennial grown as an annual. This popular and easy-to-grow bean, also known as string bean, produces long, flat pods prolifically and for a long season. Most climb to up to 3 m (10 ft), and must be supported on cane wigwams, double rows of canes, or trellis; bush and dwarf types are also available. Their scarlet flowers are ornamental and enhance a potager. Keep picking the young pods before they get tough and stringy and to stimulate further production. 'White Lady' has virtually string-less pods; 'Kelvedon Marvel' is a traditional favourite and early cropper. Cold-tolerant cultivars include 'Prize Winner'.

Butter bean *P. lunatus* Also called the Lima bean (see page 209), this can be grown for its young, edible pods. Pick regularly to encourage more pods to form.

Runner beans (*Phaseolus vulgaris*) are flat-podded, tender beans, and are popular and easy to grow.

Flageolet *P. vulgaris* This is not a separate bean, but the French bean grown specifically for the seeds, which are eaten at the immature stage. Harvest flageolets when pods start to turn rubbery, but before the seeds inside begin to harden. Cultivars best suited to picking at this stage include 'Borlotto Lingua di Fuoco', a striking bean streaked with red on an off-white background.

Climbing French bean *P. vulgaris*
These are the same beans as the haricot (see page 208), but they are grown for the young pods rather than dried seeds. They are also called green beans. These beans require support for their long climbing stems that cling by means of tendrils.

They are tender perennials grown as annuals. Deep, fertile, moist soil in a warm site gives the best crop. They are often grown on a "wigwam" framework, but can also be planted in 1 or 2 rows and supported on rows of sturdy canes that are stabilized by crossbars. They bear over a longer period than bush French beans and are a good choice where space is too limited for successive plantings. Pick the pods regularly to prolong cropping, and pinch out the tops once they reach the top of the support, to stop them getting top-heavy. They take longer to mature and some older cultivars have strings that must be removed before eating. Cultivars include

Pick broad beans (*Vicia faba*) when pods are plump, but before the outer skin becomes tough. If the seed stalk within the pod is darkened, the beans may be tough.

'Cobra', 'Hunter' and 'Blue Lake'.

Broad bean *Vicia faba* Also called fava bean, this hardy bean is usually grown for its immature white seeds or beans. It is far more frost-tolerant than other beans and can be planted with the spring peas, 4–6 weeks before last frost of spring. It is best in areas with long, cool springs. Broad beans have long taproots so need deep, well-dug and well-drained soil. The best yields occur on heavy soils or well-irrigated lighter soils. There are 3 main types: longpod (eg 'Masterpiece Green Longpod'), which have 38-cm (15-in) or longer pods with 8–10 kidney-shaped beans; Windsor sorts (eg 'Green Windsor'), with broader, shorter pods and 4–5 round seeds; dwarf varieties (eg 'The Sutton'), reach only 30 cm (18 in) so can be grown under cloches for early or late harvest. Taller cultivars may need support.

Asparagus bean *Vigna unguiculata* subsp. *sesquipedalis* Also known as yard long bean, this very tender perennial produces long, thin, crunchy pods best eaten at 20–30 cm (10–12 in). It requires a support, cannot stand cold soil or cold nights, and needs a longer growing season than regular beans—at least 75 days of warm, frost-free weather. They are not easy to grow therefore in temperate climates, so are best planted as a greenhouse annual.

Phyllostachys spp.

HARDINESS
Hardy.

DAYS TO MATURITY
Depending on
species, some
shoots can be
harvested in the
second spring.

COMMENTS
Cut stalks for
garden canes
when 3 years
old or more.

BAMBOO SHOOT

WHERE GARDEN SPACE ALLOWS, BAMBOO
PROVIDES EDIBLE YOUNG SHOOTS IN SPRING
AS WELL AS USEFUL GARDEN CANES LATER.

Position Plant in full sun in fertile,
moist, well-drained soil; pH 6.0–7.0.

Cultivation Propagate by division
in early spring. Buy potted divisions
by mail or in garden centres. Plant
in early spring and water until
established.

Pests and diseases Little troubled by
pests, except slugs and snails, which
eat the young shoots. Most bamboos
that produce edible shoots are
"spreading" bamboos that spread
by underground rhizomes. Build
a strong underground barrier or
mow frequently to keep the clump
from getting out of hand and
becoming invasive.

Harvesting and storage Cut tender
young shoots at ground level in
early to mid-spring. Stir-fry or use
fresh in salads.

Special tips Edible species vary
widely in their mature height and
hardiness. The smallest, *P. aurea*,
also called fishpole or golden
bamboo, grows to about 6 m (20 ft)
tall. *P. bambusoides*, or timber
bamboo, grows to 22 m (73 ft) tall
and 15 cm (6 in) in diameter.
The hardiest bamboos include
P. aureosulcata, *P. dulcis*, *P. nuda*
and *P. viridiglaucescens*, all up to
9–10.5 m (30–35 ft) tall.

Pisum sativum

HARDINESS
Hardy; peas grown
for early crops
over winter are
best protected
with cloches or
raised indoors.

DAYS TO MATURITY
75–100 days.
Young plants will
tolerate moderate
frost, but frost will
halt development
of autumn crops.

COMMENTS
The pods of crisp
sugar snap peas
(left) are edible.

PEA

TALL-GROWING PEAS WILL NEED A SUPPORT
OF SOME TYPE FOR THEIR CLIMBING STEMS
AND TENDRILS.

Position Plant in full sun on a site
with good air circulation. Prefers
well-structured, well-drained but
moisture-retentive soil; pH 6.0–7.0.

Cultivation To get the best yield
from peas, it is important to choose
a cultivar appropriate to the time of
year. Then, you can sow from late
winter to midsummer, for harvest
from late spring to early autumn.
Seed planted in late autumn can
overwinter and germinate in early
spring. Protect early and late sowings
under fleece or cloches, or sow
seeds indoors in a length of plastic
guttering. Transplant by gently
sliding the compost and seedlings
into a broad drill. Plant bush types
2.5 cm (1 in) deep and about
2.5 cm (1 in) apart in double rows
spaced 15 cm (6 in) apart. Planted
in this way, the plants will help to
support each other and the yield
will be greater in very little extra
space. Plant tall pea plants roughly
2.5 cm (1 in) apart in single rows
and provide a support of canes for
them to climb on. Do not thin.
Weed carefully to avoid uprooting
plants, or mulch to discourage weeds.
Peas do not need supplementary
fertilizer, especially if the soil has
been sufficiently well dug and
composted or manured during the

Pea continued

Keep your pea plants well watered during flowering and pod set and they will continue to produce for a considerable time, especially if the pods are picked regularly.

previous season. If your soil tends to be acidic, apply a light dressing of lime to correct the pH level. Practise crop rotation with root vegetables and brassicas to avoid soil-borne diseases.

Pests and diseases Birds and mice steal the seeds; sowing indoors avoids this. The seeds may be attacked by pea moth, pea aphid, pea thrips and pea seed beetle. If root rot is a problem in your area, do not plant where peas have been grown in the preceding 2 years. Autumn plantings are often plagued by powdery mildew. Good air circulation and resistant cultivars help to prevent it.

Harvesting and storage Pick shelling peas when pods are full and plump and peas are tender. Pick sugar snap peas when pods are rounded but still smooth, before the peas begin to bulge the sides of the pod. Pick mangetouts when pods are perfectly flat, showing only the tiniest hint of the pea inside. Peas are best eaten immediately or frozen promptly, as their sugars begin to turn to starch quickly. Dry and store over-mature crops as you would dried beans, for use in soups.

Special tips Make sure you provide adequate moisture when pea plants are in bloom. Even low-growing cultivars benefit from some support.

If the space available for peas is limited, plant a variety such as 'Alderman', which can be grown on a cane wigwam, or on a trellis.

Stick peasticks (hazel, birch or willow branches) into the pea row for a natural-looking support. Make sowings in late summer to extend the harvest, and remember to compost spent plants, as long as they are not diseased in any way. Time to maturity differs with the various cultivars, with the earlier ones generally producing a lower yield than those that grow taller and mature later.

Related plants

Garden pea *P. sativum* var. *sativum*
Also called shelling pea. Cultivars include 'Feltham First' (hardy, early type), 'Onward' (dwarf type, good flavour) and 'Kelvedon Wonder' (wrinkled seeds, prolific dwarf type).

Sugar snap pea *P. sativum* var. *sativum*
The fleshy pods are not fibrous like garden peas and may be eaten cooked or raw in salads. They are best if the strings are removed before cooking. Cultivars include 'Cascadia' (bush type), 'Sugar Ann' (bush type) and 'Oregon Sugar Pod' (climbing type, very sweet).

Mangetout *P. sativum* var. *macrocarpon* Also called snow pea. The thin pods are favoured in oriental cuisines. Cultivars include 'Oregon Sugar Pod' (climbing type), 'Delikata' (climbing type) and 'Carouby de Mausanne' (bush type).

Portulaca oleracea var. *sativa*

PORTULACACEAE

HARDINESS
Half-hardy.

DAYS TO MATURITY
30–70 days,
although thinnings
can be eaten
sooner.

PURSLANE, SUMMER

POPULAR AS A SALAD GREEN, CULTIVATED
PURSLANE IS TALLER AND MORE SUCCULENT
THAN ITS COUSIN, THE WEED.

Position Plant in full sun. Not fussy
about soil and will even grow in
sand; pH 6.0–7.0. Drought-resistant.

Cultivation Seed thinly in rows or
broadcast in small beds after frost
danger is past in spring. Do not
cover seeds but firm gently into the
soil with the back of a hoe. Keep
the soil moist until the seeds
germinate. Thin to 10–15 cm (4–6 in)
apart (the thinnings can be used in
salads). Sow small successive crops
up to midsummer and protect early
sowings under cloches or fleece. You
can also broadcast sow for cut-and-
come-again crops. Water frequently.

Pests and diseases Little bothered
by pests or diseases, except slugs
and snails.

Harvesting and storage Harvest fresh
leaves and stems with scissors as
needed. For cut-and-come-again
crops, leave 2.5 cm (1 in) or more
above ground to sprout new leaves.
May be harvested 4 or 5 times. Best
used fresh as it does not store well.

Special tips Common purslane is
also edible. Collect seeds of the best
wild plants to grow in the garden,
saving seed each year from plants
with the best flavour and growth
habit. Named cultivars are not
generally available, but seed suppliers
may offer variants based on leaf
size or green or gold colour.

Raphanus sativus

HARDINESS
Hardy.

DAYS TO MATURITY
21–35 days,
summer radishes;
50–60 days,
mooli types;
from 140 days,
autumn and
winter radishes.
Will withstand
moderate frost.

COMMENTS
Cultivars of the
daikon include
'Daikon' and
'Miyashige'.

RADISH

FAST-GROWING RADISHES ADD A CRISP,
COLOURFUL TOUCH TO SALADS. HARVEST
WHILE YOUNG AND TENDER.

Position Sow in sun or light shade,
in loose, moisture-retentive soil;
pH 6.5–7.5.

Cultivation Sow early radishes under
cover in mid- and late winter, then
transplant in mid-spring, 12 mm
(½ in) deep in double or triple rows.
Make the rows short. Thereafter, sow
small crops outdoors every 2 weeks
until early autumn. Thin radishes to
2.5–5 cm (1–2 in) apart, or seed
sparingly and thin by pulling radishes
as they reach eating size. Sow winter
radishes in mid- to late summer and
thin to 10–15 cm (4–6 in) apart.

Keep moist and harvest when
young to avoid strong flavour and
toughness. Mulch between rows to
keep soil moist in hot weather.

Pests and diseases Rotate winter
radishes and other root crops to
avoid clubroot. Cabbage root fly,
flea beetle, and slugs and snails
may attack the plants. Summer
radishes, especially slender French
breakfast types, become woody and
bitter when over-mature. Sow small
but frequent crops to keep tender
radishes on the table. The roots of
radishes planted in heavy soils are
apt to be misshapen and have a
number of branching side roots.

Radish continued

The mooli is a white, carrot-shaped, hot radish, up to 60 cm (2 ft) long. Also known as daikon, it is often grated as a condiment.

Harvesting and storage Pull summer and autumn crops as soon as they are large enough for use. Pull winter radishes as needed when they reach eating size; they can be left in the ground and will grow as big as a turnip. Alternatively, store in damp sand in a cool place, or pickle.

Special tips Interplant summer radishes as a catch crop with slower-growing crops such as broccoli and cabbage. Harvest the radishes before the companion crops need the space. Radishes are frequently mixed with beetroot or carrot seeds: the radishes germinate first and so mark the rows of the slower-growing crops. Because they grow quickly, they are a good crop for children to sow.

Related plants

Summer radish *R. sativus* These are round or pointed, or long and slender, small radishes and may be pink, red or white.

Black Spanish radish *R. sativus* This winter radish is up to 10 cm (4 in) in diameter, with black skin and white flesh. Pungent, keeps well.

Chinese radish *R. sativus* Winter radish. Long and white like the Japanese radish, but sweet, not pungent.

Winter radish *R. sativus* A catch-all term for radish cultivars that are suitable for at least short-term storage as a root vegetable. In addition to those above, the German beer radish, which is large, white, and turnip-shaped, is very popular in northern Europe.

Rheum x *hybridum*

HARDINESS
Hardy perennial,
but avoid frost
pockets.

DAYS TO MATURITY
Harvest sparingly
in the second year
after planting and
more heavily
thereafter.

COMMENTS
Cultivars include
'Glaskins Perpetual'
and 'Timperley
Early'. 'Victoria' is
robust and green-
stemmed rather
than red.

RHUBARB

EVEN THOUGH MANY THINK OF IT AS A FRUIT
CROP, RHUBARB IS ACTUALLY A VEGETABLE,
BECAUSE IT IS THE STEM THAT IS HARVESTED
AND EATEN RATHER THAN A FRUIT.

Position Plant in full sun in rich,
deep, well-drained soil; fairly heavy
soils suit it best; pH 5.0–6.8. It is often
planted near the compost heap, so it
benefits from the nutrient-rich run-off.

Cultivation Can be grown from seed,
but it is quicker to use dormant
crowns, or "sets", of this hardy
perennial; they are available from
mail-order suppliers or you could
obtain a division from a neighbour.
Plant in late autumn or in early
spring, 1–2 months before the last
spring frost. Dig a hole big enough

to accommodate the roots and cover
the crown with no more than 5 cm
(2 in) of soil. Mix a spadeful or two
of compost or well-rotted manure
into the soil to get the plant off to a
good start. Finish off with a deep
mulch. This plant is a heavy feeder,
so top-dress it every spring with
plenty of well-rotted compost or
manure and feed again, with a
general-purpose fertilizer or compost
tea, after the leaves die down.
Rhubarb is drought-tolerant, but be
sure to water it well to ensure an
abundant crop of tender stalks.

Pests and diseases Little troubled by
pests. Plant in well-drained soil to
avoid root rot. Honey fungus may
attack this crop.

Rhubarb continued

It is well worth forcing rhubarb: the etiolated, light-starved stems are not only very pretty, but taste very sweet without any of the sourness of older stems.

Harvesting and storage To force the first, early stems, cover the crown of an established plant in late winter with a terracotta forcing pot to exclude the light. You could use a dustbin instead—a bucket is too small. Leave in place for at least 6 weeks to blanch the emerging stems. After harvesting some forced stems, uncover the crown by mid-spring and allow to develop normally, to avoid exhausting the plant. To harvest large, outer leaf stalks, grasp them near the base and pull with a slight twisting motion. Remove the toxic leaves. Never pull all the stems and stop harvesting after midsummer. The stout stalks, cooked by themselves or with seasonal fruits, make delicious desserts. Spring stalks are more tender. Chop and freeze uncooked stems.

Special tips Cut off flower stems that rob the plant of energy, resulting in stringy leaf stalks. Although the leaves contain oxalic acid and are toxic, they can be added to the compost heap.

Rumex spp.

HARDINESS
Hardy.

DAYS TO MATURITY
60 days for first-year crop, although thinnings may be harvested sooner.

COMMENTS
Will withstand moderate frost. The leaves can be frozen for use in soup and sauces.

SORREL

A TENDER GREEN SALAD PLANT WITH A DELICIOUS LEMONY FLAVOUR. FRENCH SORREL WITHSTANDS DRY WEATHER BETTER THAN SOME OTHER SORRELS.

Position Plant in full sun or partial shade in rich, moist soil; pH 6.0–7.0.

Cultivation Sow the seeds indoors or sow directly in the garden in autumn or 2–4 weeks before last spring frost. Thin to stand 15–20 cm (6–8 in) apart, using the thinnings in salads. Hoe or mulch to discourage weeds and keep watered for best production. Top-dress the bed with well-rotted compost or manure each autumn or spring. Sorrel is a perennial plant, but will decline after 3–4 years. Start a new bed from seed or divide existing plants.

Pests and diseases Use cloches to protect plants from leaf-eating insects. Keep flower stems cut back to extend the spring harvest.

Harvesting and storage Pick fresh outer leaves as needed. Produces abundantly in spring and autumn; less productive in hot weather.

Related plants

Common sorrel *R. acetosa* Pictured above, it has longer leaves and milder flavour than French sorrel.

French sorrel *R. scutatus* This has smaller leaves than common sorrel; the "buckler-leaved" variant has arrow-shaped leaves.

Scorzonera hispanica

HARDINESS
Hardy.

DAYS TO MATURITY
175 days.

COMMENTS
This black-skinned, perennial is related and very similar to salsify (see page 233); its root may be as much as 30 cm (1 ft) long.

SCORZONERA

THIS VEGETABLE IS NOT WIDELY GROWN, PERHAPS BECAUSE OF ITS UNATTRACTIVE APPEARANCE, BUT IT HAS A SUBTLE AND DELICIOUS, PARSNIP-LIKE FLAVOUR.

Position Plant in an open position in sun and in deep, rich, stone-free soil that has not been recently manured; pH 6.8.

Cultivation Dig over the ground before sowing to create a friable soil in which the roots can develop. Add grit if needed to heavy soils. When hoeing off weeds, take care not to damage the roots in case they fork. Water if needed in dry weather.

Pests and diseases Sow seed direct outdoors in mid- to late spring or in late summer for an overwintering crop.

The plants do not transplant well.

Pests and diseases Little troubled by pests and diseases.

Harvesting and storage Lift roots very carefully from mid-autumn through the winter; they are very brittle and bleed easily. They are best used immediately, but may store for a week in a refrigerator. Leave small roots in the ground for harvest next year. Roots are best washed and boiled in salted water, then peeled, to avoid bleeding and preserve the delicate flavour. Pick young 15-cm (6-in) shoots, or "chards", and flower buds from overwintered roots in early spring for use in salads.

Solanum melongena

HARDINESS
Tender.

DAYS TO MATURITY
112–170 frost-free
days.

COMMENTS
Provide adequate
soil moisture and
calcium to prevent
blossom-end rot,
which shows up as
a soft, brown spot
at the blossom end
of the fruit.

AUBERGINE

AUBERGINES THRIVE IN HOT WEATHER AND
NEED AMPLE AMOUNTS OF WATER AND
FERTILIZER TO PRODUCE THEIR FRUITS.

Position Grow in full sun in light,
rich, well-drained, warm soil, loam-
based compost or grow-bags;
pH 5.5–6.8.

Cultivation It does not pay to start
the plants too early in the season
or put them outdoors too early;
in many areas, it is best to keep
them in the greenhouse. Sow in
spring indoors in modules and
transplant into deep pots, grow-bags
or soil beds. Pinch out the shoot tips
to create a bushy plant and start
feeding with tomato fertilizer every
10–12 days once the first fruits set.

Keep well-watered. Thin the fruits
to 1 per stem to obtain good-sized
fruits. Plants in pots may be placed
outdoors in a sheltered, sunny spot
in summer.

Pests and diseases The main pests
under cover are the usual red spider
mite, whitefly and aphids; biological
controls are effective. *Botrytis* (rot)
can be a problem in cold conditions.

Harvesting and storage Cut off the
fruit with some stem attached;
harvest often to encourage further
fruiting. Standard cultivars, such as
'Black Beauty', will bear 4–10 full-
sized fruits, or more if picked small.
Oriental cultivars bear more but
smaller fruits. It is better to harvest

The white aubergine is as delicious as it is decorative. Harvest the glossy fruits at any size and keep picking regularly to keep the plants bearing.

when a little small, as soon as the skin colours, than to let the fruit become bitter and over-mature. If frost threatens, harvest all fruits, leaving 5 cm (2 in) of stem attached, and store in a cool, moist, well-ventilated place. They will keep for a month or longer.

Related plants

Baby aubergine *S. melongena*
A gourmet item, usually slender or egg-shaped, up to 10 cm (4 in) long. Quick-maturing, good for short-season areas. Cultivars include 'Thai Yellow Egg' and 'Baby Belle'.

Italian aubergine *S. melongena* There are many fine cultivars with tender, non-bitter, white flesh and dazzling skin colour. 'Rosa Bianca' is rosy lavender and white; 'Violetta di Firenze' has dark lavender, somewhat ridged fruit.

Oriental aubergine *S. melongena* Long, thin, purple-black fruits, but also light green and white-lavender. Cultivars include 'Long Purple Brinjal'.

White aubergine *S. melongena* This type has an attractive white skin, but may be less prolific than its purple siblings. 'Snowy' and 'Listada de Gandia' bear medium-sized fruits.

Solanum tuberosum

HARDINESS
Frost-tender.

DAYS TO MATURITY
100–110 days, early crops; 110–120 days, second earlies; 125–140 days, maincrop potatoes.

COMMENTS
Plant earlies in early spring, second earlies in mid-spring, and maincrops in mid- to late spring. Salad potatoes (left) have a waxy texture that makes them ideal for use in salads.

POTATO

ALTHOUGH FROST-TENDER, POTATOES STORE WELL, SO IF YOU GROW EARLIES AND MAINCROPS, YOU CAN EAT HOME-GROWN POTATOES ALL YEAR ROUND.

Position Plant in full sun in deep, well-drained, slightly acid soil with plenty of potash; avoid frost pockets. The ideal pH is 5.2–5.7, but potatoes will also do well at pH 5.8–6.5.

Cultivation Most potatoes do not come true from seed and are planted from pieces of tuber called "seed potatoes". Each piece should be about the size of an egg and contain one or more "eyes", or dormant buds. Cut seed potatoes to size, if necessary, and let the pieces dry for 1 day to avoid having them rot in the ground. Plant earlies about 30 cm (1 ft) apart, and maincrops about 38 cm (15 in) apart, in a trench 7.5–10 cm (3–4 in) deep. Rake the soil level to cover the seed potatoes. Protect early plantings from frost under cloches or horticultural fleece. Tubers will form above the seed potato, not below it, so plants must be earthed up to get good yields. With a hoe or rake, draw soil up around the top-growth when it is 15–20 cm (6–8 in) tall, burying all but the top-most leaves. Repeat at least once, and more often if needed, as the plant grows. Earthing up also supports the plants and protects new tubers from exposure to light. On level or slightly sloping beds,

White potatoes are good for general use. For easy harvesting, incorporate loose compost, leaves and straw into the mounded ridges and the potatoes will pull up readily.

the furrow between rows can be used for irrigating. You can also grow potatoes under straw or leaf mulch, adding layers as the plant grows. In well-prepared and fertilized soil, no extra fertilizer is needed, but water regularly to promote smooth-skinned, well-developed potatoes.

Pests and diseases To avoid soil-borne pests such as potato cyst eelworm and diseases such as potato powdery scab, rotate plantings of potato and its relatives, such as tomato and aubergine. Potatoes are the best crop for soil that has recently been under turf or grassland, but prepare the area the autumn before planting and turn it over once during the winter, if possible, to destroy wireworms,

and don't leave maincrop potatoes in the ground. Do not use fresh manure on potato beds as it encourages scab. Covering plants with cloches or fleece or dusting them with ground limestone helps to deter flea beetles. Other pests that eat the tubers are cutworms and slugs. A common problem in warm, damp weather is potato blight. The first signs are brown patches on leaf edges, which quickly spread and rot the haulms, and then the tubers. At the first symptoms, remove the haulms completely to stop the rot reaching the tubers, and burn them. Don't put them on the compost heap because they will infect it with spores. Spraying with Bordeaux mixture

When flowers appear on the plants, you can harvest some small new potatoes. When the leaves die down, the mature potatoes are ready to harvest.

may help to prevent it. If exposed to light, potato tubers develop green patches that contain the toxic alkaloid solanine. Earth up or mulch deeply to prevent sunlight from reaching the tubers; store harvested potatoes in a dark place (never eat green potatoes—they are poisonous).

Harvesting and storage Flowering is usually the signal that the plant has begun to form tubers. Check by gently probing the soil around the base of the plant, taking no more than a few tubers per plant for early use. "New potatoes" are those that have been freshly harvested and eaten within a day, before the skin toughens and the sugars begin to be converted to starches. When the

foliage dies back, the potatoes are mature. Dig up as needed, but be sure to lift all the tubers before a hard frost, because potatoes that have been frozen will rot in storage. Dry, without washing, and store in well-ventilated boxes or sacks in a cool to cold, dark place, ideally about 4°C (40°F).

Special tips To speed up your harvest, try pre-sprouting, or chitting, your seed potatoes. Set whole tubers in a cool, bright spot. Once they have developed short, green shoots (in about 4–6 weeks), plant the chitted potatoes out into the garden as you would normally. If you are short of space, or want to grow potatoes for harvest in winter, try growing 1 or 2

Potato continued

Red potatoes are good for boiling or baking in their skins. Set aside any tubers that are nicked or damaged during harvesting and use them first.

seed potatoes in a bucket or large container. Plant in about 13 cm (5 in) of soil-based compost and earth up as the plant grows until the container is full. Feed with a high-potash fertilizer and water regularly. Then just tip out of the container to harvest.

Related plants

Red potatoes *S. tuberosum* A red-skinned potato, usually with moist, white flesh, but some cultivars have cream-coloured or yellow flesh. Small ones are often sold commercially as new potatoes. Cultivars include the early 'Red Duke of York', with pale yellow flesh; the firm-fleshed second early, 'Kondor'; and 'Desiree', a heavy-yielding maincrop with good drought resistance.

White potatoes *S. tuberosum* With white- or buff-coloured skin and white flesh, this variety is an all-purpose potato. 'Foremost' is a high-yielding early, oval in shape with firm flesh; 'Kestrel' is a second early with some eelworm and slug resistance; 'King Edward', an old favourite, is an oval, red-blotched maincrop potato with creamy flesh.

Salad potatoes *S. tuberosum* Yellow- or white-fleshed potatoes popular for their delicate flavour, beauty and appealing waxy texture. Popular cultivars include 'Rocket', an early with white flesh; 'Charlotte', a second early with firm, yellow flesh and good flavour; and 'Pink Fir Apple', a long, knobbly maincrop with yellow flesh.

Spinacia oleracea

HARDINESS
Hardy. Spinach
will withstand
moderate frost.

DAYS TO MATURITY
35–70 days,
although thinnings
can be harvested
sooner.

COMMENTS
Good, reliable
cultivars are
'Sigmaleaf',
'Monnopa'
and 'Tetona'.

SPINACH

FRESH OR COOKED, SPINACH IS DELICIOUS
AND NUTRITIOUS. IT NEEDS COOL WEATHER
AND PLENTY OF WATER TO PRODUCE
ABUNDANT, CRISP LEAVES.

Position Plant in full sun or partial
shade in moist, fertile, well-limed
soil; pH 6.0–7.0.

Cultivation Sow seed 13 mm (½ in)
deep, every 3 to 4 weeks from
midwinter to early autumn. Set out
or thin seedlings to 10–15 cm (4–6 in)
apart. Keep free of weeds and
water regularly. Sow several batches
from late summer to early autumn
for overwintering—some batches
may succumb to winter cold or bolt,
so it is best to spread the risk. Seed
autumn crops heavily, because

spinach germinates poorly in warm
soil. Spinach can also be sown more
thickly for use as a cut-and-come-
again salad crop, or as a catch crop
between longer-term vegetables.

Pests and diseases Use netting to
protect from birds; if downy mildew
is a problem, space out plants to
increase air circulation.

Harvesting and storage Pick larger
outside leaves or harvest the whole
plant at its base. Spinach freezes
well for use as a cooked vegetable.

Special tips Hot weather and
lengthening days can cause spinach
plants to bolt (run to seed). Choose
heat-resistant cultivars and sow spring
crops early to avoid this problem.

Tetragonia tetragonioides

AIZOACEAE

HARDINESS
Half-hardy perennial, grown as an annual.

DAYS TO MATURITY
55–70 days.

COMMENTS
Named cultivars are not generally available.

SPINACH, NEW ZEALAND

NEW ZEALAND SPINACH IS A BRANCHING, MAT-LIKE PLANT THAT THRIVES IN WEATHER THAT IS TOO HOT FOR TRUE SPINACH.

Position Plant in a sheltered site in full sun in rich, well-drained soil; pH 6.5–7.5.

Cultivation Soak seed overnight to hasten germination and sow directly in the garden after the last spring frost. Alternatively, sow indoors in modules in mid-spring, and harden off and transplant the plants 30–45 cm (12–18 in) apart when the danger of frost is past.

Pests and diseases New Zealand spinach is rarely troubled by pests, but may be eaten by birds or be prone to downy mildew in damp weather. Seed can be slow to germinate. Mark the row well to avoid weeding out young plants.

Harvesting and storage Pick about 10–15 cm (4–6 in) of the branch tips, together with the leaves, which are small and brittle. Whole plants may be cut above the ground when they are small; the stem will re-sprout. Cook as you would true spinach.

Special tips New Zealand spinach is good for hot, dry conditions where true spinach does poorly. It will tolerate saline soils.

Tragopogon porrifolius

HARDINESS
Hardy biennial
grown as an annual,
but can be grown
as a winter
vegetable.

DAYS TO MATURITY
140–150 days or
up to 252 days if
grown as a winter
vegetable.

COMMENTS
Other common
names include
oyster plant,
a reference to the
unusual flavour of
this easily grown
vegetable.

SALSIFY

A HARDY ROOT VEGETABLE, SALSIFY LOOKS
LIKE A SLENDER PARSNIP WITH NARROW,
GRASSY LEAVES, BUT HAS A DELICATE,
OYSTER-LIKE FLAVOUR.

Position Plant in full sun in deep,
light and rich soil that has few
stones; pH 6.0–8.0.

Cultivation Sow seed 13 mm (½ in)
deep in spring. Thin to 7.5–10 cm
(3–4 in) apart. Water regularly and
mulch to maintain the soil moisture
and produce smoother, more tender
roots. Salsify roots can be left in the
ground over winter to harvest the
new flowering shoots in spring.
Cut off the old leaves in autumn
and earth up or mulch to protect
the roots over winter.

Pests and diseases Salsify is little
troubled by pests or diseases. Spotty
or slow germination may indicate
that the seed is old. Purchase fresh
salsify seed each year.

Harvesting and storage Dig roots
as needed when large enough, but
mulch the bed before a hard frost.
Store the harvested roots in damp
sand in a cool place. If grown for
the young shoots (chard), cut the
shoots with unopened buds about
10 cm (4 in) long.

Valerianella locusta

HARDINESS
Hardy; often grown as a winter vegetable.

DAYS TO MATURITY
30–80 days depending on time of sowing; thinnings can be harvested earlier.

COMMENTS
Other common names are lamb's lettuce and mâche. Reliable cultivars are 'Corn Salad' and 'Vit'.

CORN SALAD

SMALL, TENDER, GREEN CORN SALAD PROVIDES A GOOD ALTERNATIVE TO LETTUCE IN AUTUMN AND WINTER. IT'S EXPENSIVE TO BUY, BUT EASY TO GROW.

Position Full sun or partial shade. Not fussy about soil, but prefers it rich with humus; pH 6.0–7.0. Will withstand light frosts.

Cultivation Sow seed from mid-spring to early autumn; just cover with fine soil and firm with the back of a hoe. Plant thickly in rows or more thinly in wide beds; keep moist. Thin to 5 cm (2 in) apart; use thinnings in salads. Avoid plantings that will mature in hot weather. Protecting late sowings under cloches or horticultural fleece will yield a better-tasting crop. Mulch lightly after a hard frost. Remove mulch in early spring.

Pests and diseases Little troubled by pests or diseases, but slugs and snails and aphids may be a problem. In colder areas, mulch more heavily over winter to avoid plants being "heaved" up above ground as the soil freezes.

Harvesting and storage Harvest entire rosettes by pinching off at ground level. Some cultivars remain sweet even when in flower, but taste to check.

Special tips In wide-bed plantings, thin and weed simultaneously by raking shallowly in two directions.

Zea mays

HARDINESS
Half-hardy.

DAYS TO MATURITY
70–105 frost-free
days. Early cultivars
include 'Earlibird'
and 'Early Extra
Sweet'. Longer-
season cultivars
include 'Tuxedo'
and the super-
sweet 'Northern
Extra Sweet'.

COMMENTS
Use short-season
cultivars for a
better chance
of a good yield.

SWEET CORN

TENDER AND SUCCULENT, FRESH SWEET CORN
IS A CLASSIC SUMMER TREAT FROM THE
GARDEN. IT'S WELL WORTH GROWING.

Position Plant in full sun, in a
sheltered site. Avoid dry or heavy,
cold soils; prefers deep, well-manured
soil with high organic content;
pH 6.0–6.8.

Cultivation Sow seed in late spring
after last spring frost, or 1–2 weeks
earlier if soil has first been warmed
by covering with black plastic for a
week or more in sunny weather.
Seed germinates poorly in cold,
wet soil and may rot. Avoid this
by sowing indoors in modules and
transplanting in early summer. Sow
2.5 cm (1 in) deep and 10 cm (4 in)
apart in blocks at least four rows
wide, rather than in long, single rows,
to ensure good wind-pollination.
Rows should be 45–60 cm (18–24 in)
apart. Thin seedlings to 20–30 cm
(8–12 in) apart; mulch or hoe
shallowly to avoid damaging roots
near the soil surface. Sweet corn
grows rapidly and needs adequate
feeding and water. Apply diluted
seaweed solution or compost tea
after 1 month and again when the
tassels appear. Water is most critical
when sweet corn is in tassel. Plant 3
successive crops of the same cultivar
every 2 weeks in spring, or 1 sowing
each of an early, mid-season and
late cultivar, to extend the harvest.
Modern sweet corn cultivars include

Sweet corn continued

Colourful ears of ornamental corn are very easy to grow. Hang them upside-down to finish drying and use for dramatic decorative effects.

some known as "supersweet", which have been genetically modified to slow the conversion of sugar to starch. But if these cultivars cross-pollinate with other sweet corn cultivars, tough kernels will result. It is recommended that corn plots be separated by 7.5 m (25 ft) or more, but this is not always practical in home gardens. Instead, time the plantings to ensure that at least 10 days elapse between pollination periods for the cultivars. For example, you could plant a supersweet cultivar that matures in 82 days at the same time as a regular cultivar that matures in 72 days. Or you could plant an 82-day supersweet cultivar next to an 82-day regular

cultivar, as long as you sow it 10 days earlier or later.

Pests and diseases Plant in warm soil to avoid wireworms, which destroy seed. Mice also eat the seed; place chicken wire over the soil until the seedlings appear. Rotate sweet corn plantings and shred crop debris to reduce overwintering pests, such as frit flies, and sweetcorn smut. Patchy spots on kernels, or poorly filled ears, indicate poor pollination. Birds, badgers and squirrels may eat the ripe sweet corn.

Harvesting and storage Harvest when silks have turned brown and dry and ears feel full, usually about 3 weeks after the silks appear.

Plant corn in blocks rather than rows to get more effective pollination. To hand-pollinate corn, strip the pollen from the tassels and sprinkle it onto the silks.

Check by pulling back a husk and pressing a thumbnail into a kernel. It should squirt a milky liquid. Holding the stalk firmly, snap the ear downwards, then up. Freeze corn that cannot be eaten immediately after picking, as it begins to turn starchy within hours.

Special tips If space is limited, interplant a fast-growing catch crop such as lettuce between rows of sweetcorn. The lettuce can be used before the sweetcorn casts too much shade.

Related plants

Miniature sweet corn *Z. mays* var. *rugosa* Pick baby ears a day or two after silks appear and use whole in stir-fries or for pickling. 'Minipop' and 'Minor' are grown specifically for miniature corn, but any sweet corn cultivar will do.

Ornamental sweet corn *Z. mays* var. *indurata* Also called Indian corn. These cultivars of field sweet corn have colourful kernels.

Popcorn *Z. mays* var. *praecox* The dense kernels explode into crisp puffs when heated. Harvest as dry as possible, pull back the husks, and hang in an airy place to "cure". Test-pop a few kernels to determine when the corn is dry enough to be hulled and stored in bags or jars. Cultivars include 'Strawberry Popcorn'.

Sprouts

DAYS TO MATURITY
This varies with the type of seed you are sprouting and the temperature.

COMMENTS
Many vegetable seeds are excellent for sprouting, including alfalfa, adzuki bean, mung bean, beetroot, salad cress, rape, mustard, peas, lentils, sunflowers, beans, radishes and broccoli. Flavour and texture vary; experiment to find which you like best.

SPROUTS

A WIDE VARIETY OF SEEDS, INCLUDING ALFALFA AND LENTILS, ARE EASY TO SPROUT WITHOUT SOIL. THEY ARE TASTY EATEN RAW IN SALADS AND SANDWICHES, OR SPRINKLED OVER STIR-FRIES AT THE LAST MINUTE.

Position Sprouts are grown indoors and no soil is required.

Cultivation Use only seeds that have not been treated with fungicides or other chemicals; natural food stores often sell seeds packaged especially for sprouting. Use fresh seeds to ensure good germination. Soak large seeds overnight in water, or smaller ones for an hour or two. Pick out any broken seeds and rinse the rest several times in warm water in a sieve or colander. (Don't waste the rinse water. Some pot plants, for example African violets, thrive on it, but test with small diluted amounts until you are sure.) You will find several styles of sprouting systems at natural food stores, but you can simply put the seeds in a wide-mouthed jar, cover it with muslin or cheesecloth and invert it over a dish to catch any remaining rinse water. Good air circulation is very important. Keep the container in a warm place, rinsing the seeds twice daily with tepid water to stop the seeds fermenting or going mouldy. In hot weather, rinse more often.

Harvesting and storage Sprouts are ready to eat in 3–5 days, or slightly longer if you are sprouting some of

SOME OF THE MANY SYSTEMS FOR GROWING SPROUTS

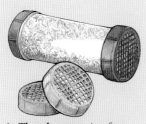

1. The tube system is, after a screw-top jar, perhaps the simplest of all. It has three screen lids and one solid lid for transportation. Made from clear plastic, it affords excellent drainage and air circulation.

2. Tiered trays allow you to grow a good quantity of sprouts and keep them clean. Excellent drainage and air circulation and perhaps the best choice if you like to have a few types of sprouts on the go at the same time.

3. The hemp bag system has excellent drainage and air circulation. It is very good for beans, grains and the larger seeds, but it's fine for smaller seeds, too. It really comes into its own when you are travelling.

4. The miniature garden is perfect for baby greens. It's so small you can keep it on your desk at work to supply fresh sprouts for your lunch. Simply sprinkle small seeds on the moist felt pads for a mini-crop.

the hard-seeded vegetables. Store sprouted seeds in the refrigerator and use promptly; many sprouts become mouldy quite quickly.

Special tips Old seeds may not germinate or do so only slowly. Visit www.sproutpeople.com for more information on the types of sprouting systems that are available.

Herbs for the Kitchen Garden

No vegetable or fruit garden is complete without a planting of at least the basic herbs, to season the dishes cooked from your fresh or preserved produce. You could grow your herbs in a dedicated herb garden, in rows along with your vegetables, mixed in with flowers in an ornamental potager, or in containers. They shouldn't be too far from the kitchen door, though, to make it easy to pick them.

Grow some herbs in containers by the kitchen door, so that they are always to hand. Use a light, gritty compost to provide well-drained conditions.

Where to grow herbs

Most common culinary herbs are easy to grow. Many Mediterranean herbs, like bay, marjoram, oregano and sage, prefer very well-drained, light soils and warm, sheltered sites in full sun. The flavour is often more intense in plants grown in slightly poorer soils. A few herbs, such as mint and meadowsweet, prefer moister soil and do not mind shade.

Herbs are very easy to grow in containers.

How to grow herbs

Herbs grown as annuals, such as basil, chives, dill, chervil, fennel and parsley are best grown from seed. Other herbs, like woody shrubs bay, hyssop, rosemary, sage and thyme, or perennials like lemon balm, sweet Cicely and French tarragon, are best bought as small pot plants, since you won't need many of each. Once they reach a decent size, keep the plants bushy and productive by regular pinching out or pruning of the shoot tips.

Mentha spp.

HARDINESS
Hardy or frost
hardy; depending
on species.

DAYS TO MATURITY
90–150 days.

COMMENTS
Mints range in
height up to 1 m
(36 in). Popular
varieties include
apple mint
(*M. suaveolens*),
peppermint
(*M.* x *piperita*),
pineapple mint
(*M. suaveolens*
'Variegata') and
spearmint (*M.
spicata*).

MINT

THE MINTS ARE HERBACEOUS PERENNIALS
THAT THRIVE IN MOST LOCATIONS. THE FRESH
AND DRIED FOLIAGE PROVIDES FLAVOURING
FOR BOTH SWEET AND SAVOURY DISHES.

Position Plant in full sun to partial
shade, in rich, moist, well-drained
soil; pH 6.5–8.3.

Cultivation Propagate from new
plantlets that spring up along the
roots, or by division in spring or
autumn. Allow 30–45 cm (12–18 in)
between plants. Mint is a rampant
spreader: to control it, plant in
bottomless buckets that are 25 cm
(10 in) deep, or in large pots. Cut
frequently and severely, or the plant
will become woody after several

years. Top-dress with well-rotted
compost or manure in autumn.

Pests and diseases Thin clumps for
good air circulation to avoid root
and foliage diseases. Watch for aphids,
which stipple leaves; control them
with a strong spray of water.

Harvesting and storage Harvest fresh
leaves as needed. Just before
flowering, cut the stalks and hang
in bunches to dry; store in airtight
containers. Leaves can also be
frozen or infused in oil or vinegar.

Special tips Mints have hairy leaves
that can cause skin irritations and
rashes. Mint tea should not be drunk
continuously over a long period.

Ocimum basilicum   LAMIACEAE

HARDINESS
Tender; best grown
in containers under
cover.

DAYS TO MATURITY
60 days, until just
before flowering.

COMMENTS
Short-lived
perennial grown as
annual. Plant near
tomatoes and
peppers to enhance
their growth. Sow
successive batches
for a plentiful
supply when older
plants get woody.

BASIL, SWEET

BASIL IS POPULAR FOR ITS STRONG FLAVOUR
(WITH HINTS OF LIQUORICE AND PEPPER)
AND ITS NATURAL AFFINITY WITH TOMATOES,
WHICH IS SO USEFUL IN THE KITCHEN.

Position Plant in a warm, sheltered
site, in rich, well-drained but moist
soil or compost; thrives in hot sun;
pH 6.4–8.

Cultivation Sow seed indoors in seed
trays in warmth, 6 weeks before last
frost in early to mid-spring. Transplant
the seedlings to small pots before
hardening them off and setting
outdoors after all risk of frost has
passed, in a warm, sheltered spot.
Top-dress with more compost in
mid-season to enhance production.
Basil is easily damaged by low

temperatures, so in many areas, it is
best to keep the pots in the greenhouse or conservatory. Always water
basil in the morning; it does not like
being wet in the cool of the night.

Pests and diseases A good companion
plant because it repels aphids, red
spider mites and other pests.

Harvesting and storage Pinch off
leaves weekly, to get the plant to
bush out. Use it fresh or dried—
dried foliage loses colour and
flavour. Best preserved chopped
and frozen, or as pesto. If freezing
pesto, leave out garlic until ready
to use it: garlic becomes bitter after
a few months. Basil keeps well in
a jar if covered with olive oil.

Petroselinum crispum

HARDINESS
Hardy.

DAYS TO MATURITY
120 days.

COMMENTS
Biennial usually grown as an annual; about 30 cm (1 ft). It goes to seed in the second year and also prematurely if the taproot is damaged during transplanting.

PARSLEY

PARSLEY IS REQUIRED IN SO MANY RECIPES THAT IT IS A FEATURE OF MOST HERB GARDENS. GROW IN THE GARDEN OR ON A SUNNY PATIO OR WINDOWSILL.

Position Plant in full sun; tolerates partial shade. It thrives in moderately rich, well-drained soil; pH 6.0–7.0.

Cultivation Sow seed shallowly outdoors in successive batches from early spring when soil reaches 10°C (50°F), thinning to 20 cm (8 in) apart; germinates slowly. Alternatively, soak seeds overnight in warm water before sowing in biodegradable pots indoors in early spring; transplants poorly. Remove all flower stalks and prune away dead leaves. For productive plants, top-dress with well-rotted compost in mid season. To attract beneficial insects to the garden, let a few plants flower and go to seed. Pot up plants from late sowings to bring indoors for winter supplies.

Pests and diseases Carrot root fly larvae may attack the roots and celery fly larvae the leaves. Aphids may also transmit viruses.

Harvesting and storage Cut leaf stalks at the base for fresh foliage all summer. Hang in bunches to dry in shade; freeze whole or chopped.

Related plants
Italian parsley *P. crispum* var. *neopolitanum* has flat, dark green foliage and a strong flavour. Plants are more resistant and larger than curly-leaved varieties.

Rosmarinus officinalis

ROSEMARY

THE FLOWERS AND LEAVES OF THIS HIGHLY SCENTED HERB ARE USED TO SEASON AND GARNISH MEAT, FISH AND POULTRY. FRESH SPRIGS ARE USED TO FLAVOUR OIL, VINEGAR AND WINE.

Position Plant in full sun to partial shade in light, well-drained soil; pH 7.0–8.3.

Cultivation Sow shallowly indoors in early spring, then transplant to pots outdoors; plant out in the garden for a second season, spacing 90 cm (3 ft) apart. Or take cuttings from new growth in late summer. Overwintering success varies with local conditions and cultivar; larger plants may overwinter better outdoors than small ones. Potted plants may be brought into a sunny greenhouse for the winter; or keep them at 7°C (45°F) in a conservatory, watering only occasionally. Prune after flowering to encourage bushy growth.

Pests and diseases Indoors, watch for scale insects—wipe them from foliage with a cloth soaked with methylated spirit. Can also be susceptible to mildew; provide good air circulation, especially in winter. Root rot may affect outdoor plants in cold, wet winters; take cuttings to replace the parent plant.

Harvesting and storage Snip off fresh foliage as needed all year; the leaves are more tender from spring to midsummer. Freeze or dry sprigs.

Thymus spp.

HARDINESS
Hardy; but dislike winter wet.

DAYS TO MATURITY
150–350 days.

COMMENTS
Variable shrub; height to 45 cm (18 in). Most species are evergreen and flower in summer; flower colours (lilac, rose-purple, mauve, white, pink, purple), depend on the species and cultivar.

THYME

EASY-TO-GROW THYME IS A FAVOURITE OF COOKS AND GARDENERS. PRETTY IN LEAF AND FLOWER, A CARPET OF THYME MAKES A BEAUTIFUL UNDERPLANTING FOR ROSES.

Position Plant in full sun to partial shade, in ordinary, well-drained soil; pH 7.0–8.5.

Cultivation Sow shallowly in late winter indoors, keeping the soil at 21°C (70°F) for best germination. Plant outdoors in late spring in clumps, 30 cm (1 ft) apart. Divide older plants in spring or autumn or take cuttings in late summer. Add grit to heavy soils, or as a top-dressing, to stop winter wet rotting the roots. Replace plants every 3–4 years to control woody growth.

There are more than 350 species. Grow shrubs for low hedging and mat-forming types for aromatic carpets.

Pests and diseases Usually free from pests and diseases, if soil is well drained.

Harvesting and storage Trim foliage as needed during the summer, or harvest entirely twice per season, leaving at least 7.5 cm (3 in) of growth. Best harvested while in bloom. Bunch sprigs together and hang to dry. Thyme foliage freezes well. Place in airtight containers for use during winter months.

Part Six

PLANT DIRECTORY

FRUIT

Actinidia deliciosa

HARDINESS
Half-hardy, but need warm temperatures to fruit well. Protect plants from late-spring frosts.

HEIGHT
1.2–1.8 m (4–6 ft)

SPREAD
4.5 m (15 ft)

COMMENTS
You'll need to control enthusiastic kiwi growth so the climber won't tangle or shade itself out. Kiwis are also called Chinese gooseberries.

KIWI FRUIT

KIWIS MAKE EXCELLENT COVERING FOR TRELLISES AND ARBOURS. WHILE YOU ENJOY THE SHADE, REACH UP TO PICK THE FRUIT.

Position Plant in full sun on a south- or west-facing wall in average to poor, deep and well-drained soil; pH 6–7.

Cultivation With the exception of a few self-fertile cultivars, such as 'Issai' and 'Jenny', kiwis have either male or female flowers. For pollination, plant a male within about 12 m (40 ft) of females—closer if possible. One male will pollinate up to 8 female vines. Keep the soil moist up to harvest time, but water less as winter approaches. Mulch well, but feed lightly, if at all.

Pruning Before planting, install a sturdy post-and-wire support (as you would for grapes). Insert a stake next to the climber at planting time, and cut out all but one stem. Prune off sideshoots from the remaining stem and train it up the stake.

Propagation Propagate using cuttings or by grafting.

Pests and diseases Surround young plants with a circle of wire mesh fencing to prevent cats from rolling or chewing on leaves and stems.

Harvesting and storage From the third or fourth year, pick kiwi fruit in autumn, when the seeds are black and most of the fruit is still firm.

Ananas comosus

HARDINESS
Tender.

HEIGHT
90–180 cm (3–6 ft)

SPREAD
90–180 cm (3–6 ft)

COMMENTS
Although this is a tropical fruit, it is possible to grow it if you give it the shelter, attention and warm soil that it needs. They cannot stand cold draughts.

PINEAPPLE

PINEAPPLE FLOWERS FUSE TO FORM A WARTY, GREEN-AND-YELLOW SKIN OVER THE FRUIT.

Position Pineapples need full sun and warm, well-drained, acid soil or compost; pH 4.5–6.5. They are fairly tolerant of dry conditions.

Cultivation Pineapples need 70 per cent humidity and maximum light. Try creating a tent, within the greenhouse, of clear plastic or a hot bed. This was used by the Victorians, who placed cold frames over pits of fresh manure. The rotting manure provides heat to the pineapple roots. No pollination needed. Grow plants in containers, in compost with extra sand or perlite for drainage. Avoid overwatering. When plant is 2–3 years old, induce flowering by covering the crown for a few days with a paper bag containing a slice of apple.

Pruning Prune 1–2 months after harvest: cut off sideshoots at the base and at base of fruit stalk. If needed, thin sideshoots along stem.

Propagation Plant sideshoots, or twist off the top crown of leaves, let it dry for a few days, and plant it.

Pests and diseases Control red spider mite, scale insects, thrips or mealybugs with biological controls.

Harvesting and storage Cut or snap fruit from stem when colour changes; slight softening and aroma indicate ripeness. Store above 10°C (50°F).

Averrhoa carambola OXALIDACEAE

HARDINESS
Tender.

HEIGHT
6–9 m (20–30 ft)

SPREAD
4.5–7.5 m (15–25 ft)

COMMENTS
Star fruit come in sweet or sour types. For jam, use slightly under-ripe sweet types or fully ripe sour types. Ripe star fruit can be cooked in tarts and puddings or added to curries.

STAR FRUIT, CARAMBOLA

CARAMBOLA TREES PRODUCE FLESHY FRUITS THAT ARE STAR-SHAPED IN CROSS SECTION AND ENCLOSED WITHIN A WAXY, YELLOW SKIN. BOTH THE SKIN AND THE CRISP FLESH ARE EDIBLE.

Position Plant in full sun and well-drained, slightly acid compost with low salt content.

Cultivation This slow-growing, tropical plant is best grown in a container in a greenhouse or conservatory, where it should reach about 1.5 m (5 ft) after 5 years. Water and feed well during the growing season, but keep dry while the tree is dormant.

Pruning Star fruit needs little pruning beyond the removal of vigorous, upright shoots.

Propagation For temperate climates, grafted plants are the best option; they bear more quickly, and their fruit quality is more predictable.

Pests and diseases Plants have no significant pest or disease problems.

Harvesting and storage Pick the fruits when they are pale green with some yellow. Ripe fruits often fall to the ground. Fruits will keep for a few weeks at 10°C (50°F). Pickle under-ripe fruits or cook them as you would a vegetable.

Berberis spp.

HARDINESS
Hardy to frost hardy.

HEIGHT
90–360 cm (3–12 ft)

SPREAD
90–360 cm (3–12 ft)

COMMENTS
Common barberry *Berberis vulgaris* and species such as *B. asiatica* and *B. aristata* are used for their fruits. Be careful: all parts of barberry, except ripe fruits, are harmful if eaten.

BARBERRY

BARBERRIES PRODUCE RED, YELLOW OR BLACK BERRIES; BOTH THE FLESH AND SKIN OF THE BERRIES ARE EDIBLE. THE FLAVOUR IS USUALLY TART, BUT IN SOME SPECIES THE FRUITS HAVE ENOUGH SUGAR TO BE DRIED INTO "RAISINS".

Position Barberries prefer full sun and moist, well-drained soil. (Evergreen species are generally less hardy than deciduous species.)

Cultivation Set out container-grown plants any time the soil isn't frozen or waterlogged, or plant bare-root shrubs in spring or autumn, while they are dormant. Space plants 90–360 cm (3–12 ft) apart, depending on how big the particular species gets.

Pruning Cut a few of the oldest stems to the ground in winter. Also shorten spindly stems and thin out suckers if the stems are crowded.

Propagation Mix seed with moist peat-free compost and refrigerate it for 2–3 months before sowing in a warm, bright place. Or dig up suckers from the base and transplant.

Pests and diseases Generally no significant problems, but powdery mildew and aphids may attack.

Harvesting and storage Harvest the berries after they are fully coloured. Make the fruit into jams or pickles, or dry and store in airtight jars.

Castanea sativa

HARDINESS
Hardy.

HEIGHT
30 m (100 ft)

SPREAD
15 m (50 ft)

COMMENTS
This tree is often coppiced for its durable wood, which makes good stakes and fencing poles. Trees from seed take up to 20 years to fruit, but grafted trees, eg 'Marron de Lyon', may produce nuts after 5 years.

CHESTNUT, SWEET

THE EDIBLE NUTS OF THIS HANDSOME TREE ARE POPULAR AS ROASTED OR GLAZED TREATS AND IN STUFFING, BUT MAY ALSO BE BOILED AS A VEGETABLE, GROUND INTO A FLOUR FOR BAKING AND SAUCES, AND PICKLED OR PURÉED.

Position Plant in sun or partial shade, in well-drained, deep, loamy to sandy soil that is lime-free; pH 6.5.

Cultivation Sweet chestnuts need to be cross-pollinated, so grow at least 2 trees near each other. Chestnuts are drought-resistant, but appreciate regular watering when young and to produce a good crop.

Pruning Needs little pruning.

Propagation Sow ripe seed in autumn before it dries out, in a seedbed or in pots in a cold frame. Graft cultivars in late winter.

Pests and diseases May suffer from honey fungus or *Phytophthora* root rot; the only remedy is to dig up and dispose of the tree and its soil.

Harvesting and storage Fruits may not ripen after cold summers. Gather fruits in mid- to late autumn as they fall. The husks start to split when the seeds or nuts are ripe; protect your hands with gloves when peeling off. Each husk contains up to 3 chestnuts. Dry slowly in a cool, dry place for 1–2 weeks to sweeten; peeled or unpeeled nuts keep for many months in an airtight jar or refrigerator. Boiled, skinned nuts may be frozen.

x *Citrofortunella microcarpa*

RUTACEAE

HARDINESS
Half-hardy, but will not fruit well outdoors in the UK.

HEIGHT
1.8–7.2 m (6–24 ft), smaller in pots.

SPREAD
90–360 cm (3–12 ft), less in containers.

COMMENTS
The sweet, edible rind easily peels from the flesh, which is juicy, but too tart to eat plain. Use fruits to make marmalade.

CALAMONDIN

CALAMONDINS GROW AS BUSHES OR SMALL TREES, PRODUCING BOUNTIFUL HARVESTS OF SMALL, ROUND, REDDISH ORANGE FRUITS.

Position Give calamondins full sun and soil-based, well-drained potting compost.

Cultivation Calamondins are self-fertile, so you need only one plant. They are easy to grow in containers under cover. Put the container in a bright spot with good air circulation, but shade it from very hot sun. While the tree is growing, keep it humid by misting daily and water your tree regularly to keep the soil evenly moist, especially during bloom. Feed fortnightly with an all-purpose liquid fertilizer. In winter, water to keep the compost just moist and pot on or top-dress with fresh compost.

Pruning Calamondins don't need regular pruning, except to keep the plant small enough for the container and greenhouse.

Propagation Propagate calamondins by taking semi-ripe stem cuttings, or layering.

Pests and diseases Problems are usually minimal if compost drainage is good, but watch for scale, mealy-bugs, red spider mites and whiteflies.

Harvesting and storage Harvest when fruits are fully coloured, or let them hang on the tree until you are ready to use them.

Citrus spp.

CITRUS

ONE FACTOR COMMON TO ALL CITRUS
FRUITS IS THEIR RICH VITAMIN C CONTENT.
LEMONS AND LIMES HAVE THE POWER TO
PERK UP THE FLAVOUR OF MOST DISHES;
ORANGES AND GRAPEFRUIT ARE REFRESHING
AS SNACKS AND IN SALADS.

Position Frost will damage the fruit
of any citrus plants and sometimes
the rest of the tree. These trees are
best grown in containers in a
greenhouse or conservatory, in a
bright, well-ventilated spot, away
from cold and draughts. Use a rich,
soil-based compost. Citrus trees can
be moved outdoors once all risk of
frost is past.

Cultivation Citrus trees are nearly
all self-fertile, so you need only one
to get a good harvest. Once growth
starts, keep humid by misting or
watering the greenhouse floor as
needed. Keep the compost moist to
prevent early fruit drop. Feed lightly
but often to encourage good tree
vigour. In winter, pot on or top-
dress to refresh the compost and
water sparingly.

Pruning Remove damaged or
diseased branches and upright-
growing shoots (suckers) that
emerge from the roots. Trim back
long branches to shape the plant.
Wear gloves when pruning thorny
types to protect your hands.

Propagation Propagate by bud
grafting onto disease-resistant stock.

Citrus continued

HARDINESS
Frost tender, but
can withstand brief
spells of light frost.

HEIGHT
3–9 m (10–30 ft)

SPREAD
3–9 m (10–30 ft)

COMMENTS
For containers,
choose a tree that
has been grafted
onto a dwarfing
rootstock, or look
for dwarf cultivars
such as 'Meyer'
lemons or 'Valencia'
oranges.

These evergreen shrubs and trees are often spiny, so take care where you place them; they also have sweetly scented flowers that sometimes appear at the same time as the fruits.

Pests and diseases Start with virus-free, disease-resistant plants and provide good growing conditions to minimize problems. Keep an eye out for scale insect (small, hard-shelled insects on leaves and stems), whiteflies (small, white flies on leaf undersides), thrips (tiny insects that cause scarring on leaves and fruits), and red spider mites (tiny insects that cause yellow-stippled leaves). Use biological controls, sticky traps and fatty acids to prevent infestations and control diseases.

Harvesting and storage Most citrus trees produce fruit 3–4 years after planting. Finding out when the fruit is ripe can be tricky, since you can't rely on the skin colour as an indicator. For example, some oranges remain green when they are ripe unless the temperature falls to below 7°C (45°F). Other cultivars colour up early, well before the fruit is ready. The only way to really know if the fruit is ripe is to taste it. Even when they're ripe, many citrus fruits can linger on the tree for weeks without loss of quality. The exception is mandarin oranges; pick these fruits promptly before the flavour deteriorates. Store citrus fruit in the refrigerator for up to 2 weeks.

Cornus mas

HARDINESS
Hardy.

HEIGHT
4.5–7.5 m (15–25 ft)

SPREAD
3–6 m (10–20 ft)

COMMENTS
Although grown mainly as an ornamental shrub, in hot summers, it will bear edible ripe fruit. You can enjoy the fruits as they are, make a drink, preserves, or a thickened, sweet syrup called *rob de cornis*.

CHERRY, CORNELIAN

THE RED FRUITS OF CORNELIAN CHERRY LOOK LIKE TRUE CHERRIES. THE FLAVOUR IS TART—RATHER LIKE A SOUR CHERRY. YOU CAN EAT THE WHOLE FRUIT, BUT NOT THE SEED.

Position Give plants full sun and average, well-drained soil.

Cultivation Set out container-grown plants anytime, as long as the ground is not frozen, or plant bare-root stock in spring or autumn, while it is still dormant. Space plants 3–6 m (10–20 ft) apart. The flowers are partially self-fertile, but cross-pollination increases yields.

Pruning No regular pruning needed.

Propagation Cornelian cherry is easy to graft onto seedling rootstock.

To grow seedlings, either nick the seed with a knife or keep it warm and moist for 4 months. Then pot the seed and move to a cool, moist spot for 1–4 months before putting the pots in a warm, bright place so the seeds will germinate.

Pests and diseases Generally no significant problems, except for anthracnose.

Harvesting and storage Harvest the fruits any time after they are fully coloured. (Most turn red; a few kinds ripen yellow or white.) The longer they hang on the tree, the more mellow they become in flavour. Harvested fruits also mellow if kept at room temperature.

Corylus spp.

HARDINESS
Hardy.

HEIGHT
5–6 m (16–20 ft)

SPREAD
Up to 6 m (20 ft)

COMMENTS
Cobnuts
(*C. avellana*) have
short husks so the
nuts are visible;
filberts (*C. maxima*)
have long husks
that cover the nuts
completely.

HAZELNUT

HAZELNUTS ARE SMALL, PLUMP NUTS
PRODUCED ON TREES AND SHRUBS.

Position Hazelnuts do best in full
sun in well-drained, light soil; if the
soil is too fertile, the plant produces
more leaf than nut.

Cultivation Mulch in spring to
reduce weeds and keep soil moist.
Water mature trees during dry times.

Pruning Hazels naturally grow into
dense bushes that make good hedges;
thin out the older wood each winter
to encourage new growth. In late
summer, snap over-vigorous shoots
half-way (brutting) to promote fruit
buds and restrict growth. The next
spring, shorten brutted stems to 3 or
4 buds. Cut tall leading shoots back
to lower sideshoots.

Propagation Grow from seed, or by
layering or grafting.

Pests and diseases Nut weevils and
powdery mildew may affect hazels.
Net shrubs to keep squirrels away.

Harvesting and storage Hazels begin
bearing nuts in 2–3 years. They
ripen in autumn and are ready to
pick when nuts come free from the
husks easily. 'Barcelona' drops its
nuts without tapping. Let the nuts
dry until crunchy. Store in a cool
place for up to a year.

Cucumis melo

MELON, SWEET

VINE-RIPENED MELONS ARE A GREAT TREAT, WELL WORTH THE EXTRA CARE THEY DEMAND FOR A SUCCESSFUL CROP.

Position Full sun in a very warm, sheltered site with good air circulation; it's usually best to grow them in a greenhouse or under cloches or fleece. Plant in well-drained, well-manured soil, not too acid; pH 6.0–7.0.

Cultivation Set out plants 2–3 weeks after germination into soil that has first been warmed with black plastic mulch. Use cloches or fleece to increase warmth and protect from bean seed fly; remove covers when the plants bloom. Hoe shallowly to reduce competition from weeds until plants begin to climb. Water weekly with compost tea or diluted seaweed solution to maintain growth.

Pruning To make a bushy plant, pinch out the growing tip of the main stem once it has 3–5 leaves. Tip-prune the sideshoots once they have 5–7 leaves and tip-prune the sideshoots coming from those. Thereafter, allow the shoots to fruit. If you are training melons up a support, let 1 or 2 main shoots grow and tie them into the support. Pinch out the tips when they reach 2 m (6 ft) to prompt more sideshoots, and tip-prune those when they have 4–5 leaves. When fruits start to form, support them in netting slings or mesh bags.

HARDINESS
Tender; grow short-season cultivars. Melons do not tolerate frost.

SPREAD
If space is limited, melons can be supported on a cane wigwam or trellis.

COMMENTS
Most cantaloupes and musk melons mature in about 68 days; winter melons, including honeydews, take up to 95 days.

Musk melons (*Cucumis melo*), like other melons, do not ripen after picking, so for the best flavour leave the fruit on the vine until fully ripe.

Propagation In mild areas, sow seed directly into the ground when the soil is thoroughly warm. Plant 3 or 4 seeds to a mound and site mounds 1.2–1.5 m (4–5 ft) apart. Elsewhere, sow indoors in individual pots, 2 seeds to a pot, around the time of the last frost.

Pests and diseases Plant radishes or basil in the mound with melons to help deter bean seed fly. Or protect plants with cloches or fleece; remove covers when plants start to flower to aid pollination. Spray foliage thoroughly with a fungicide such as sulphur to control powdery mildew. Rotate plantings of melons and its relatives, such as squashes and cucumber, to reduce pest populations.

Other problems include cucumber mosaic virus, stem and root rots, slugs and snails, red spider mite, aphids and whitefly. Do not allow plants to become stressed from lack of water or nutrients.

Harvesting and storage Pick musk melons when cracks appear where fruit is attached to the stem. They should "slip" from the stem easily with a slight tug. Let them sit for 1–2 days at room temperature to ripen perfectly. When ripe, hard-rind melons, such as honeydews and true cantaloupes, will show a subtle change of rind colour. Most melons have a short storage life; some late-season melons will keep up to 2 months in a cool, dry place.

Melon continued

If you are allowing the plant to sprawl along the ground, it is best to keep developing fruits clear of the soil, for example on tiles or low-slung netting, to avoid any rot.

Related plants

Cantaloupe *C. melo,* **Cantalupensis Group**
True cantaloupes are hard-skinned, with greyish-green, rough, grooved rinds that are relatively thick. They have pale green or orange flesh and are best suited to cooler climates. Most commercial cantaloupes are actually musk melons (see below). True cantaloupes don't have a netted rind. Try 'Charentais', a very sweet, heirloom cultivar; 'Ogen', very reliable, with dark green rind and green flesh; 'Sweetheart', a fast-maturing and medium-sized melon, with grey-green rind.

Honeydew melon *C. melo,* **Inodorus Group**
These winter melons have smooth rind, usually pale green or ivory, with green flesh. They are generally late-maturing; early cultivars include 'Honeydew', with orange flesh.

Musk melon *C. melo,* **Reticulatus Group**
Also called, incorrectly, cantaloupe. These melons are usually smaller than cantaloupe or winter melons. They fruit best if grown in a greenhouse. Rind is netted and usually ridged, flesh is orange or green, sweet and fragrant. Cultivars include 'Blenheim Orange' (old favourite) and 'Emir'.

Cydonia oblonga

HARDINESS
Hardy, but frost can damage the blossom.

HEIGHT
4.5–6 m (15–20 ft)

SPREAD
4.5–6 m (15–20 ft)

COMMENTS
The skin and aromatic, white or yellowish flesh are edible cooked, but the flesh is too astringent to be eaten raw.

QUINCE

QUINCE TREES PRODUCE HARD, YELLOW FRUIT COVERED WITH DOWNY HAIRS.

Position Plant in a warm, sheltered site in full sun, in well-drained and moderately fertile soil. Avoid frost pockets.

Cultivation Plant container-grown stock anytime, as long as the ground is not frozen or waterlogged; or set out bare-root plants in spring or autumn, while they are dormant. Space plants 4.5–6 m (15–20 ft) apart. Quinces are self-fertile, so you need only one plant.

Pruning Train as a small tree or large shrub. Each winter, prune off enough wood to keep the plant open to sunlight and air, removing any diseased or misplaced branches.

Propagation Graft cultivars onto quince rootstock, propagated by layering or from seed.

Pests and diseases Quince is relatively untroubled by pests, but may sometimes be affected by diseases such as quince leaf blight, fireblight, brown rot or mildew.

Harvesting and storage Pick fruits when they are scented and fully coloured. Handle ripe fruit gently. It can be stored for 2–3 months at temperatures near freezing with high humidity, such as in a refrigerator. Alternatively, make it into a fine, clear, pink jelly or quince cheese.

Cyphomandra betacea   SOLANACEAE

HARDINESS
Frost tender.

HEIGHT
3–5 m (10–15 ft)

SPREAD
1.5–2.5 m (5–8 ft)

COMMENTS
This is a relative of the tomato and is also known as the tree tomato. It will tolerate winter temperatures of 5°C (40°F) if kept nearly dry, but will not withstand frost.

TAMARILLO

THIS SUBTROPICAL, SHORT-LIVED TREE CAN BE GROWN IN THE UK ONLY IN A GREENHOUSE OR CONSERVATORY AND NEEDS A LONG SUMMER TO FRUIT.

Position Plant in a large container in a warm, sunny place under cover, in rich, but well-drained, soil-based potting compost or in a greenhouse bed in fertile, moist but well-drained soil.

Cultivation Water regularly during the growing season and feed monthly with dilute seaweed solution or tomato feed. The plant can be moved outdoors for the summer. Top-dress with fresh compost and an all-purpose fertilizer in spring.

Pruning Prune in late winter to keep to a manageable size; take out the growing tip to encourage the plant to bush out.

Propagation Sow seed under cover in spring or take softwood cuttings in summer and grow on in pots.

Pests and diseases Aphids, thrips, whitefly and red spider mites may occur under cover; use biological controls. Keep the greenhouse humid to deter red spider mites.

Harvesting and storage The fruits, which look like long tomatoes, ripen to yellow, orange or red. Cut the stalks and use fresh, store for 1–2 weeks or make into jam or chutney. Unripe fruits are not palatable.

Eriobotrya japonica

HARDINESS
Frost hardy;
but needs warm
temperatures to
fruit well.

HEIGHT
6–9 m (20–30 ft)

SPREAD
7.5–10.5 m (25–35 ft)

COMMENTS
Loquats are not easy
to grow to fruiting
stage, but they are
worth a try as a
greenhouse plant.
Eat loquats fresh,
cook them into a
sauce or cut them
in half and dry them.

LOQUAT

LOQUAT TREES PRODUCE YELLOW, PLUM-SIZED, ROUND, OVAL OR PEAR-SHAPED FRUIT WITH SCENTED WHITE PULP THAT IS SWEET WITH A BIT OF A TANG. REMOVE THE SKIN AND SEEDS BEFORE EATING LOQUATS.

Position Plant in full sun in greenhouse beds or in a container in well-drained, soil-based compost with added fertilzer. Loquats are somewhat drought-resistant.

Cultivation To grow loquats in a container, choose a dwarf cultivar and repot annually. Most cultivars are self-fertile. Plant a seedling in the container or bed when it is about 30 cm (18 in) tall. Through the growing season, keep it well watered and warm, at least 18°C (64°F), and feed regularly.

Pruning Thin the young fruits in winter by clipping off single fruitlets or clusters. Shorten additional stems to let in light.

Propagation Graft cultivars onto seedling loquat rootstock. Both quince and pyracantha have been used as dwarfing rootstocks.

Pests and diseases Under cover, loquats may suffer from red spider mites, mealybugs, whiteflies or thrips —use biological controls. Enclose fruits in paper bags to protect them from sunburn if plants are growing in full sun.

Harvesting and storage Cut off fruits when fully coloured and slightly soft.

Ficus carica

FIG

FIGS ARE PRODUCTIVE AND EASY TO GROW. THEY ARE SELDOM TROUBLED BY PESTS OUTDOORS, EXCEPT FOR BIRDS. NET THE TREE TO DISCOURAGE THESE GREEDY FIG-LOVERS.

Position Plant in full sun in average, well-drained soil. Overly rich soil will promote foliage growth at the expense of fruit. In very frost-prone areas, plant figs in large containers in gritty compost and move them inside for winter.

Cultivation Select self-pollinating cultivars. In very mild or sheltered areas, grow freestanding trees; space large cultivars up to 8 m (25 ft) apart; smaller trees can be as close as 1.5 m (5 ft) apart. Figs can also be trained against a warm, sunny south- or west-facing wall, or in a container so they can be taken indoors over winter. If planting outdoors, it is best to contain the roots to promote fruiting: dig a planting pit about 60 cm (2 ft) deep and square, line it with thick plastic or paving slabs and refill with soil. After planting, top-dress every spring with high-potash fertilizer. Through the growing season, water well and feed regularly with tomato fertilizer. Mulch generously with compost as needed. Repot container-grown figs every 2 years to refresh the compost. Over winter, protect fruitlets from frost by using fleece or moving containers under cover.

Pruning Thin out excess growth as

Fig continued

HARDINESS
Hardy, but needs
frost protection
to preserve the
embryo fruits.

HEIGHT
3–8 m (10–25 ft)

SPREAD
3–8 m (10–25 ft)

COMMENTS
Good cultivars
for the UK climate
include 'Brown
Turkey', 'Brunswick'
and 'White
Marseilles'.

Figs need a long, warm summer to ripen properly, so choose a sheltered spot for your tree.

needed to control plant size and allow for good light penetration into the centre of the plant. You can also train espaliers to grow on sun-warmed walls. The best form is a fan: in the first winter, cut the leader to leave 2 sideshoots, then cut them down by a third to encourage sublaterals. In the second winter, cut the leaders back again and remove all but 3 sublaterals on each. From the third winter, cut all the shoots back by a third to spur fruiting. Figs take 2 years to form ripe fruits; sometimes, 2 sets of fruits form in one season. If the second set hasn't ripened, remove them in autumn to concentrate energy on the larger fruits for next year.

Propagation Propagate by cutting rooted suckers off the roots or taking hardwood cuttings.

Pests and diseases Place netting over trees to discourage birds, or grow green-fruited cultivars, which are less appealing to birds. Under cover, deal with pests such as scale insects and red spider mite using biological controls. Look out also for coral spot, which infects through pruning cuts.

Harvesting and storage Fig trees produce their first crop a year after planting. Ripe figs are soft, with a slightly flexible "neck"; sometimes the skin splits. You can keep figs for a few days in the refrigerator, or cut them in halves and dry them.

Fortunella spp.

HARDINESS
Frost tender, but
may withstand
short, light frosts
occasionally.

HEIGHT
2.4–4.5 m (8–15 ft)

SPREAD
1.8–3.6 m (6–12 ft)

COMMENTS
Fruits are tasty
fresh, crystallized
or cooked into a
marmalade or
a sauce. They
keep well in
the refrigerator.

KUMQUAT

THE FRUIT OF THE KUMQUAT LOOKS LIKE A
MINIATURE ORANGE—ABOUT THE SIZE OF A
CHERRY AND EITHER ROUND OR ELONGATED.
THE SKIN IS EDIBLE AND SWEET, AND THE
JUICY FLESH RANGES FROM TART TO SWEET.

Position Plant in full sun in large
containers filled with well-drained,
slightly acid, rich, soil-based compost.
Kumquat tolerates winter weather as
cold as –7.7°C (18°F), but without
sufficient heat in summer, the fruits
will be few and of poor quality,
so they need the protection of a
greenhouse or a conservatory.

Cultivation Kumquats make beautiful
potted plants that fruit reliably.
To obtain fruit, keep the plant at a
minimum of 20°C (68°F) and 75 per

cent humidity. Keep well watered
and feed every month with liquid
fertilizer. Put in a cool, sunny room
in winter and repot every year.

Pruning Kumquats need no pruning
other than to shape the plants and
thin out crowded branches.

Pests and diseases Problems are
usually minimal if soil drainage is
good, but look out for scale insects,
mealybugs, red spider mites and
whiteflies.

Harvesting and storage Harvest fruits
when fully coloured.

Fragaria spp.

HARDINESS
Hardy.

HEIGHT
25 cm (10 in)

SPREAD
30–60 cm (1-2 ft)

COMMENTS
Strawberries are self-fertile. For the longest possible harvest, grow plants of more than one type (summer-bearers, perpetuals and container-grown plants under cover).

STRAWBERRY

YOU'LL AVOID MOST PROBLEMS BY STARTING WITH CERTIFIED DISEASE-FREE PLANTS OF DISEASE-RESISTANT CULTIVARS.

Position To extend the harvest, grow a combination of strawberry types. Try summer-bearers for the beginning ('Elvira'), middle ('Cambridge Favourite'), and later part of the summer ('Florence'), and late-bearing perpetual cultivars like 'Mara des Bois'. You can also grow strawberries under glass to get even earlier and later fruits. Plant in an area of full sun free from late-spring frosts. The soil should be fertile and well drained. If possible, avoid areas previously used to grow sweet peppers, tomatoes, potatoes, aubergine, melons, okra, mints, raspberries or blackberries, chrysanthemums or roses—crops that may leave behind problems that can attack strawberries. Add extra organic matter before planting to make the soil rich and moist.

Cultivation For an easy-care strawberry bed, mound your garden soil in a bed about 15 cm (6 in) tall and 60 cm (2 ft) wide, install drip irrigation, and cover it all with landscape fabric or black plastic before planting. Cut X-shaped slits in the fabric, and plant through the slits into the soil. This system is especially good for perpetual strawberries. If planting in a flat bed, space plants 30–60 cm (1–2 ft) apart and keep the soil moist until

Strawberry continued

Strawberries do well in containers, such as special strawberry pots or hanging baskets. A bonus with such ways of growing is that the fruits are easier to protect from birds.

berries are almost ripe. In early winter, cover plants with 5 cm (2 in) of straw to prevent cold damage. Pull back the mulch as soon as plants begin to grow again in spring. If frost threatens the new growth, cover the plants overnight with a fleece.

Pruning Weed, pinch out unwanted runners and mow along edge of bed as needed to keep paths clear.

Propagation Propagate by trans-planting disease-free rooted runners.

Pests and diseases Pick ripe fruit regularly and avoid overhead watering to keep grey mould (*Botrytis*) at bay. Remove and destroy damaged flowers and fruits as you spot them. If plants wilt,

dig up a few. If there are few or no side roots and the roots are reddish inside when cut lengthways, red core is the problem. If the roots are black and rotting, the culprit is root rot. Destroy all wilted plants. Vine weevil larvae also eat the roots. hand-pick slugs and snails and watch for red spider mite and aphids.

Harvesting and storage Pick berries, leaving some stems on for better storage, when fully coloured, tender and sweet. Eat fruit fresh, make into jam or freeze immediately.

Fragaria vesca

HARDINESS
Hardy.

HEIGHT
15 cm (6 in)

SPREAD
15–30 cm (6–12 in)

COMMENTS
Plants will fruit generously, even in small pots. Eat the fruits fresh as they do not store well. Alpine strawberries make good ground cover as they spread readily, or edging to edible beds.

STRAWBERRY, ALPINE

ALPINE STRAWBERRIES PRODUCE POINTED FRUITS ON LOW, CLUMP-FORMING PLANTS. THE RIPE FRUITS ARE USUALLY RED, ALTHOUGH SOME WHITE CULTIVARS EXIST. THE WHOLE FRUIT IS EDIBLE.

Position Plant in full sun, with well-drained soil that is rich in humus.

Cultivation Set out container-grown plants any time the ground isn't frozen, while the plants are dormant or sow seed indoors in spring or autumn. Set plants 15–30 cm (6-12 in) apart, so that the soil is just below the lowest leaves on the crown. Alpine strawberries are self-fertile, so you will get fruit from just one plant.

Pruning None is necessary.

Propagation To divide old plants, dig them up and cut off young crown pieces (with attached roots) from the outside of the clump. Throw away the old centre and replant the divisions immediately. To grow alpine strawberries from seed, scatter the fine seed on the surface of potting compost in a container. Transplant seedlings when large enough to handle.

Pests and diseases Keep birds at bay with netting, or grow white-fruited cultivars, which birds leave alone. Watch out for slugs and snails.

Harvesting and storage Harvest the fruits when soft and scented.

Helianthus annuus

HARDINESS
Hardy.

HEIGHT
90–300 cm (3–10 ft)

SPREAD
60 cm (3 ft)

COMMENTS
Each flowerhead of this giant annual may be up to 30 cm (1 ft) across and contain more than 1,000 seeds.

SUNFLOWER

ALTHOUGH IT IS GROWN MAINLY FOR ITS HUGE, BRIGHTLY COLOURED FLOWERS, THE SUNFLOWER PRODUCES LARGE SEEDS, WHICH ARE RICH IN OIL AND MAKE A HEALTHY SNACK.

Position Plant in a sheltered spot in full sun, in well-drained, reasonably fertile soil.

Cultivation Thin seedlings to 45–60 cm (18–24 in) apart. Support stems of tall varieties with stakes or canes. Keep well watered; regular watering produces larger seedheads. Avoid planting near potatoes because they may stunt the sunflowers' growth.

Propagation Sow seeds singly in spring, where they are to grow, 12 mm (½ in) deep and 15 cm (6 in) apart. They do not transplant well.

Pests and diseases Provide good air circulation to avoid mildew. Stems may collapse from *Sclerotinia* rot.

Harvesting and storage Collect ripe seeds in late summer or early autumn when the flowerheads begin to droop. Cut off the flowerheads and break them apart; rub the heads to dislodge the seeds. Seeds are used either fresh or roasted, in cereals and breads. Store in airtight containers in a cool place.

Special tips Sunflowers bloom relatively quickly, but take a long time to ripen their seeds. Very heavy heads may need support.

Juglans regia and *J. nigra*

JUGLANDACEAE

HARDINESS
Hardy.

HEIGHT
18–20 m (60–70 ft)

SPREAD
15–20 m (50–70 ft)

COMMENTS
The English walnut
Juglans regia (also
called Persian
walnut) is less
vigorous than the
black walnut
J. nigra, but has
better-quality nuts.

WALNUT

WALNUTS ARE LARGE TREES THAT PRODUCE
EDIBLE NUTS ENCASED IN A HUSK AND SHELL.
THE HARD SHELL IS ROUND. THE MEAT
WITHIN IS RICH AND BUTTERY.

Position Full sun and deep, moist
but well-drained, rich soil is best, but
plants will tolerate soils on limestone.

Cultivation Transplant 3- or 4-year-
old trees in winter when they are
dormant, and avoid pot-bound plants
since they have long taproots. Stake
the plant to allow it to establish well.

Pruning Train young trees to form a
sturdy framework of well-spaced,
wide-angled branches. On mature
trees, just cut out diseased or dead
wood and untidy branches.

Propagation Mix seed with damp
sand and refrigerate for 3–4 months
before sowing in a warm, bright
place. Graft cultivars onto black
walnut rootstock.

Pests and diseases Relatively trouble-
free, except for walnut blotch and
walnut leaf blight.

Harvesting and storage Harvest nuts
when the husks begin to split. Clean
the shells (wear gloves to avoid
stained fingers) and dry the nuts in
the sun. Store in a cool, dry place
such as a shed.

Malus x *domestica*

APPLE

TO GET HIGH YIELDS FROM YOUR APPLES,
YOU'LL NEED TO GROW AT LEAST TWO
CULTIVARS THAT FLOWER AT THE SAME TIME
SO THEY CAN CROSS-POLLINATE, AS WELL
AS PRUNE THEM APPROPRIATELY TO
ENCOURAGE FRUITING.

Position Plant apple trees in full sun,
away from frost pockets and exposed
sites, and in rich, well-drained soil.

Cultivation There are more than
1,000 different apple cultivars
available. For extra-high yields,
you can choose spur-bearing trees,
which can be pruned to be heavily
loaded with short fruit-bearing
branches (spurs), so that they stay
about 25 per cent smaller than the
same cultivar without spurs.

You can also choose grafted trees
with different combinations of
rootstocks and top-growth to make
just about any kind of apple tree
you can imagine. Plant full-sized
apple trees 7.5–9 m (25–30 ft) apart,
semi-dwarfs 3.6–4.5 m (12–15 ft)
apart and dwarfs 1.8–2.4 m (6–8 ft)
apart. Provide plenty of moisture
and nutrients to keep young trees
growing quickly. Mulch with
compost in spring, and make sure
the soil is moist around mature trees
when they're in bloom. A late spring
frost that damages the blossom may
affect the fruit yield later in the year.

Pruning Apple trees can be grown
in a variety of forms, from the usual
freestanding bush or narrower

Apple continued

HARDINESS
Hardy.

HEIGHT
2.4–9 m (8–30 ft)

SPREAD
2.4–9 m (8–30 ft)

COMMENTS
Support the brittle trunks of young apple trees by tying them carefully to a strong stake. Remember to loosen the ties as they grow.

A mulch of marigold roots has been found to suppress populations of parasitic nematodes in the soil around apple trees.

pyramid shape to highly trained espaliers and cordons. They need pruning in the initial years after planting to form them into the shape of tree you require. Thereafter, it is best to prune them regularly in order to keep them healthy and to obtain a decent crop of good-sized fruits. Start initial pruning of young trees on spring planting or in the spring following autumn planting. As well as pruning the tree, thin the fruitlets each summer. If you allow a tree to set a heavy crop, it may begin bearing biennially, ie every other year. Also, crowded fruits may be smaller than usual and of poor quality. Start thinning the fruits from midsummer; trees will often have

dropped some fruitlets naturally. From a cluster, remove the king fruit (the one in the centre, which is often misshapen) and some of the smaller ones or any that are already damaged. Leave a couple of eating apples every 10 cm (4 in) or so and cooking apples every 15 cm (6 in) along the branches.

Pruning a bush apple To form a tree with a short trunk and low canopy, which is easy to pick, start by cutting back the single stem of the year-old sapling. Leave about 75 cm (30 in) for a normal bush and 60 cm (24 in) for a dwarf bush. The next winter, choose 4–5 of the new side branches to form a 'bowl' shape and cut back to one-third of their length, to an

Apple continued

Once they ripen, many apple fruits are very ornamental, bringing autumn colour to the garden as well as a delectable crop.

outward-facing bud. The third winter, prune all main stems and well-placed sideshoots by about one-third; trim other sideshoots to 2–4 buds. In the fourth year, cut back the new leading stems to two-thirds and longer sideshoots to 10 cm (4 in). Whenever you are pruning, also take out any crossing, dead or damaged growth.

To keep the mature tree fruiting well, prune each winter. Most apple trees are spur-bearers, that is, fruiting from fruit buds on short, knobbly stems or spurs; others are tip-bearers, ie they produce fruits at the tips of their stems. If the tree is a spur-bearer, cut back half of the new growth on leading stems and sideshoots to 4–6 fruit buds to create spurs. If the tree is a tip-bearer, leave the youngest and vigorous sideshoots unpruned to bear fruits, but cut back just the tips of older and leading shoots to encourage new fruiting sideshoots.

Propagation Propagate by grafting.

Pests and diseases Some problems that might occur include apple sawfly, codling moth, aphids, scab, canker, mildew and brown rot. You can prevent many problems by planting disease-resistant cultivars. Among these, 'Lord Lambourne' and 'Cheddar Cross' are early ripening; 'Discovery' and 'Grenadier' ripen in mid-season; and 'King of the Pippins'

'Egremont Russet' is an old, but still popular, dessert cultivar, an early cropper producing apples with a nutty flavour and dry, firm flesh. They go very well with cheese.

ripens late. When mildew or scab do strike, carefully rake up and dispose of all dropped leaves in autumn. If the diseases were a major problem last year, spray with an approved fungicide. In autumn, apply grease bands to the trunk of the tree, and any stakes, to stop winter moths crawling into the tree.

Harvesting and storage Depending on the rootstock, apples will start producing fruit in 2–5 years. Pick apples when they develop full colour and flavour, but are still crunchy and crisp. To avoid damaging the apple, cup it in your hand and twist gently; if ripe, it should come away easily from the tree. Never tug apples from the branch; you may tear off

the bark and next year's fruit buds. Mid- and late-season apples often benefit from being stored to develop their full flavour. Use any bruised fruit at once. Store unblemished apples at 0°C (32°F) and 90 per cent humidity in a cool, well-ventilated, dark place such as a shed or garage. Space them out so they are not touching, in trays or slatted boxes; it is best to wrap each one in paper. Check them regularly and remove any that show signs of rot to stop it spreading to other apples.

Malus spp.

ROSACEAE

HARDINESS
Hardy.

HEIGHT
2.4–7.5 m (8–25 ft)

SPREAD
2.4–7.5 m (8–25 ft)

COMMENTS
Fruits of most crab apples are used for cooking. Many of them are also very ornamental.

CRAB APPLE

THE SMALL, BRIGHTLY COLOURED FRUITS, IN REDS, YELLOWS OR RUSSETS, NOT ONLY PROVIDE US WITH THE OLD FAVOURITE, CRAB APPLE JELLY, BUT ALSO FORM VERY PRETTY TREES FOR THE ORNAMENTAL GARDEN.

Position Plant in full sun, away from frost pockets, and in well-drained soil.

Cultivation Plant container-grown stock any time the ground isn't frozen, or set out bare-root plants in spring or autumn, while dormant. Space plants 2.4–7.5 m (8–25 ft) apart. The plants need cross-pollination, but the pollinator can be an apple or a crab apple.

Pruning Train young plants to a sturdy framework of wide-angled, well-spaced main limbs. Mature plants need little pruning beyond removing water shoots and thinning congested growth.

Propagation Graft or bud cultivars onto seedling apple or crab apple rootstocks. Seed, for seedling rootstocks, germinates readily if kept cool and moist for 2–3 months.

Pests and diseases Crab apples can have the same pest and disease problems as apples (see previous page) but are usually less troubled by them.

Harvesting and storage Pick fruits when they are fully coloured and pull off the plant easily. Store, refrigerated, in a plastic bag with air holes in it.

Mespilus germanica

HARDINESS
Hardy.

HEIGHT
2.7–6 m (9–20 ft)

SPREAD
2.7–6 m (9–20 ft)

COMMENTS
The ripening
(bletting) process
takes more than
2 weeks in cool
temperatures.
Eat the flesh,
but not the seeds
or the skin.

MEDLAR

A MEDLAR FRUIT LOOKS LIKE A SMALL,
RUSSETED APPLE, TINGED WITH DULL YELLOW
OR RED. THE FLESH IS SOFT AND BROWN
AND TASTES LIKE THICK APPLE SAUCE.

Position Give medlars full sun and
moderately rich, well-drained soil.

Cultivation Plant container-grown
stock any time the ground isn't
frozen or waterlogged, or set out
bare-root plants in spring or autumn,
while they are dormant. Space plants
3.6–7.5 m (12–25 ft) apart. Plant with
the graft union below ground level
so the scion also takes root. Medlars
are self-fertile, and virtually every
blossom sets fruit. On young trees,
pinch off some blossoms to channel
more energy into shoot growth.

Pruning This tree needs very little
pruning; simply trim as needed to
shape and to remove odd dead or
diseased branches. For a smaller
tree, the best form is a standard
or half-standard.

Propagation Graft medlar onto pear,
hawthorn, quince or medlar
seedling rootstock.

Pests and diseases No pest or
disease problems worth noting.

Harvesting and storage Harvest the
fruits as the leaves begin to drop in
autumn. Although the fruits may
feel rock-hard, handle them
carefully to avoid bruising. Place
them on a shelf in a cool, dark
room to "blett", or soften.

Morus spp.

HARDINESS
Hardy.

HEIGHT
4.5–9 m (15–30 ft)

SPREAD
3–6 m (10–20 ft)

COMMENTS
Do not plant
mulberries where
falling fruits will
cause problems
with staining.
For cooking, pick
the fruit when it
is still firm and
slightly under-ripe.

MULBERRY

MULBERRY TREES PRODUCE BLACK, RED OR
WHITE BLACKBERRY-SHAPED FRUITS. FLAVOUR
RANGES FROM SWEET WITH A SHARP TANG
TO PURELY SWEET. EAT THE WHOLE FRUIT.

Position Plant in full sun and
average, well-drained soil.

Cultivation Plant container-grown
stock any time the ground isn't
frozen or waterlogged, or set out
bare-root plants in spring or autumn,
while dormant. Space plants 3–9 m
(10–30 ft) apart. Cultivars selected
for fruit production generally do not
need cross-pollination.

Pruning No regular pruning needed.

Propagation Russian mulberry
M. alba 'Tartarica' makes a good
rootstock for most other mulberries.
Softwood or hardwood cuttings of
most species usually root readily.
With hardwood cuttings, either
split the lower end or take a small
"heel" of 2-year-old wood along
with the 1-year-old wood used for
the cutting.

Pests and diseases Relatively
problem-free.

Harvesting and storage Mulberries
take 5 years or more to start bearing
fruit, and fruiting is variable.
To harvest in quantity, spread a
clean sheet under the tree and
shake the branches. Ripe fruits do
not keep well fresh, but can be
frozen or dried.

Olea europaea subsp. *europaea*

HARDINESS
Frost hardy, but damaged by prolonged cold.

HEIGHT
9 m (30 ft)

SPREAD
Up to 9 m (30 ft)

COMMENTS
The best way to grow olives is in a container, so they can be kept under cover over winter. In long, hot summers, they may fruit successfully.

OLIVE

OLIVE TREES PRODUCE GRAPE-SIZED FRUIT WITH EDIBLE FLESH AND SKIN (DON'T EAT THE SEEDS). THE FRUITS HAVE A RICH, OILY TASTE, ESPECIALLY WHEN THEY ARE RIPE.

Position Give olives a large pot of soil-based compost, with some slow-release fertilizer. Keep in a cool greenhouse or conservatory and move outside, once all risk of frost has passed, for the summer.

Cultivation Plant container-grown stock anytime, or bare-root plants in spring or autumn, while dormant. Cross-pollination usually increases yield, so it helps to grow at least 2 trees together. During the growing season, keep the plants well watered, but water sparingly in winter. Olives need a period of winter cold to produce flower buds. Where fruits are close together on a stem, thin by just cutting back the stem, or removing excess fruits individually.

Pruning Young trees need little pruning. Prune mature trees to keep them from growing too large.

Propagation Propagate olives by hardwood or softwood cuttings.

Pests and diseases Red spider mite, whitefly and thrips may affect olives under cover; use biological controls.

Harvesting and storage Harvest fruit when it is green (unripe) or black (ripe). Don't expose olives intended for eating to cool temperatures. Olives are usually brined for storage after bitterness has been removed.

Opuntia ficus-indica

HARDINESS
Tender.

HEIGHT
30–450 cm (1–15 ft)

SPREAD
90–450 cm (3–15 ft)

COMMENTS
Eat the fruits raw.
Slice the pads and
cook as you would
string beans.

PRICKLY PEAR

IF YOU HAVE A HEATED GREENHOUSE OR
CONSERVATORY, IT IS WORTH TRYING TO GET
FRUIT FROM THIS VIGOROUS CACTUS.

Position Prickly pear needs full sun
and minimum temperatures of 18°C
(64°F) all year round and very well-
drained, gritty compost.

Cultivation Plant seedlings or rooted
cuttings in spring in containers.

Pruning No pruning is necessary.

Propagation Sow seed and keep it
in the dark until seedlings appear.
You can also use the fleshy pads to
start new plants. Cut a pad from the
parent plant and let it dry for a few
days before setting it upright with
the base in well-drained compost.

Water sparingly until roots form and
growth begins.

Pests and diseases Greenhouse pests,
such as red spider mite, mealybug,
and scale insects can be a problem,
as is mildew and rot in cold conditions.

Harvesting and storage Wear thick
leather gloves to harvest the flat,
green pads, then remove the spines
(and the tiny, hair-like needles at the
bases of the spines) by rubbing them
off with a rough cloth or peeling
them off with a vegetable peeler.
Wear gloves to harvest the egg-sized
fruits, which are ripe when fully
coloured. Rub off the needles and
peel off the skin before eating the
usually red pulp.

Lycium barbarum

HARDINESS
Hardy; mature
plants withstand
-15°C (5°F).

HEIGHT
3.5 m (11 ft)

SPREAD
5 m (15 ft)

COMMENTS
Goji berries were
grown by the
Victorians and
are known also
as boxthorn,
Duke of Argyll's
tea tree and
matrimony vine.

GOJI BERRY

THIS EASY-TO-GROW SOFT FRUIT COMES
FROM THE HIMALAYA AND IS REGAINING
POPULARITY AS A SNACK FOOD, AND IN
MUESLI, TEA AND JUICE: ITS BERRIES ARE
RICH IN VITAMIN C.

Position Plant in full sun in well-
drained soil; tolerates dry or light,
sandy soils.

Cultivation Goji berry bushes are
self-pollinating. Plant in early spring
and water regularly until established
and in dry conditions. Plants do not
survive waterlogging, especially in
winter. Mulch in spring and keep
weed-free. Bushes may also be
grown in containers, in a well-
drained compost.

Pruning Little pruning is necessary,
except to remove dead wood or
shorten overly long stems in late
winter. To renew older shrubs, cut
them hard back every 4 years or so.

Propagation Sow seed in autumn
or take cuttings: hardwood cuttings
in winter or softwood cuttings
in summer.

Pests and diseases Trouble-free.

Harvesting and storage To harvest
the small, red-orange berries from
late summer to early autumn, simply
shake the bush; avoid handling them
as they will turn black. They can be
eaten fresh, but are best dried.

Passiflora spp.

HARDINESS
Frost tender.

SPREAD
A sprawling climber, spreading 6 m (20 ft) or more in a season, unless pruned.

COMMENTS
Passion fruit are filled with many seeds, each in a membrane with a sweet-tart, tangy flavour. You can eat both the seeds and the pulp.

PASSION FRUIT

A GRAFTED PLANT WILL BEAR FRUIT, AS IT HAS BOTH MALE AND FEMALE CHARACTERISTICS.

Position Grow in full sun in average, well-drained soil, rich in humus. A sunny wall or a greenhouse will help fruit to ripen.

Cultivation Set out container-grown plants anytime, spacing them about 3 m (9 ft) apart. Some need cross-pollination, so it's smart to plant at least two seedlings or cultivars to be on the safe side. The plants need some support, such as a fence or trellis, on which to climb. The species *P. edulis* is often grown for fruits, but is not cold-hardy; grow it in a well-drained compost in a container. The plants can overwinter without full sun in a cool room; in spring, trim and provide full sun.

Pruning Regular pruning is not a necessity, but it will help to keep the plant untangled. For the neatest growth, train one or two permanent "arms" along the top of the support. Each winter, cut all sideshoots back to 2 buds.

Propagation Sow fresh seed, take cuttings (or buy a grafted plant).

Pests and diseases Generally no significant problems.

Harvesting and storage Pick up ripe fruits from the ground. Fruit can be stored for a few weeks in a plastic bag at about 10°C (50°F).

Physalis ixocarpa

HARDINESS
Frost tender.

HEIGHT
90–120 cm (3–4 ft)

SPREAD
60–90 cm (2–3 ft)

COMMENTS
This is a perennial, grown as an annual; it is also known as Mexican green tomato.

TOMATILLO

THIS RELATIVE OF THE CAPE GOOSEBERRY HAS STICKY, GOLF-BALL-SIZED FRUITS THAT ARE TART AND GOOD TO EAT RAW, IN SALSA, OR COOKED INTO JAMS AND PIES.

Position Plant in full sun, in rich, well-drained, lime-free soil.

Cultivation Tomatillos are not self-fertile, so you need to grow at least 2 plants together. Plant in containers or grow-bags under cover or outdoors in a warm, sheltered spot. Transplant seedlings to be grown outdoors in early summer, spacing them about 90 cm (3 ft) apart. Water regularly and, once fruit buds form, feed weekly with tomato fertilizer.

Pruning Trim to keep from sprawling too far.

Propagation Sow seeds in early spring in pots to grow on in warmth under cover, or sow in mid-spring for outdoor crops.

Harvesting and storage Harvest fruits from late summer to early autumn when the papery husks begin to open. Do not use unripe, green fruits as they contain toxins. The fruits store well for a couple of weeks in the refrigerator and may also be frozen whole.

Physalis pruinosa

HARDINESS
Hardy, but young stems can be damaged by frost.

HEIGHT
90–180 cm (3–6 ft). There is a larger-growing variety, *Physalis peruviana*.

SPREAD
90–180 cm (3–6 ft)

COMMENTS
Eat the ripe fruit fresh, cook the berries into jams, or dry them like raisins. Unripe fruit is poisonous.

CAPE GOOSEBERRY, DWARF

THE PALE YELLOW BERRIES OF DWARF CAPE GOOSEBERRY RIPEN WITHIN HUSKS ON A SMALL, SPREADING BUSH.

Position Cape gooseberry is a perennial in the tropics, but you can grow it as an annual wherever you can grow tomatoes. It needs full sun and well-drained soil that is not overly rich in nitrogen.

Cultivation Sow seed indoors about 8 weeks before the average date of your last spring frost. Transplant outdoors 1 week after that last frost date. Space plants 90 cm (3 ft) apart.

Pruning No pruning is necessary.

Propagation Grow from seed sown indoors in early spring. Even where

Cape gooseberries are perennial, yields are better if you start new plants every 2–3 years.

Pests and diseases Plants usually have no significant problems in temperate climates.

Harvesting and storage Harvest fruits when the husks are dry and papery. Pick them individually, or shake the plant and gather those that drop. Fruit can be stored for months if kept dry and intact in their husks. The husk is not edible.

Pinus spp.

HARDINESS
Fully hardy to frost tender, depending on the species.

HEIGHT
7.5–45 m (25–150 ft)

SPREAD
3–22.5 m (10–75 ft). Eventual size varies with species.

COMMENTS
Pines with edible seeds include the stone pine *P. pinea*, *P. sibirica* and *P. koraiensis*.

PINE NUT

MANY PINE SPECIES YIELD EDIBLE SEEDS OR KERNELS, HELD WITHIN THE CONES.

Position Plant in full sun in well-drained soil. Grows best in rich soil, but will tolerate infertile conditions.

Cultivation Plant container-grown stock any time the ground isn't frozen or waterlogged, or set out small bare-root plants between spring and autumn where winters are mild, or in spring where winters are severe. Space plants 3–22.5 m (10–75 ft) apart, depending on the eventual size of the plant, which varies with species.

Pruning Pines need little pruning. If desired, pinch out the shoot tips in spring for bushier growth.

Propagation Enhance germination by keeping sown seed warm for 2–3 months, then cool for a few months. Graft pines using a side graft indoors in winter.

Pests and diseases Generally no significant problems.

Harvesting and storage The dry-textured, delicate-flavoured, cream-coloured kernels are usually about 13 mm (½ in) long. Gather cones of species that drop ripe seed just before the cones open. With other pines, open the fallen cones either by heating them gently in the oven or smashing them with a hammer. Store the pine nuts in cool, dry conditions.

Prunus armeniaca

HARDINESS
Hardy, but early blossoms vulnerable to frost.

HEIGHT
2.4–7.2 m (8–24 ft)

SPREAD
4.8–7.2 m (16–24 ft)

COMMENTS
In frost-prone areas, select later-blooming cultivars, such as 'Petite Muscat' or the more frost-tolerant 'Alfred' and 'Blenheim'.

APRICOT

FULLY RIPE APRICOTS ARE SO SOFT THAT THEY DON'T SHIP WELL, SO THE BEST WAY TO ENJOY THEM AT THEIR PEAK IS TO GROW YOUR OWN.

Position Plant in full sun in average to poor, well-drained soil. Early-opening flowers should be protected from frost with fleece or netting.

Cultivation Many apricots are self-fertile and will produce some fruit if planted alone. But with most, yields will increase if you plant a second cultivar for cross-pollination. Plant dwarf or trained trees 3.6–4.5 m (12–15 ft) apart and full-sized trees 7.5 m (25 ft) apart. Mulch with compost to keep the soil moist in spring and feed and water as needed.

Pruning Some cultivars will fruit only every other year unless the fruits are thinned out to leave them 5 cm (2 in) apart. Apricot trees are best trained as a fan against a south- or west-facing wall, with several "arms" to each side of the main stem.

Propagation Propagate by bud graft.

Pests and diseases Apricot, like its relative plum, can suffer from silver leaf disease, which enters through wounds or pruning cuts, as well as bacterial canker, dieback and scale insects.

Harvesting and storage Pluck the fruits when they are soft and sweet. Can be made into jam or frozen.

Prunus avium

HARDINESS
Hardy, but blossom does not withstand frost.

HEIGHT
4.5–9 m (15–30 ft)

SPREAD
4.5–9 m (15–30 ft)

COMMENTS
Some sweet cherries need a compatible partner for cross-pollination, but the best choice is a self-fertile cultivar.

CHERRY, SWEET

CHERRIES ARE IN SEASON FOR ONLY ABOUT 6 WEEKS SO CAN BE VERY EXPENSIVE. IT'S A LUXURY TO HAVE A TREE IN THE GARDEN.

Position Plant in full sun in a warm, sheltered site, in average, well-drained soil. Cherries prefer warm, dry climates, so avoid frost pockets.

Cultivation Space standard sweet cherry trees 6–9 m (20–30 ft) apart and dwarf or trained cherries 3 m (10 ft) apart. Mulch with compost in early spring. In spring, if necessary, protect the blossom under a "tent" of fine netting or fleece.

Pruning Train free-standing cherry trees to an open-centred form. A fan-trained cherry is easily kept to size and easier to protect from frost or birds. Once established, shorten new stems by a half each year for more fruiting spurs.

Propagation Propagate by grafting.

Pests and diseases The main predator with cherries is birds. Be prepared to net the trees once the fruit starts to ripen to keep the birds away. Other problems include canker, cherry slugworm, fruit fly, silver leaf and brown rot.

Harvesting and storage Cherries begin to bear fruit 3–7 years after planting. If it is dry, let cherries ripen on the trees for best flavour.

Prunus cerasus

HARDINESS
Hardy.

HEIGHT
3–3.5 m (10–12 ft),
depending on the
rootstock.

SPREAD
3–3.5 m (10–12 ft)

COMMENTS
These cherries are
self-fertile; one tree
produces a good
crop of fruits.
Popular cultivars
are 'Morello'
and 'Nabella'.

CHERRY, ACID OR SOUR

THE TART FLAVOUR OF THESE FRUITS BECOMES
DELICIOUS WHEN THEY ARE COOKED AND
USED IN DESSERTS, MADE INTO WINES OR
JAMS, OR PRESERVED IN ALCOHOL.

Position Plant in sun or partial shade
against a wall, in well-drained but
moist soil.

Cultivation Plant trained forms
against a sunny or cool wall. Mulch
in early spring and protect from
frost with horticultural fleece. When
fruits begin to ripen, net the tree to
stop birds taking the crop.

Pruning Train as a fan to make it
easy to protect the blossom from
frost and the fruits from birds.
Cherries are borne on one-year-old
wood, so winter pruning aims to

create new fruiting shoots for the
following year.

Propagation Increase by grafting.

Pests and diseases Acid cherries
suffer the same pests as sweet
cherries (see page 287).

Harvesting and storage When the
cherries are dark and soft, cut the
stalks with scissors or secateurs to
avoid damaging the bark.

Prunus domestica

HARDINESS
Hardy, but blossom
is vulnerable to late
spring frosts.

HEIGHT
2.4–6 m (8–20 ft)

SPREAD
2.4–6 m (8–20 ft)

COMMENTS
Close relatives
of the plum are
damsons, gages,
and bullaces
(*P. institica*) and
they are grown in
the same way.

PLUM

PLUMS COME IN A WIDE RANGE OF COLOURS,
FLAVOURS AND SIZES, SOME FRUITING EARLIER
THAN OTHERS. SPEND SOME TIME CHOOSING
THE ONE BEST SUITED TO YOUR NEEDS.

Position Plant plum trees in full sun
in well-drained, average to rich soil.

Cultivation Many plums and damsons
will self-pollinate, so one tree is
enough. But if you plant two
compatible cultivars, they may set
more fruit. If you live in an area
prone to late frosts, choose a cultivar
that flowers late in the season or
train the tree on a sheltered wall or
under cover; otherwise the blossom
will be damaged and the tree will
not crop well. Space full-sized plum
trees 6–7.5 m (20–25 ft) apart and
dwarf trees 2.4–3.6 m (8–12 ft) apart.

Mulch with compost in spring and
keep the soil moist through the
growing season. Apply a general
fertilizer when the petals drop.

Pruning Plum trees are often seen
in gardens as standards or informal
trees with tall trunks, but it is simpler
to prune them as bush forms to make
picking the fruit easier. You can also
train freestanding trees as pyramids;
fans are best for wall-trained plums,
especially in colder areas. To train a
plum as a bush, wait until buds start
breaking in spring on the newly
planted sapling and cut down the
main stem to about 75 cm (30 in)
above ground. If it has any side
branches; choose 4 about 1 m (3 ft)
high and remove any others

Plum continued

Plum trees are one of the most popular fruit trees in the UK, for their spring blossom as well as their juicy fruit, which can be eaten fresh or in jams and desserts.

completely. The following spring, prune the side branches by half to outward-facing buds and remove any shoots from the trunk. After that, the tree needs little pruning, except to remove dead, crossing or damaged shoots in summer. Plum branches are very brittle and tend to snap if laden with fruits, so it is important to thin the crop. In early summer, plum trees often shed some fruitlets spontaneously: this is known as the "June drop". About this time, remove most of the fruitlets to leave 1 every 5–7.5 cm (2–3 in). The remaining fruits will be much larger and juicier. If necessary, you could also support fruiting branches temporarily with fork-topped posts.

Propagation Propagate by bud graft.

Pests and diseases Like all *Prunus*, plums can be badly affected by silver leaf disease, so don't prune in autumn or winter when they are dormant. It may help to use wound sealant on pruning cuts, to stop the airborne fungal spores entering the tree. Other problems include canker, brown rot, aphids, plum fruit moth and red spider mite. Pheromone traps are available for fruit moths; when hung in the tree in early summer, they attract male moths, which then get stuck in glue.

Harvesting and storage Plum trees start to bear 3–4 years after planting. Pick the fruit when soft and sweet.

Prunus dulcis

HARDINESS
Hardy, but blossom is often damaged by frost.

HEIGHT
4.5–9 m (15–30 ft)

SPREAD
4.5–9 m (15–30 ft)

COMMENTS
Almonds need a long, hot summer to crop well, so there are only a few cultivars worth growing in the cool UK climate, such as 'Ingrid' and 'Robijn'.

ALMOND, SWEET

MOST ALMONDS NEED CROSS-POLLINATION TO SET THEIR CROP, SO CHECK CATALOGUE DESCRIPTIONS TO MAKE SURE YOU PLANT THE BEST COMPANIONS.

Position Grow in full sun in average to fertile, but well-drained soil.

Cultivation Most almonds require another tree to pollinate them. Plant trees 7.5 m (25 ft) apart, or pollinate a single tree using a soft brush. Mulch with compost each spring. Water plants regularly when the weather is hot.

Pruning Train freestanding almonds as a bush, but as you prune each year, do more heading and less thinning than you would for trees such as peaches. The aim is to develop a thick branch network, which will promote better fruiting. For the best chance of ripe fruit, train as a fan against a south- or west-facing wall.

Propagation Propagate by grafting.

Pests and diseases Suffers the same problems as peaches (see page 292) as well as squirrels. Pick up all fallen nuts and destroy bad ones.

Harvesting and storage Most almond trees begin to produce nuts after 3–4 years. Use a padded stick to knock the nuts off the tree.

Prunus persica and *P. persica* var. *nectarina* ROSACEAE

Peach and nectarine

Both peaches and nectarines fruit reliably outdoors in the UK only when wall-trained as fans. Growing them on a wall also gives them extra warmth.

Position Plant in warm, sheltered sites in full sun; peaches tolerate most soils if they are well drained and fairly deep and moist.

Cultivation Most peaches and nectarines are self-pollinating, so you can get a crop from 1 tree. Wall-trained trees are easy to protect from frost, winter wet and silver leaf spores by covering them over with fleece or a clear plastic sheet over winter. Remember to remove it once blossom appears, otherwise insects will not be able to pollinate them.

Feed in early spring with an organic fertilizer and mulch. Spray the leaves with dilute seaweed solution every 3–4 weeks during the growing season. Water regularly if necessary; lack of moisture may check the growth of the tree and cause split stone. Although peaches and nectarines are usually self-fertile, it is worth brushing the fully open flowers with a soft paintbrush to help pollination along.

Pruning Train peach trees in the early spring after planting as a fan, with 2 "arms", by cutting down the main stem to about 30 cm (1 ft) tall and removing all but 2 side branches. When pruning peaches and nectarines, cut above the thinner, pointed growth buds, rather than

HARDINESS
Hardy, but blossom can be damaged by frost.

HEIGHT
2.4–4.5 m (8–15 ft)

SPREAD
3–6 m (10–20 ft)

COMMENTS
These fruits need a long, warm summer, so grow them in a greenhouse, conservatory or on a warm wall.

Shop peaches and nectarines are usually picked before they are fully ripe, so never achieve the flavour and juiciness of a fruit picked fresh from the tree.

solitary, fatter fruit buds. In the summer, choose 4 shoots from each arm to extend the fan shape and tie them into the supports; cut all other sideshoots to 1 bud. In successive years, in early summer, thin out sideshoots on the main stems to about 10 cm (4 in) apart and train more leading shoots to form 4–6 arms on both sides of the fan. At each pruning, remove any shoots that are growing away or towards the wall. On mature fans, cut half the fruiting sideshoots to 1 bud to prompt formation of productive new wood. Once the tree starts fruiting regularly, thin heavy crops when the fruitlets are about the size of marbles. Thin fruits on fan-trained peaches to 23 cm

(9 in) apart and on fan-trained nectarines to 15 cm (6 in) apart.

Propagation Propagate by bud graft.

Pests and diseases Like all *Prunus*, silver leaf disease can enter through wounds or pruning cuts. Peach leaf curl is a common problem. Also may suffer from aphids, red spider mite, canker, brown rot, scale insects, and split stone.

Harvesting and storage Peach and nectarine trees begin fruiting 2–4 years after planting. Harvest when fruit is soft and sweet. Can be made into jam or frozen.

Pyrus communis

Pear

Position Plant in a sheltered, frost-free site in full sun in moisture-retentive, well-drained soil.

Cultivation Space full-sized trees 4.5–6 m (15–20 ft) apart and dwarf or wall-trained pears 2.4–3.6 m (8–12 ft) apart. Water and mulch as necessary to keep the soil moist and avoid any damage to foliage and fruit. Pear trees are long-lived, but the quality of the fruit is past its best after 30 or so years.

Pruning Like apples, pears may be spur-bearing or tip-bearing. The former produce fruits on old wood, but the latter fruit on new wood at the shoot tips, so should be pruned only lightly once established. Pears may be grown in a range of forms, from bushes and pyramids to cordons and fans. The espalier form, with parallel, horizontal "arms", makes it easy to protect the blossom from frosts and birds. Create a support of horizontal wires set at least 15 cm (6 in) apart and starting about 45 cm (18 in) above the ground. In the first winter, cut down the main stem to just above the bottom wire and, in the following winter, train the side branches into the wires. Prune out any surplus side branches and cut back the main stem again to

HARDINESS
Hardy, but blossom is vulnerable to frost damage.

HEIGHT
2.4–6 m (8–20 ft)

SPREAD
2.4–6 m (8–20 ft)

COMMENTS
Plant cultivars that mature at different times for an extended harvest. For example, 'Beth' and 'Onward' (ripen mid-August), 'Beurre Superfin' and 'Conference' (early autumn).

Test whether pears are ready for picking by cupping each one in your hand: if it is ready, it will come away from the branch quite easily and with its stalk intact.

encourage more side branches to train in the second year. In the second summer, begin cutting back sideshoots on the framework branches to 3 buds to encourage fruiting buds. Once the espalier is full sized, prune in winter to thin out crowded stems and reduce over-large spurs to 1–2 buds. Heavy-bearing trees will need some fruit thinning. In early to midsummer, remove the smaller fruits, leaving 1 or 2 of the best fruits per cluster.

Propagation Propagate by grafting.

Pests and diseases Pears suffer a number of pests, such as pear midge larvae, which distort the fruitlets, aphids, pear leaf blister mite and birds. Diseases include canker, pear scab, brown rot and blossom wilt.

Harvesting and storage Pear trees generally begin to produce fruit 3–5 years after planting. Pears tend to be at their best for quite a short time, and go over quickly, so you should check the ripening fruits regularly. If picked too early, pears may shrivel up; if left too long on the tree, the flavour declines and they often rot at the core. Pick the pears when they are firm, but not quite ripe; the skins usually change colour slightly and the fruits will come away readily from the tree. Store the pears in a cool, dark, well-ventilated place for 1–3 weeks until soft and sweet.

Ribes spp.

GROSSULARIACEAE

HARDINESS
Hardy.

HEIGHT
90–210 cm (3–7 ft)

SPREAD
90–210 cm (3–7 ft)

COMMENTS
Blackcurrants
(*Ribes nigrum*)
tolerate an alkaline
soil better than red-
or whitecurrants
(*R. rubrum*).

CURRANT

THE TART BERRIES OF CURRANTS ARE
EXCELLENT FOR JAMS OR JUICE. IF POSSIBLE,
PLANT TWO OR MORE CULTIVARS, AS CROSS-
POLLINATION WILL INCREASE YIELDS.

Position Plant red- or whitecurrants
in sun or shade in well-drained,
average soil; blackcurrants prefer
richer, moister soil and full sun.

Cultivation Most currants are self-
pollinating. Space blackcurrants 1.8 m
(6 ft) apart, red- and whitecurrants
a little closer, and mulch well.
Top-dress with garden compost and
a potassium-rich fertilizer in early
spring. Water regularly in dry weather.

Pruning Blackcurrants are pruned
hard into bushes, to obtain as many
new shoots as possible to fruit the

next year. Bushes do not fruit
in the first year. In the third and
following autumns, remove up to
one-third of the oldest stems at the
base, to renew the fruiting growth.
Prune red- and whitecurrants like
gooseberries (see opposite).

Propagation By hardwood cuttings.

Pests and diseases Aphids, fungal
leaf spots and gooseberry sawfly;
buy mildew-resistant cultivars.

Harvesting and storage For cooking
or making jam, pick currants when
they are not quite ripe. For fresh
eating, let them ripen on the bush.

Ribes uva-crispa

HARDINESS
Hardy.

HEIGHT
60–180 cm (2–6 ft)

SPREAD
60–180 cm (2–6 ft)

COMMENTS
Modern cultivars
are more resistant
to fungal infections
and some, such as
'Pax', are spineless.

GOOSEBERRY

THE GOOSEBERRY PRODUCES FRUIT BEFORE
OTHER SOFT-FRUIT CROPS; THE BERRIES MAY
BE GREEN, RED OR YELLOW AND ARE GOOD
FOR COOKING OR FOR FRESH EATING.

Position Plant in full sun or light
shade in average soil; will tolerate
alkaline soil.

Cultivation Most gooseberries are
self-pollinating; however, they will
produce higher yields if interplanted
with 2 or 3 other cultivars. Space
the plants 1.2–1.5 m (4–5 ft) apart
and mulch. Top-dress with garden
compost and a potassium-rich
fertilizer in early spring. Water
regularly in dry weather.

Pruning At planting time, select one
branch as the main trunk or "leg",

and remove the rest. Each winter,
remove all shoots that are more than
3 years old; then remove all but 6
of the remaining shoots.

Propagation By hardwood cuttings.

Pests and diseases Powdery mildew
affects gooseberries; dust with sulphur
or use disease-resistant cultivars.

Harvesting and storage Pick slightly
unripe, alternate fruits in early
summer for cooking and leave
the rest to pick when ripe.

Rubus fruticosus

HARDINESS
Hardy.

HEIGHT
1.2–2.1 m (4–7 ft)

SPREAD
90–180 cm (3–6 ft)

COMMENTS
Look for thornless, highly productive cultivars, such as 'Loch Ness' and 'Waldo'.

BLACKBERRY

THE FLAVOUR OF BLACKBERRIES IS AT ITS BEST WHEN THE FRUITS TURN DARK AND LOSE SOME OF THEIR GLOSSINESS. SOME THORNLESS CULTIVARS NEED SUPPORT.

Position Plant in full sun in average to rich soil.

Cultivation Buy blackberries as bare-root plants, called "stools". They need plenty of space and good air circulation. Plant thorny cultivars 90–120 cm (3–4 ft) apart and thornless cultivars 1.2–1.8 m (4–6 ft) apart. Make paths between the rows for good sun exposure and adequate air circulation. Keep the soil evenly moist and mulch with well-rotted garden compost in early spring.

Pruning Cut fruit-bearing canes to the ground right after harvest and thin the new canes to leave only the strong canes to fruit next year. Shorten side branches to about 30 cm (1 ft) long. For maximum yields, train blackberries to a trellis.

Propagation By division or layering.

Pests and diseases Watch for distorted growth, sterile canes or orange-spotted leaves that drop early. These are all symptoms of incurable viral or orange rust diseases. Destroy infected plants.

Harvesting and storage Eat soft, sweet blackberries as soon as possible after picking, or freeze.

Rubus idaeus

HARDINESS
Hardy.

HEIGHT
1.2–1.8 m (4–6 ft)

SPREAD
60–120 cm (2–4 ft)

COMMENTS
Raspberries ripen from summer on. Summer-bearing cultivars, such as 'Glen Moy', fruit on 2-year-old canes. 'Allgold' and 'Autumn Bliss' bear a second autumn crop on new canes.

RASPBERRY

IF BIRDS ARE BEATING YOU TO YOUR BERRIES, COVER THE PLANTS WITH NETTING. ROLL BACK THE COVER AS NEEDED TO HARVEST.

Position Plant in full sun in fertile, lime-free soil.

Cultivation If possible, buy bare-root certified virus-free plants, or stools, and plant them 60 cm (2 ft) apart in a row. They'll fill in within a year or two. Top-dress with well-rotted garden compost and a little balanced organic fertilizer in late winter, if needed, for good growth. Water in dry spells and mulch to discourage weeds and keep soil evenly moist.

Pruning Cut off all the old canes at ground level when they have finished fruiting. Leave 8–10 of the strongest canes per metre (3 ft) of the new canes on summer-bearing plants to produce berries next year.

Propagation Propagate by division or layering, but only if you are sure your plants are healthy.

Pests and diseases Several fungal diseases may attack raspberries: *Botrytis*, raspberry spur blight and cane blight. Spray with Bordeaux mixture when the buds begin to turn green. Remove and destroy plants affected by disease. Several pests attack the plants, such as raspberry beetle and leaf and bud mite.

Harvesting and storage Harvest berries when they're sweet and ripe. Eat fresh or freeze for later.

Rubus x *loganobaccus*

HARDINESS
Hardy.

HEIGHT
2.4–3.6 m (8–12 ft)

SPREAD
2.4–3.6 m (8–12 ft)

COMMENTS
Completely ripe fruits have a delectable flavour and aroma. Use quickly, as they are very soft and fragile.

BOYSENBERRY

RIPE BOYSENBERRY FRUITS ARE LARGE, MAROON AND ALMOST SEEDLESS.

Position Plant canes in full sun in well-drained soil, rich in humus.

Cultivation Plant container-grown stock any time the ground isn't frozen or waterlogged, or set out bare-root plants in spring or autumn, while dormant. Boysenberries are self-fertile, so you can get fruit from just one plant. Space plants 90–180 cm (3–6 ft) apart. Set up a stake next to each plant or erect a one- or two-wire trellis on which to support the canes. The canes are biennial, bearing fruit in their second season.

Pruning In winter, cut canes that fruited the previous summer to the ground—they are dead anyway. Thin remaining canes, leaving 8 to 10 of the most vigorous ones per plant. Shorten these to 2.1 m (7 ft), and cut back any sideshoots to 30–45 cm (12–18 in).

Propagation Propagate by layering.

Pests and diseases Given good growing conditions, boysenberries usually have few major problems.

Harvesting and storage For full flavour, harvest when the fruit practically drops off into your hand. Even at cool temperatures and high humidity, fruit keeps only 2–3 days.

Sambucus spp.

HARDINESS
Hardy.

HEIGHT
1.8–3 m (6–10 ft)

SPREAD
90–180 cm (3–6 ft)

COMMENTS
The edible species usually grown is *S. nigra*. But other species (such as *S. ebulus*) have poisonous berries.

ELDERBERRY

ELDERBERRIES PRODUCE CLUSTERS OF SMALL BLUE-BLACK BERRIES. THE FLAVOUR IS VERY MILD, SO ELDERBERRIES TASTE BEST COOKED WITH SUGAR AND ANOTHER, MORE ACIDIC FRUIT. THE WHOLE FRUIT IS EDIBLE.

Position Plant in full sun or partial shade and humus-rich, evenly moist soil.

Cultivation Plant container-grown shrubs anytime, or set out bare-root plants in spring or autumn, while they are dormant. Space plants 1.8 m (6 ft) apart. Plant 2 seedlings or 2 different cultivars for best yields.

Pruning On established bushes, cut stems that are more than 3 years old to ground level each winter.

Also prune away suckers to control the spread of the plants.

Propagation Dig up and transplant suckers from the base of the plant, take cuttings or sow seed.

Pests and diseases If needed, net bushes to keep birds at bay.

Harvesting and storage Harvest the berries when they are fully coloured. An easy way to pick fruit from the clusters is to pop them off with the tines of a dinner fork. Store the fruit in the refrigerator. The fruit is most often used in jams, tarts and preserves, as well as cordials and wines. (Elder flowers are also collected for cordials and wines.)

Vaccinium corymbosum

HARDINESS
Hardy, highbush
types.

HEIGHT
60–450 cm (2–15 ft)

SPREAD
90–300 cm (3–10 ft)

COMMENTS
Only highbush
blueberries can be
grown in the UK.
They need acid
soil.

BLUEBERRY

HIGHBUSH BLUEBERRIES ARE ONLY PARTLY
SELF-FERTILE SO NEED CROSS-POLLINATION.
CHECK CATALOGUE DESCRIPTIONS TO GET
APPROPRIATE PARTNERS.

Position Plant in full sun or light
shade in light, acid, well-drained soil
or soil-based ericaceous compost.

Cultivation Plant in containers or
raised beds, or if you have acid soil,
direct outdoors, 1.5 m (5 ft) apart.
Apply a thick layer of mulch in spring
of acid material such as pine needles
or bark to keep the soil evenly moist.
Water only with rainwater—tap water
is too alkaline. Repot container-grown
plants every couple of years to
refresh the compost.

Pruning Pinch off all the flowers on
a young blueberry bush the first
year after planting, so the bush will
grow strong. The next year you'll
have to remove only dead or
damaged wood. Let plenty of sun
and air penetrate the entire plant.

Propagation Propagate by hardwood
or softwood cuttings, or by division,
depending on cultivar.

Pests and diseases Blueberries are
relatively trouble-free, but suffer
from chlorosis in soils that are not
sufficiently acid. Net ripening bushes
to stop birds eating the berries.

Harvesting and storage Harvest after
the berries turn blue. Don't pick
under-ripe berries; they won't ripen.
Eat immediately or freeze.

Vaccinium macrocarpon

HARDINESS
Hardy.

HEIGHT
Up to 30 cm (1 ft)

SPREAD
Unlimited. (The sprawling stems root where they touch the ground and continue to grow outwards.)

COMMENTS
The tart berries are completely edible. Cultivars include 'Early Black' and 'McFarlin'.

CRANBERRY

CRANBERRIES GROW AS LOW, CREEPING BUSHES. THEIR WHITE FLOWERS ARE FOLLOWED BY HARD, RED BERRIES, EACH ABOUT THE SIZE OF A THUMBNAIL.

Position Cranberries thrive in sun and moist, well-drained, humus-rich and very acid soil; pH 4.0–5.5. The plants do not tolerate dry or alkaline soil, but they can withstand flooding in cold weather and are also happy in a bog garden.

Cultivation Plant in spring or, where winters are severe, autumn. Space plants 30–60 cm (1–2 ft) apart. Mix plenty of ericaceous compost into the soil before planting. Mulch with coarse, lime-free sand, renewing the mulch every couple of years.

Pruning Cut away some of the sprawling stems and some of the upright, fruiting stems when they become overcrowded.

Propagation Semi-ripe stem cuttings and layered stems root readily. Where winters are mild, set rooted cuttings outdoors in autumn; otherwise, set them out as early as possible in spring.

Pests and diseases Generally no significant problems.

Harvesting and storage Pick berries in autumn, after they are fully coloured. Cranberries will keep for 2–4 months at high humidity and temperatures just above freezing. They can also be dried.

Vaccinium vitis–idaea

HARDINESS
Hardy.

HEIGHT
15–60 cm (6–24 in)

SPREAD
Unlimited. (Plants send up shoots from creeping underground stems.)

COMMENTS
The round, red berries are a little larger than peas and have a flavour similar to, but less sharp than, that of true cranberries.

LINGONBERRY OR COWBERRY

LINGONBERRY IS A LOW, CREEPING BUSH THAT PRODUCES WHOLLY EDIBLE FRUIT.

Position Give lingonberries full sun or partial shade and well-drained, humus-rich, acid soil; pH 4.5–5.5.

Cultivation Set out container-grown plants any time the ground isn't frozen or waterlogged, or plant bare-root stock in spring or autumn, while dormant. Space plants of the species *V. vitis-idaea* 45 cm (18 in) apart and those of the variety *V. vitis-idaea* subsp. *minor* 25 cm (10 in) apart. Lingonberries compete poorly with weeds, so weed thoroughly before planting. Also dig in plenty of ericaceous compost. Mulch with coarse, lime-free sand to suppress weeds further and to keep the shallow roots cool and moist. Plants are partially self-fertile, but planting at least two seedlings or cultivars may increase yields.

Pruning Once plants are a few years old, mow a different third or quarter of the planting yearly in late autumn (so each part gets mown every 3–4 years) to about 2.5 cm (1 in) tall.

Propagation Take cuttings in spring.

Pests and diseases Generally no significant problems.

Harvesting and storage Delay harvest until fruit is thoroughly red and ripe. Store fruit at temperatures just above freezing with high humidity.

Viburnum trilobum

HARDINESS
Hardy.

HEIGHT
2.4–3.6 m (8–12 ft)

SPREAD
2.4–3.6 m (8–12 ft)

COMMENTS
The seeds must be strained when you make jam or jelly. There is an offensive odour while the fruit is cooking, but it is not present in the finished product.

CRANBERRY, HIGHBUSH

THE SHINY, BRIGHT RED BERRIES OF THE HIGHBUSH CRANBERRY RIPEN IN DROOPING CLUSTERS. THE TART FRUITS CONTAIN A SINGLE, LARGE SEED. EAT THE WHOLE FRUIT, EXCEPT FOR THE SEED.

Position Plant in full sun or partial shade in moist, well-drained soil.

Cultivation Plant container-grown shrubs any time the ground isn't frozen or waterlogged, or set out bare-root plants in spring or autumn, while they are dormant. Space plants 1.8–2.7 m (6–9 ft) apart. Plant several of them close together for a bright display when they are in fruit, along a border as an informal hedge, or grow just one as a specimen shrub.

Pruning Cut off old, non-productive stems at ground level in winter.

Propagation Take hardwood or softwood cuttings. Seed does not germinate until it has been kept warm and moist for 4 months, then cool and moist for 3 months.

Pests and diseases Generally no significant problems.

Harvesting and storage Harvest any time after the berries turn fully red. Fruits not harvested hang on the bush well into winter, shrivelling with time. Store at cool temperatures and high humidity, such as in a covered container in the refrigerator.

Vitis vinifera

GRAPE

TO PREVENT GROWING CLUSTERS FROM
RIPENING UNEVENLY, THIN IN EARLY SUMMER,
WHEN FRUITS ARE SMALL AND HARD.

Position Plant in full sun in a
well-ventilated site and in average
well-drained, slightly alkaline soil
that is deep enough for the large
roots and not too rich—you'll get
more leaf than fruit if so.

Cultivation Set up a support system
before planting for the vines to cling
to. Unless you live in a very mild
area or have a sunny, sheltered,
south-facing wall, the best fruit is
gained from plants grown in a
greenhouse. Vines are often planted
with the roots outside (they need a
period of winter chill) and the top-

growth under cover to ripen the fruit.
Grape vines are self-fertile, so you
need only one. Plant in winter and
position the plant to get the most
space for the leading stems to grow
if training as a cordon. Work in
coarse grit to improve drainage on
heavy soils. After planting, keep the
soil moist and mulch well. Feed with
a high-potash fertilizer in spring and
keep feeding indoor vines through
the summer. Stroke the flowers of
indoor vines to aid pollination.

Pruning Train the vine over wire
strung between posts. Vines can be
trained in a variety of ways; they
fruit on new wood, so have to be
pruned regularly for a good crop.
Cordons may have 1, 2 or more

For the best and sweetest flavour, leave the fruits on the grape vine until they have ripened fully, before harvesting them.

leading stems with fruiting sideshoots. To create a single-stemmed cordon, in late winter, cut the vine back to a stump with 2 buds. When the buds start growing, leave the stronger shoot and remove the other one. In the summer, shorten all the sideshoots to 5–6 leaves or buds and any sublaterals to 1 bud. Each year, cut down the leader by up to two-thirds to ripened, mature wood and repeat the process. After a few years, the leader stems will not need much cutting back, but the sideshoots always need thinning and shortening. For a multiple cordon, leave 2 or more leader stems to develop.

Propagation Propagate by cuttings, grafting or, for some types, layering.

Pests and diseases Birds take the fruits from outdoor vines. Pests under cover include scale insects, mealybug and red spider mite; scrape off loose bark in winter to prevent the insects overwintering. Ventilate to avoid grey mould (*Botrytis*).

Harvesting and storage Harvest the bunches of grapes by cutting them off the vine with clean secateurs.

INDEX

Page references in *italics* indicate photos and illustrations.

A

Abelmoschus esculentus 114, *114*
Actinidia deliciosa 248, *248*
Actinidiaceae 248, *248*
Aizoaceae 232, *232*
Alliaceae 115–22, *115–22*
Allium spp. 115–22, *115–22*
A. *ampeloprasum* 122
A. *cepa*
   Aggregatum Group 118, *118*
   Proliferum Group 117
A. *porrum* 119–20, *119–20*
A. *sativum* 121–2, *121–2*
   var. *ophioscorodon* 122
A. *schoenoprasum* 120
A. *tuberosum* 120
Almond, sweet 24, 72, 291, *291*
Amaranth 123, *123*
Amaranthaceae 123, *123*
Amaranthus tricolor 123, *123*
Ananas comosus 249, *249*
Apiaceae 124–6, *124–6*, 180–81,
   180–81, 183, *183*, 203, *203*,
   243, *243*
Apium graveolens
   var. *dulce* 124–5, *124–5*
Apple 22, *23*, 72, *91*, 272–5, *272–5*
Apricot 72, 74, 286, *286*
Arachis hypogaea 127, *127*
Arctium lappa 128, *128*

Armoracia rusticana 129, *129*
Artichoke *71*, 179, *179*, 185, *185*
Asparagaceae 130–31, *130–31*
Asparagus officinalis 14, *14*, 86,
   130–31, *130–31*
Asparagus bean 213, *213*
Asparagus pea 195, *195*
Asteraceae 128, *128*, 163–6, *163–6*,
   178–9, *178–9*, 185, *185*, 189–92,
   189–92, 224, *224*, 233, *233*,
   270, *270*
Atriplex hortensis 132
   var. *rubra* 132, *132*
Aubergine *12*, 51, 57, 62, 103, 160,
   198, 225–6, *225–6*
   baby 226
   Italian 226
   Oriental 226
   white 226, *226*
Autumn 74, 84–5
Averrhoa carambola 250, *250*

B

Bamboo shoot 58, 214, *214*
Barbarea verna 194
Barberry 251, *251*
Bare-root plants 60–1, 74–9, *76–7*
Basella alba 133, *133*

Basellaceae 133, *133*
Basil, sweet 240, 242, *242*, 259
Bean 12, 43, 56–7, 66, 70, 89, 206–13,
    206–13
  adzuki 238
  asparagus (yard long) 213
  broad 210, 213, *213*
  butter 209, 211, *211*
  dried 206–209
  flageolet 210, 212
  French 208, 212–13
  fresh 210–13
  haricot 208
  hyacinth *206*, 208–9
  kidney 208
  lablab *206*, 208–9
  lima 12, 209, 211, *211*
  mung 238
  pinto 208, *208*
  scarlet runner 12, 56, *210*, 211
  soya 184, *184*
Beetroot 14, 56–7, 61, 71, 86, 135–7,
    135–7
  cylindrical 137
  golden 137
Berberidaceae 251, *251*
Berberis spp. 251, *251*
Beta vulgaris
  subsp. *cicla* 134, *134*
  subsp. *vulgaris* 135–7, *135–7*

Betulaceae 257, *257*
Blackberry 22, 72, 79, 90, 298, *298*
Blueberry 22, 25, 72, 90–1, *90*, 93,
    302, *302*
Boysenberry 300, *300*
Brassica spp. 157–8, *157–8*
B. campestris subsp. *chinensis* var.
    utilis 152
B. hirta 158
B. juncea 158
  var. *foliosa* 158, *158*
B. napus 158
  Napobrassica Group 138, *138*
B. nigra 158
B. oleracea
  Acephala Group 139–40, *139–40*,
    145–6
  Albroglabra Group 148
  Botrytis Group 141–3, *141–3*
  Capitata Group 144–6, *144–6*
  Gemmifera Group 147, *147*
  Gongylodes Group 148, *148*
  Italica Group 149–51, *149–51*
B. rapa
  Rapifera Group 155, *155*
  Ruvo Group 151
  var. *chinensis* 152, *152*
  var. *nipposinica* 153, *153*
  var. *pekinensis* 154, *154*
  var. *perviridis* 156, *156*

Brassicaceae 129, *129*, 138–58, *138–58*, 167, *167*, 182, *182*, 194, *194*, 202, *202*, 219–20
Broccoli 14, *14*, 89, 149–51, *149–51*
    Calabrese 151
    Chinese 149, 150
    purple sprouting 149, 150, *151*
    raab 149, 151
    Romanesco 149, 151
    white sprouting 149, 150
Bromeliaceae 249, *249*
Brussels sprouts 14, 147, *147*
Bullace *see* plum
Burdock, Greater 128, *128*

Caprifoliaceae 301, *301*, 305, *305*
Capsicum annuum 159–62, *159–62*
    Conoides Group 161, *162*
    Grossum Group *161*, 161–2
    Longum Group *160*, 161
Carambola *see* Star fruit
Cardoon 178, *178*
Carrot 57, 62, *86*, 89, 180–81, *180–81*
Castanea sativa 252, *252*
Cauliflower 14, 57, 141–3, *141–3*
    green 143
    mini 143
Celeriac 58, 126, *126*
Celery *86*, 124–5, *124–5*
Celtuce 58, 192, *192*
Chenopodiaceae 132, *132*, 134–7, *134–7*, 231, *231*
Cherry 24
    acid or sour 72, 288, *288*
    cornelian 256, *256*
    sweet 72, 287, *287*
Chestnut, sweet 252, *252*
Chicory 14, 58, 61, 165–6, *165–6*
    leaf 165
    red 166
    Witloof 166
Chilli pepper *see* peppers
Chinese cabbage *see* cabbage, Chinese
Chinese gooseberries *see* kiwi
Chives 120
    Chinese 120
Chop-suey greens 58, 163, *163*
Choy sum 152
Chrysanthemum coronarium var. *spatiosum* 163, *163*

C

Cabbage 14, *42*, 144–6, *144–6*
    Chinese 14, 61, 150, 154, *154*
    michihi 154
    ornamental *19*, 145–6
    pointed-headed 146
    red *19*, 146, *146*
    round-headed 146
    Savoy 144–46
Cactaceae 280, *280*
Calabrese 149
Calamondin 253, *253*
Calcium 48–9
Cantaloupe 259–260
Cape gooseberry, dwarf 284, *284*

Cichorium endivia 164, *164*
C. intybus 165–6, *165–6*
x *Citrofortunella microcarpa*,
    253, *253*
Citrus spp. 72, 254–5, *254–5*
Climate 12–15
Cloches 68–71, *68*

Cobnut *see* hazelnut
Cold frames 68–9, *68–9*, 104, *105*
Compost 34–9, *34–9*
    tea 34
Containers 22, 62, *62*, 64, 79, *79*,
    82, *82*
Convolvulaceae 186–8, *186–8*
Corn salad 14, 58, 61, 234, *234*
Cornaceae 256, *256*
Cornelian cherry 256, *256*
Cornichon 170
Cornus mas 256, *256*
Corylus 257, *257*
    avellana 257
    maxima 257
Courgette 57, *57*, 171–2, *172*
Cowberry *see* lingonberry
Crab apple 276, *276*
Crambe maritima 167, *167*
Cranberry 303, *303*
    highbush 305, *305*
Cress 58, 61, 194, *194*
    Land 194

Crop rotation 17, 18
Cucumber 12, 57, 89, 168–70, *168–70*
    cornichons 170
    gherkin 170
    greenhouse 168–70, *170*
    Japanese 170
    outdoor *169*, 170
Cucumis melo 258–60, *258–60*
    Cantalupensis Group 260
    Inodorus Group 260
    Reticulatus Group *259*, 260
C. sativus 168–70, *168–70*
Cucurbita spp. 173–7, *173–7*
C. maxima 177
C. pepo 171–2, *171–2*, 175–7, *175–7*
C. scolymus 179, *179*
Cucurbitaceae 168–77, *168–77*, 193,
    193, 196, *196*, 258–60, *258–60*
Currant 22, 25, 72, 296, *296*
    black 296
    red 296, *296*
    white 296
Cydonia oblonga 261, *261*
Cynara cardunculus 178, *178*
Cynara scolymus 179, *179*
Cyphomandra betacea 262, *262*

D

Damson *see* plum
Dandelion 58, 106
Daucus carota subsp. *sativus*
   180–81, *180–81*
Diseases 100–101
Drip irrigation 94–5, *94*
Dwarf trees 76, *76*

E

Elderberry 22, *25*, 301, *301*
Endive 14, 58, 164, *164*
   Belgian 166
   broad-leaved 164
   frisée 164, *164*
Ericaceae 302–4, *302–4*
Eriobotrya japonica 263, *263*
Eruca vesicaria subsp. *sativa* 182, *182*
Eschscholzia *83*
Espalier training 20–1, *20–1*, 25, 92,
   92

F

Fabaceae 127, *127*, 184, *184*, 195, *195*,
   206–13, *206–13*, 215–17, *215–17*

Fagaceae 252, *252*
Fennel, Florence 58, 183, *183*
Fertilizer 40–9, 88–9, *88–9*
Ficus carica 264–5, *264–5*
Fig 72, 93, *93*, 264–5, *264–5*
Filbert *see* hazelnut
Foeniculum vulgare var. *azoricum*
   183, *183*
Fortunella spp. 266, *266*
Fragaria spp. 267–8, *267–8*
F. vesca 91, 269, *269*
Fruit 246–307, *246–307*
   see also by name
Fruit garden 22–5, *23*
   weeding 110–11, *110–11*
Fruit trees 22–3, 74–9, 110–11
   see also by name

G

Gage (greengage) *see* plum
Garlic 56–7, 86, 121–2, *121–2*
  chives 120
  elephant 122
  hard-neck 122
  soft-neck 122
Gherkin 170
Glycine max 184, *184*
Goji berry 281, *281*
Gooseberries 22, 72, 74, *76*, 297, *297*
  Cape, dwarf 284, *284*
Gourd, bottle 193, *193*
Grape 25, 72, 77, 79, 93, 306–307, *306–307*
  weeding 110, *110*
Grapefruit 254
Green manure 42, *42*, 43
Grossulariaceae 296, *296*, 297, *297*

Hoeing 106, *106*, 108
Horseradish 14, 129, *129*

I

Ipomoea aquatica 186, *186*
I. batatas 187–8, *187–8*
I. purpurea 188

J

Jerusalem artichoke 185, *185*
Juglandaceae 271, *271*
Juglans 271, *271*
  nigra 271
  regia 271

K

Kale 14, 139, *139*
  Chinese 150
  curly 140, *140*
  sea 167, *167*
Kiwi 25, 72, 248, *248*
Kohlrabi 14, 40, *40*, 61, 148, *148*
Kumquat 266, *266*

H

Hamburg parsley 205, *205*
Hazelnut 22, 72, 257, *257*
Helianthus annuus 270, *270*
Helianthus tuberosus 185, *185*
Herbs 240–45, *240–45*
  Basil, sweet 242, *242*
  Mint 241, *241*
  Parsley 243, *243*
  Rosemary 244, *244*
  Thyme 245, *245*

L

Lablab purpureus 206, 208–9
Lactuca sativa 189–91, *189–91*
  var. *augustana* 192, *192*
Lagenaria siceraria 193, *193*
Lamb's lettuce *see* corn salad
Lamiaceae 241–2, *241–2*, 244–5, *244–5*
Leek 57, 119–20, *119–20*

Lemon 254, *254*, 255
Lepidium sativum 194, *194*
Lettuce 12, 14, 56–7, 61, *70*, 89,
    189–91, *189–91*
  asparagus 192, *192*
  butterhead *190*, 191
  cos 191
  crisphead 191
  iceberg *189*
  loose-leaf 191, *191*
Lime 254
Lingonberry 304, *304*
Loofah 196, *196*
Loquat 263, *263*
Lotus tetragonolobus 195, *195*
Luffa acutangula 196, *196*
L. cylindrica 196, *196*
Lycium barbarum 281, *281*
Lycopersicon esculentum 197–201,
    197–201
  var. *cerasiforme* 198, 200
  var. *pyriforme* 201
L. pimpinellifolium 201

M

Mâche *see* corn salad
Magnesium 49
Malus spp. 276, *276*
M. x *domestica* 272–5, *272–5*
Malvaceae 114, *114*
Marrow 172, *see also* courgette

Medlar 277, *277*
Melon, sweet 12, 57, 258–60, *258–60*
  cantaloupe 260, *260*
  honeydew 258, 260
  musk melon *259*, 260
Mentha spp. 241, *241*
Mespilus germanica 277, *277*
Michihi cabbage 154
Mint 241, *241*
Mizuna greens 58, 61, 153, *153*
Moraceae 264–5, *264–5*, 278, *278*
Morus spp. 278, *278*
Mountain spinach 132, *132*

Mulberry 72, 278, *278*
Mulching 50–3, 110–11, *111*
  inorganic 53
  organic 50–3
Mustards, Oriental 14, 58, 61, 157–8,
    157–8
  and cress 157
  black 158
  brown 158
  red 158, *158*
  white 158

N

Nasturtium officinale 202, *202*
Nectarine *92*, 93, 292–3, *292*
Nitrogen 37, 42–3
Nuts *see also by name*
  aftercare 79

O

Ocimum basilicum 242, *242*
Okra 12, 114, *114*
Olea europaea subsp. *europaea*
   279, *279*
Oleaceae 279, *279*
Olive 279, *279*
Onion 14, *14*, 56–7, 115–17, *115–17*
   bulb 115–7, *115*, *116*
   Egyptian (tree) 117
   pickling (pearl) 116
   red (Spanish) 116, *117*
   slicing 117
   spring 117
   Welsh (Japanese bunching) 117
Opuntia ficus-indica 280, *280*
Orach 132, *132*
Oranges 254
Oxalidaceae 250, *250*

P

Pak choi 12, 152, *152*
Parsley 243, *243*
   Hamburg 205, *205*
Parsnip 14, 203, *203*
Passiflora spp. 282, *282*
Passifloraceae 282, *282*
Passion fruit 282, *282*

Pastinaca sativa 203, *203*
Peach 22, 72, 77, *92*, 93, 292–3, *292–3*
Peanut 12, 127, *127*
Pear 22, 72, 294–5, *294–5*
Pea 14, 43, 57, 61, 89, 215–17, *215–17*
   asparagus 195, *195*
   garden (shelling) 216, 217, *217*
   mangetout (snow) 216, 217
   sugar snap *215*, 216, 217
Peppers, sweet and chilli 159–62,
   159–62
   chilli 12, *160*, 161
   Italian (cone) *161*, 162
   pickling 161, *162*
   sweet 12, 57, 88, *159*, 159–162
Persicaria odorata 204, *204*
Pests 100–101, *100*
Petroselinum crispum 243, *243*
   var. *tuberosum* 205, *205*

Phaseolus spp. 206–10, 211
   coccineus 210, 211
   lunatus 209, 211, *211*
   vulgaris 208, 208–9, 210, 212, *212*
Phosphorus 44–5
Phyllostachys spp. 214, *214*
Physalis
   ixocarpa 283, *283*
   pruinosa 284, *284*
   peruviana 284
Pinaceae 285, *285*
Pine nut 285, *285*
Pineapple 249, *249*
Pinus spp. 285, *285*
Pisum sativum 215–17, *215–17*
   var. *macrocarpon 216*, 217
   var. *sativum 215*, 217, *217*

Planning 16–19, *16–19*
Planting 74–9
   bare-root plants 75–8, *77*, 77
   choosing plants 56–63
   containers, from 79, *79*
   containers, in 22, 62, *62*, 64, 82, *82*
   protection, frost 68–71, *68–71*
Plum 22, 24, 72, 289–90, *289–90*
Poaceae 214, *214*, 235–7, *235–7*
Polygonaceae 204, *204*, 221–3, *221–3*
Portulaca oleracea var. *sativa*
   218, *218*

Portulacaceae 218
Potassium 46–7
Potato 12, *47*, 227–30, *227–30*
   see also Sweet potato
   red 230, *230*
   salad *227*, 230
   white *228*, 230
Prickly pear 280, *280*
Pruning 96–8, *97–8*
   tools 96, *96*, 98–9, *99*
Prunus armeniaca 286, *286*
P. avium 287, *287*
P. cerasus 288, *288*
P. domestica 289–90, *289–90*
P. dulcis 291, *291*
P. insititia 289
P. persica 293, *293*
   var. *nectarina* 292, *292–3*
Pumpkin 12, 57, 173–4, *173–4*
Purslane, summer 218, *218*
Pyrus communis 294–5, *294–5*

Q

Quartering 78, *78*
Quince 261, *261*

R

Radicchio 165, 166
Radish 14, *14*, 56, 61, 71, 219–20,
   219–20
   black Spanish 220
   Chinese 220
   mooli (daikon) *220*
   winter 221
Rape, oilseed 158
Raphanus sativus 219–20, *219–20*
Raspberry 22, 72, 90, 299, *299*
Rheum x *hybridum* 222, *222*

Rhubarb 14, 221–2, *221–2*
Ribes spp. 296, *296*
Ribes uva–crispa 297, *297*
Rocket 14, 58, 182, *182*
Rosaceae 261, *261*, 263, *263*,
    267–9, *267–9*, 272–7, *272–7*,
    286–95, *286–95*, 298–9, *298–9*,
    300, *300*
Rosemary 244, *244*
Rosmarinus officinalis 244, *244*
Rubus fruticosus 298, *298*
R. idaeus 299, *299*
R. x *loganobaccus* 300, *300*
Rumex spp. 223, *223*
    acetosa 223
    scutatus 223
Rutaceae 253–5, *253–5*, 266, *266*

S

Salsify 233, *233*
Sambucus spp. 301, *301*
Scorzonera hispanica 224, *224*
Sea kale 167, *167*
Seeds 62–7, *63*
    buying 62
    choosing 56
    sowing *63*, 64
    successive sowing 71
Shade 84
Shallot 118, *118*
Soft fruit 22–5, *25*, 74–9, 110, *111*
    see also by name
Soil 28–33, *28–33*

nutrients 31–2
organic matter 30–31
pH 29
preparation 32–3, *32*, 86–8
Solanaceae 159–62, *159–62*, 197–201,
    197–201, 225–30, *225–30*, 262,
    262, 281, *281*, 283–4, *283–4*
Solanum melongena 225–6, *225–6*
S. tuberosum 227–30, *227–30*
Sorrel 58
    common 223, *223*
    French 223
Soya bean 184, *184*
Spinach *12*, 14, 58, 61, 231, *231*
    Malabar 133, *133*
    New Zealand 232, *232*
    water 186, *186*
Spinacia oleracea 231, *231*
Spring 82–4
Sprouts 58, 238–9, *238–9*
Sprouting broccoli 149–51, *151*
    purple 149, 150, *151*
    white 149, 150
Squash 57, *57*, 89
    acorn 176
    buttercup 177
    butternut 177
    delicata 176
    Hubbard 177
    spaghetti 176
    summer *12*, 56, 171–2, *172*
    winter 175–7, *175–7*
Star fruit 250, *250*
Strawberries *22*, 25, 72, 74–5, 91–3,
    110, *111*, 267–8, *267–8*
    alpine 269, *269*
Sulphur 49
Summer 84
Sunflower 270, *270*
Swede 138, *138*
Sweet corn *12*, 57, 89, 235–7, *235–7*
    miniature 237
    ornamental *236*, 237
    popcorn 237
Sweet pepper *see* peppers
Sweet potato 12, 187–8, *187–8*
Swiss chard 12, 14, 56, 134, *134*

T

Tamarillo 262, *262*
Tetragonia tetragonioides 232, *232*
Thinning 98, *98*
Thyme 245, *245*
Thymus spp. 245, *245*
Tomatillo 283, *283*
Tomato *12*, *43*, 57, 197–201, *197–201*
　beefsteak 199–200, *201*
　cherry 56, *198*, 200
　currant 201
　low-acid *197*, 200
　plum *199*, 200
　pear 201
　standard 201
　trailing 201
Topography 16–17
Tragopogon porrifolius 233, *233*
Transplanting 65, *65*,
Turnip 14, 155, *155*

U

Umbelliferae 205, *205*

V

Vaccinium corymbosum 302, *302*
V. macrocarpon 303, *303*
V. vitis-idaea 304, *304*
Valerianaceae 234, *234*
Valerianella locusta 234, *234*
Vegetables 86–9, *86–9*, 112–239,
　　112–239 see also by name

　feeding 88–9, *89*
　weeding 108–9
Viburnum trilobum 305, *305*
Vicia spp. 210
V. faba 213, *213*
Vietnamese coriander 204, *204*
Vigna spp. 210–11
V. unguiculata subsp. *sesquipedalis*
　213
Vitaceae 306–7, *306–7*
Vitis vinifera 306–7, *306–7*

W

Walnut *23*, 79, 271, *271*
　black 271
　English 271
　Persian 271
Watercress 58, 202, *202*
Watering 94–5, *94–5*
　water conservation 95
Weeds 102–7, *102–7*
　fruit garden 110–11, *110–11*
　hoeing 106, *106*, 108
　smothering 108–9, *108*
　vegetable garden 108–9
Winter 82
Worm bin 39, *39*

Z

Zea mays 235–7, *235–7*
　var. *indurata* 236, 237
　var. *praecox* 237
　var. *rugosa* 237

ACKNOWLEDGMENTS

KEY l=left, r=right, c=centre t=top, b=bottom

APL=Australian Picture Library; AZ=A–Z Botanical Collection; BCL=Bruce Coleman Ltd; CBT=Corbis; CM=Cheryl Maddocks; CN= Clive Nichols; DF=Derek Fell; DW=David Wallace; GDR=G.R. "Dick" Roberts; GP. com=gardenphotos.com; GPL=Garden Picture Library; HA=Heather Angel; HSC=Harry Smith Collection; HSI=Holt Studios International; IH=Ivy Hansen; iS=istockphoto.com; JP=Jerry Pavia; JY=James Young; LC=Leigh Clapp; LR=Lorna Rose; OSF=Oxford Scientific Films; PD=PhotoDisc; PH=Photos Horticultural; SM=Stirling Macoboy; SOM=S. & O. Mathews; TE=Thomas Eltzroth; TPL=photolibrary.com; WO=Weldon Owen; WR=Weldon Russell

1t OSF/Steffen Hauser; c WO/JY; b WR/John Callanan 2c WO 5c LC 6t WO/JY; c WO/JY; b APL/ Corbis/Lynda Richardson 7t JY; c OSF/Richard Kolar; b GPL/Howard Rice 10c APL/Corbis/Michael Boys 13b GPL/Eric Crichton 15b LR 16tl DF 17tr PH 20tr HSC 21bl TE 23c GPL/Howard Rice 24t iS 25b PH 26c APL/Corbis/Michael Boys 28–29b WR 30b GPL/Joanne Pavia 31t GPL/Michael Howes 33c, b DW 37t DF 38b WO 39tl WO; br GP.com/Judy White 41c HSC 42t PH; b HSI/Nigel Cattlin 43b PH 44t HSI/Nigel Cattlin 45tr PH 46b TE 47t WO 48t HSI/Nigel Cattlin 49b BCL/Jane Burton 50br WR 51br PH 52t APL/Corbis/Patrick Johns; c TE; b iS 53l WR 54c GPL/John Glover 56tl WO; br WR 57r WO/Kevin Candland 59t PD 61b PD 62bl John Callanan 63 DW 67 DW 70t Andrew Lawson; b TE 71b CN 74–75b PH 75tr TPL 76tl GPL/John Glover; br GPL/Stephen Robson 77t TE 78b TPL 80c LC 82tl Denise Greig 83c CN 84t APL/Corbis/Eric Crichton 84–85b GPL/Juliette Wade 86–87b APL/Corbis/Eric Crichton 87t GPL/John Glover 88t, b TE 89t APL/Corbis/Bohemian Nomad Picture Makers 90tl TE 91b GPL/Howard Rice 92bl GPL/Mayer/Le Scanff 93tr TE 95t GPL/Michael Howes 96b GPL/Mel Watson 97tr Corbis 99t GPL/Mel Watson 100cl SH; bl GPL/Robert Estall 102tl GPL/Marijke Heuff 103b 105t APL/Corbis/Michael Boys 106t PH 106–107b Denise Greig 107t AZ/Anthony Cooper 108t PH 109t Artville; b GPL/Ron Sutherland 110tr AZ/Bjorn Svensson 110–111b GPL/JP 111t PH 112t GPL/JP 114t JY 115t PH 116t JP 117t GPL/Sunniva Harte 118t TE 119t DW 120t GDR 121t DF 122t GDR 123t WO/JY 124t WR 125t TPL 126t PH 127t Ardea London/Don Hadden 128t HA 129t HA 130t WR 131t CM 132t PH 133t DF 134t WO/JY 135t GDR 136t DW 137t BCL 138t GDR 139t DF 140t 141t TE 142t GDR 143t GPL/John Glover 144t GDR 145t DW 146t JY 147t GPL/Jacqui Hurst 148t GDR 149t DW 150t WO 151t GDR 152t DW 153t GPL/Christi Carter 154t WR 155t TE 156t TPL 157t WO/Michael Freeman 158t TE 159t WO/JY 160t WR 161t WO/JY 162t WO/JY 163t AZ 164t DW 165t TE 166t WO/JY 167t BCL 168t JY 169t PH 170t GPL/John Glover 171t JY 172t GDR 173t DW 174t WO 175t DW 176t GPL/Lamontagne 177t CBT 178t HA 179t CM 180t SM 181t PH 182t DW 183t GDR 184t DW 185t DW 186t DW 187t HSC 188t IH 189t DW 190t WO/JY 191t WO 192t PH 193t DW 194t HSC 195t GP.com/Judy White 196t DW 197t TE 198t GPL/Lamontagne

199t Auscape/C. Andrew Henley **200t** PH **201t** JY **202t** DW **203t** TE **204t** LR **205t** DW **206t** DW **207t** TPL **208t** SM **209t** TPL **210t** CM **211t** DW **212t** Rodale Stock Images **213t** GDR **214t** DW **215t** DW **216t** GDR **217t** TPL/Maximilian Stock Ltd/AGSTOCK **218t** DW **219t** SM **220t** DW **221t** DW **222t** SH **223t** DW **224t** TPL **225t** DF **226t** DW **227t** TE **228t** APL/Hackenberg/Zefa **229t** GPL/John Glover **230t** WR/DW **231t** HSC **232t** DW **233t** CM **234t** DW **235t** OSF/John McCammon **236t** APL/Corbis/Robert Maass **237t** DW **238t** TPL/Wen Jia Feng **240br** APL/Gerry Whitmont **241t** DW **242t** JY **243t** GDR **244t** JP **245t** DW **246c** GP.com/Judy White **248t** PH **249t** OSF/Harold Taylor **250t** TE **251t** HSC **252t** iS **253t** SOM **254t** WO **255t** SH **256t** TE **257t** APL/Corbis/Maurice Nimmo **258t** TPL **259t** GPL/Christi Carter **260t** iS **261t** HSC **262t** TPL **263t** TE **264t** SH **265t** TE **266t** TE **267t** PH **268t** GPL/John Glover **269t** PH **270t** BCL/Hans Reinhard **271t** SH **272t** GDR **273t** GDR **274t** SH **275t** iS **276t** GDR **277t** HSI/Nigel Cattlin **278t** TE **279t** TE **280t** TE **281t** TPL **282t** GP.com/Judy White **283t** iS **284t** SOM **285t** PH **286t** GDR **287t** HSC **288t** iS **289t** TE **290t** SH **291t** GDR **292t** SH **293t** DF **294t** SH **295t** DF **296t** GPL/John Glover **297t** SH **298t** PH **299t** PH **300t** TE **301t** SOM **302t** PH **303t** BCL/Charlie Orr **304t** GPL/John Glover **305t** TE **306t** iS **307t** GPL/Neil Holmes

Illustrations by Tony Britt-Lewis, Edwina Riddell, Barbara Rodanska, Jan Smith, Kathie Smith.